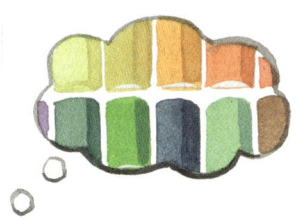

THINKING IN
WATERCOLOR

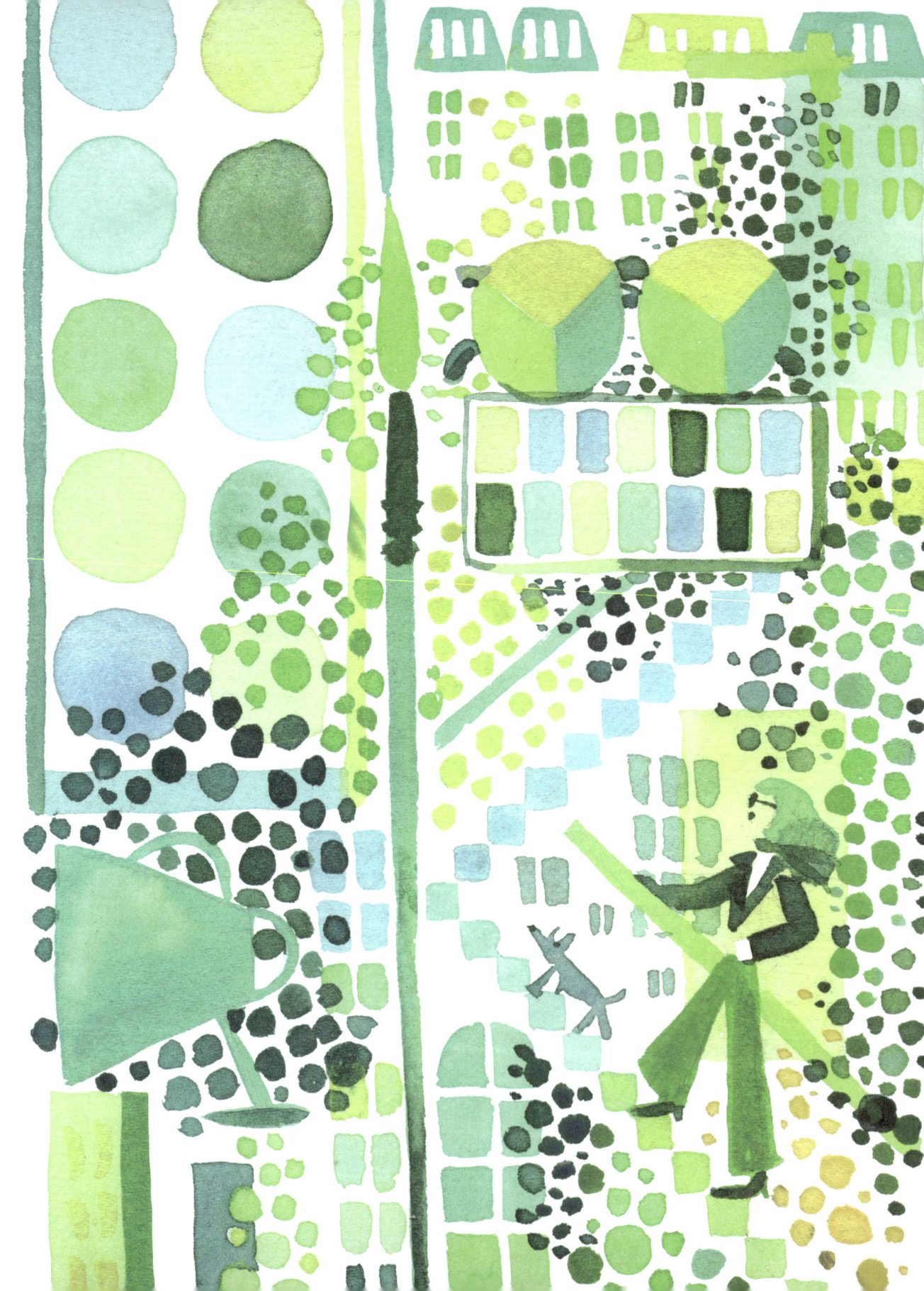

THINKING IN WATERCOLOR

A Daily Practice to Unlock Your Creativity & Discover Your Inner Artist

Jessie Kanelos Weiner

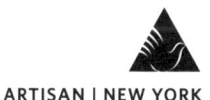

ARTISAN | NEW YORK

Library of Congress Cataloging-in-Publication Data
Names: Weiner, Jessie Kanelos, author.
Title: Thinking in watercolor : a daily practice to unlock your creativity & discover your
    inner artist /Jessie Kanelos Weiner.
Description: New York : Artisan, [2025]
Identifiers: LCCN 2024025204 | ISBN 9781648293320 (trade paperback)
Subjects: LCSH: Watercolor painting—Technique.
Classification: LCC ND2420 .W387 2025 | DDC 751.42/2—dc23/eng/20240722
LC record available at https://lccn.loc.gov/2024025204

Book design by Jane Treuhaft
Cover design by Remy Chwae and Jane Treuhaft

Artisan books may be purchased in bulk for business, educational, or promotional use. For information, please contact your local bookseller or the Hachette Book Group Special Markets Department at special.markets@hbgusa.com.

The publisher is not responsible for websites (or their content) that are not owned by the publisher.

The Hachette Speakers Bureau provides a wide range of authors for speaking events. To find out more, go to hachettespeakersbureau.com or email HachetteSpeakers@hbgusa.com.

Published by Artisan,
an imprint of Workman Publishing,
a division of Hachette Book Group, Inc.
1290 Avenue of the Americas
New York, NY 10104
artisanbooks.com

The Artisan name and logo are registered trademarks of Hachette Book Group, Inc.

Printed in China (IMSF) on responsibly sourced paper

10 9 8 7 6 5 4 3 2

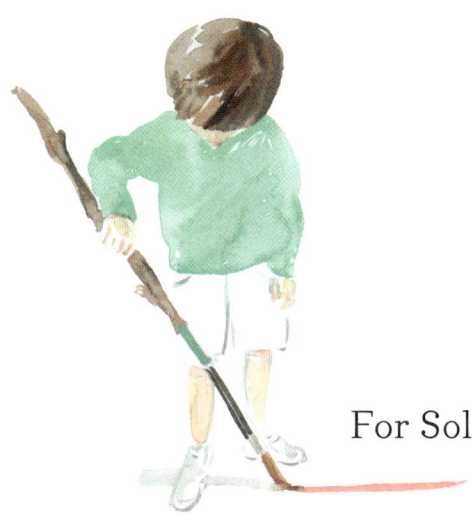

For Sol

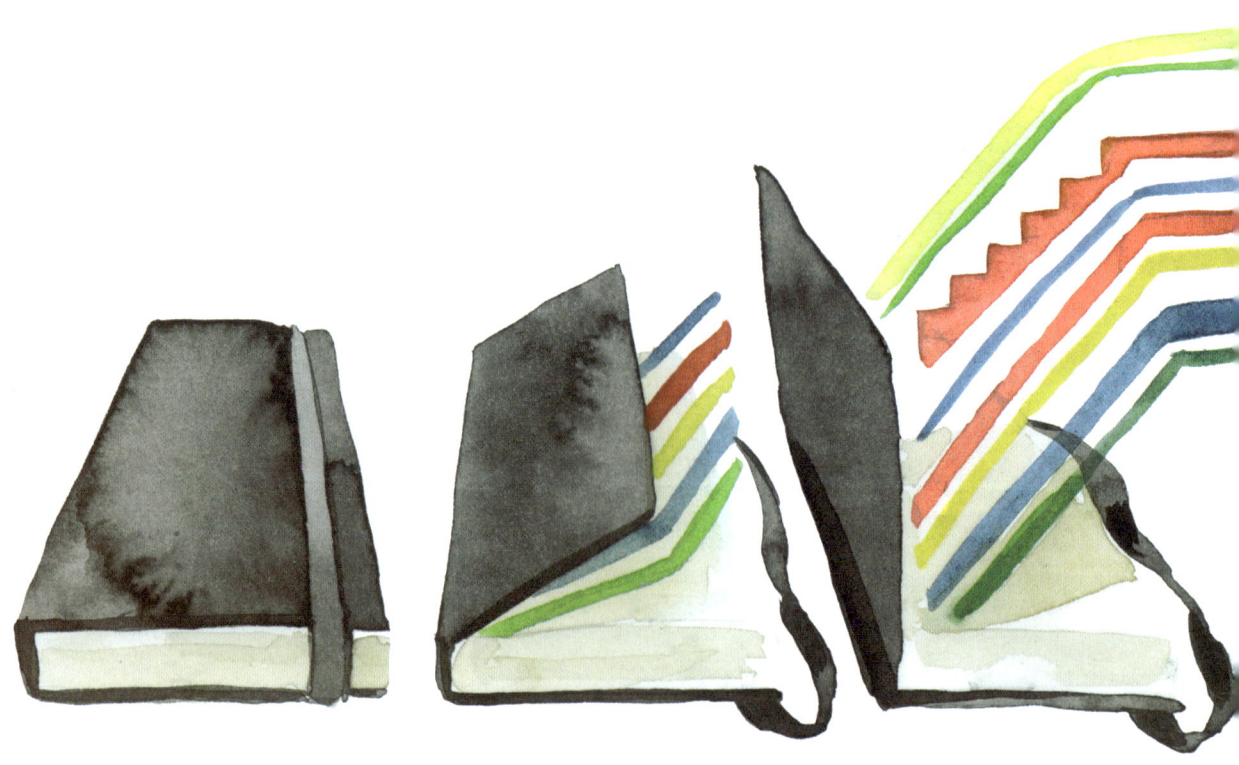

CONTENTS

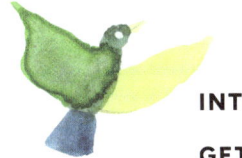

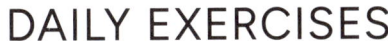

INTRODUCTION

Whenever I tell someone I paint with watercolor, I get one of two responses: "That must be so relaxing!" (from those who have never tried it), or "That's so difficult!" (from those who have dabbled in it themselves). Watercolor has a reputation for being finicky and unpredictable. But what's frustrating about it is also what pulls you in: the bright, lifelike colors; the visual record of how water travels on the page; the abstraction of life into its essential core.

Watercolor is an act of the present. It's a tool I've used for more than fifteen years to understand my surroundings, spread joy across the world, and heal. It's how I dissect my current realities and how I dream of the future. It's a portal to wonderment, a magic that happens when paint hits paper, and the only thing you can do is trust the process. And it packs a punch—a small kit of watercolors can be transported anywhere, and just a few brushstrokes can lead to maximum impact.

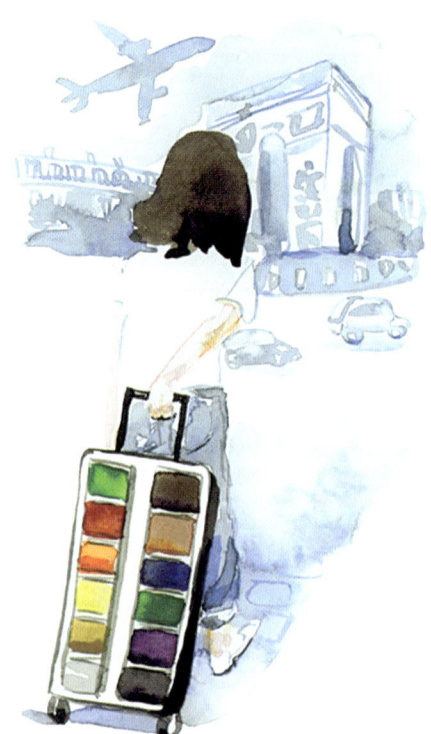

I recently pulled out my first Winsor & Newton watercolor kit. It was a fifty-plus-euro fortune when I bought it more than fifteen years ago, a broke professional babysitter with aspiring artistic tendencies. I had moved to Paris for what I thought would be a one-year Audrey Hepburn fantasy of glamour and high culture. Instead, my new mission in life was to care for a verbally abusive French four-year-old, fueled only by a one-per-day Nespresso capsule allotment. The watercolor set is stained from evenings spent painting with coffee and Perrier in Parisian cafés, trying to comprehend the rapid-fire French around me and killing time to avoid going back to my non-home. I was longing to find a voice as a young artist, but I was stumped—I couldn't paint anything other than what was in front of me. I loved watercolor but didn't know *what* to paint.

At the time, I thought I was just a twenty-two-year-old loser with no direction in life, but in reality I was well on the meandering path to becoming a professional illustrator and author. I had the gift of time, and the ability to observe and create in the present, thanks to that dear set of watercolors. I loved the looseness and detail I could get capturing a scene in just a few moments. I would often paint something on-site, lay a café napkin on top, and hope it would still resemble what I had painted by the time I got home. Sometimes the paint would smoosh itself down into an unrecognizable crinkly mess, but I could still remember the exact moment in distinct detail. Even though I wasn't always creating work, I was seeing in an intense way. Why was the golden hour in Paris so breathtaking? Why was the color of the Mediterranean so much more intoxicating than that of Lake Michigan at home? With my senses heightened, I was able to start seeing like an artist, even though I was still very early in my path to becoming a professional one.

Fast-forward, and a couple of years living in Paris meant I had enough cultural faux pas and ludicrous stories under my belt to start a blog. (It's what we did back then!) Reluctant to use the mediocre photos I took with my phone, I started illustrating my stories in watercolor.

There was the time autocorrect translated a friendly goodbye, gros bisou ("big kiss"), into "gross bisexual." It was not the kind of text a boss likes receiving. Another time, I was cooking for a family who informed me that the guest of honor at that night's dinner was a judge on the French version of *Top Chef*. The chef's red, white, and blue Meilleur Ouvrier de France collar (a lauded Best in France cooking award) became the mouth of a frowning face.

Not only was this blog a great source of catharsis, but it was also the catalyst for me to finally merge my technique with my life to create engaging illustrations. I was able to

go from just *painting* something to *saying* something with my work. Little by little, I built up my portfolio, started shakily calling art directors, and began to get work as a professional illustrator creating watercolor illustrations at the intersection of food, Paris, and travel.

But before I was getting clients like the *New York Times*, *New Yorker*, and Penguin Random House, I had to start where I was and paint what I saw and what I knew. And over the course of the next thirty days, I'll show you how to do just that.

This book is structured into thirty days of exercises, teaching you watercolor techniques and storytelling devices from the simplest to the most complex to get you to visually synthesize your own unique world. On the following pages, I will lay out everything you need to get started: must-have supplies, foolproof watercolor techniques, and a primer in color theory.

Whether you are totally new to the art form, are already quite proficient at watercolor, or have dabbled in the past and want to get better and break free from the fears that have kept you from making it a regular practice, this book will encourage you to start where you are and paint what you know best: your own story. Call me your watercolor evangelist. Are you ready to love watercolor?

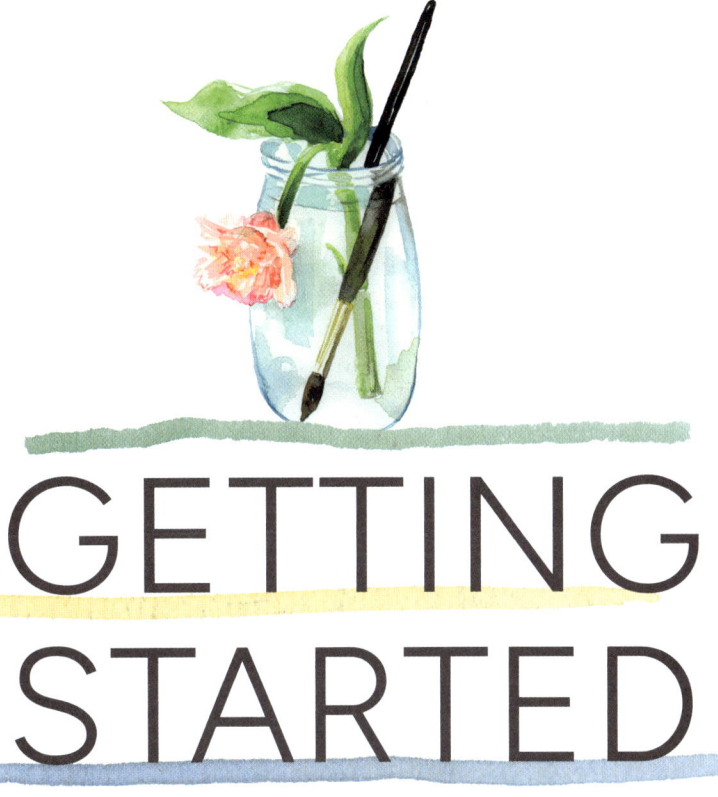

GETTING STARTED

This book has two objectives: helping you to build a watercolor practice and to develop your own visual ideas. But before we begin, let's get you up to speed on the watercolor essentials you need to set your ideas in motion: everything you need to know to set up your workspace, choose your art supplies, and make them last; key watercolor techniques and their varying visual characteristics; and the foundations of color theory to get you understanding the infinite number of colors that you can mix using watercolor.

WHAT YOU'LL NEED

I like to say that watercolor painting can be compared to cooking: You can always add more, but you can't take away, and the final result is as good as the ingredients you use. Once I learned which materials worked for me, I found it easier to execute my vision because I wasn't fighting against my paint and paper. Here's how to set yourself up for success.

PAPER

Most watercolor haters can be converted if they are simply introduced to good paper. The least-expensive watercolor paper is made of wood pulp. Sturdier, better-quality paper is made of cotton. This better-quality paper absorbs watercolor, giving you greater control and more time to play around when painting. The less-expensive paper has a tendency to get pools on the surface, resulting in watercolor marks, splotching, and warping. (The best metaphor I can think of is the difference between sopping up spilled milk with a paper towel versus a bath towel; it is a whole other level of absorption.) Since many beginning watercolorists struggle with using too much water, which can lead to dull colors as well as warped and crinkled paper, buy the best-quality and heaviest-weight paper you can to start with.

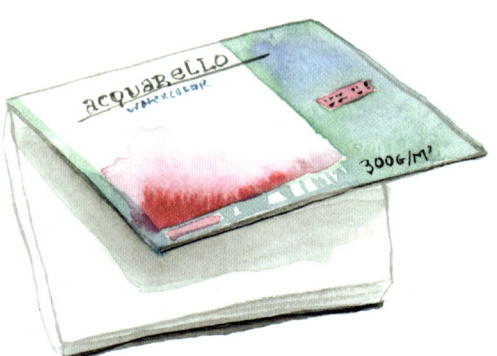

Here are a few things to look for before purchasing paper:

Weight. Buy a paper that is at least 140 lb (300 gsm). It won't warp as much even if you struggle with water-control issues. I've upgraded to 300 lb (640 gsm). I like to say that if you hold a piece of paper by one corner and shake it back and forth, it should sound like thunder; that's the sign of a sturdy enough paper.

Texture. Watercolor paper comes in different grains, or textures, ranging from smooth to rough. Because I digitally scan my watercolors, I use a fully smooth satin finish, which results in minimal retouching.

Color. If you've ever hemmed and hawed over choosing a shade of white paint, you know that they are not all created equal. Be aware that watercolor paper comes in warm and cool shades of white, which can dramatically impact how your colors look later on. I painted a super-detailed illustration for this book, but its warm colors looked dull and flat. At first, I couldn't figure out what the problem was. Then I finally realized it was because the paper was cream instead of pure white.

BRUSHES

I recommend keeping it simple and mastering what you can with a few good-quality natural-fiber brushes. I also have a few synthetic brushes on hand because they keep their shape longer. I love a round brush because it can create great detail with its fine tip but is also long enough to absorb a good amount of paint to cover a decent surface area. In my own practice, I find that I can achieve any effect I'm after with just a few sizes of round brushes. My favorite is the Winsor & Newton Series 7 Kolinsky Sable Brush, pointed round, size 2.

PAINT

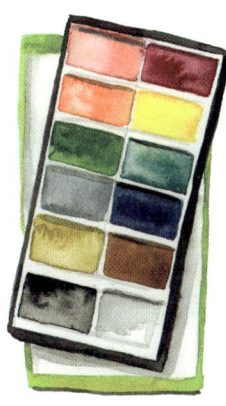

Watercolor comes in two forms: tubes and pans. As a newbie, you can easily get started with a classic set of pans and add tube colors as you go along if you desire a more saturated hue or if you find that you often need to replace a certain color. They can be used interchangeably.

When purchasing a watercolor kit, make sure it has at least ten colors: the primary and secondary colors (more on these on pages 24–25), black, white, and a few extras. I recommend buying your paint at an art supply store. It is formulated with the principles of mixing and color theory in mind, unlike the general, kid-friendly craft art watercolors you can find at grocery or office supply stores.

If you are buying individual watercolors, invest in the most expensive primary colors you can afford. Not all paints are made the same: Better-quality paints mix much better than their cheaper counterparts. When we get to color theory (pages 24–31), you will see that the purer the primary colors are, the brighter the secondary hues will be upon mixing. The Winsor & Newton Cotman Watercolor Field Travel Set, which includes twelve colors, is great for beginners. As your practice grows and evolves, you may find your needs will change. All of the illustrations in this book were painted with Kuretake Gansai Tambi pan watercolors, my personal favorite because the colors are as saturated as acrylic and easier to control than tube watercolor paints.

HOT TIP

HOW TO REMOVE A SHEET FROM THE BLOCK

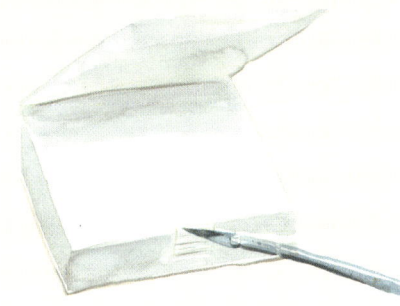

You may notice that some watercolor paper comes not in pads but in blocks with all four sides of the paper glued together. This ensures that the paper will stay flat rather than warping. I highly recommend blocks for newbies with water-control issues. But how do you remove your watercolor from the block when you're finished? Look around the four sides of the block and you should see a 1-inch (2.5 cm) section that is not glued together. Place the block on a flat surface, insert an X-Acto or palette knife horizontally into the glue-free spot, and gently run the knife around the edges to carefully remove the sheet of paper. The sheet may have some glue remnants on its sides, but these can easily be scraped off with a fingernail or a palette knife.

MAKING YOUR SUPPLIES LAST

Art supplies can cost a pretty penny (especially the good stuff), so here are some dos and don'ts for taking care of them and making them last.

- **DO** let your paint dry on your palette and reuse it at any time. Once the paint has dried, it can be reactivated by swirling a wet paintbrush on top. This is ideal if you need to put a painting on pause and don't want to remix all the colors from scratch.

- **DO** clean your brushes with a brush cleaner or baby shampoo after each painting session. Rinse the brush vigorously in water, swirl it in the brush cleaner, and gently massage the cleaner into the bristles with your index finger and thumb. Rinse until it is completely clean. Always reshape the tip of the brush with your fingertips to avoid warping and let it dry standing with the bristles up.

- **DON'T** get into the habit of letting your paintbrush sit in your water vessel while painting. This will deform the bristles and point of the paintbrush. Place it on a tabletop or upright in a cup like a bouquet of flowers until you need to use it again.

- **DO** pack your brushes in a roll-up brush holder when transporting them to protect the tips from warping during travel.

- **DO** clean your hands and work surface with soap and warm water before painting with watercolor.

WATER

Since you are essentially painting with water, you want to keep that water as clean as possible. I've seen a lot of students' work get muddied very quickly simply because they are using the tiny water cup that comes with a set of travel watercolors. I use a 1-liter glass jar or a giant clear vase so I don't have to change the water as often, but the second it doesn't look transparent, I dump it out and refill it with clean water.

A PALETTE OR OTHER MIXING SURFACE

Another way to avoid the muddy brown-black zone is to use a big enough palette to give your colors room to breathe. Feel free to use the palette built into your watercolor set, or purchase a separate plastic or porcelain one—but be sure to clean it often to avoid mixing muddy colors. I sometimes use a large dinner plate, but I mostly mix directly on a glass or marble tabletop, which I meticulously clean before I begin a day's work (because oil and water aren't friends, a post-lunch table or greasy hands can destroy a pristine watercolor). Another option is palette paper, a synthetic paper on which paint can be mixed, dried, and reactivated.

SKETCHING SUPPLIES

Watercolor requires a good amount of preparation before the paint can be applied. When I have an idea to explore, I rely on loose printer paper and waterproof Micron pens to flesh out a concept before transferring the sketch to watercolor paper.

When sketching on watercolor paper, use an H pencil and draw with the lightest hand possible. If you've taken art classes in the past, you know that not all pencils are created equal. They are marked from H (hard) to B (black, or softer), with 8H being the lightest in color and 8B being the darkest. If you have a set of six graphite pencils, they are usually organized from lightest to darkest: 6H, 2H, H, HB, 2B, 6B. H pencils leave a fine line on the watercolor paper that can be seen while you're working but then easily removed later with an eraser.

Once I have my definitive pencil sketch in place, I go back and lightly erase the line until it is barely visible. Pink erasers can make marks on watercolor paper that are nearly impossible to remove, so stick to a white or clear eraser. And a word from the unwise: Always wait for your watercolor to dry completely before erasing the pencil lines. Erasing a slightly wet watercolor will smear the paint and ruin your work.

Some watercolorists like adding a pen outline before laying on the watercolor. I find that it can flatten the volume that I've worked so hard building up with watercolor, so I don't do this myself. But add an outline if you like, just be sure that you do so with a waterproof pen to avoid bleeding.

PAPER TOWELS

Paper towels are indispensable when I'm painting. (A piece of scrap paper or a clean kitchen towel is an eco-friendly stand-in.) I fold one in half and blot my brush on it to check my colors before applying them to my precious watercolor paper. I also use it to dab off any excess water and pigment from my paintbrush. A paper towel can soak up any missteps, and it can be a good buffer if I need to rest my hand on a watercolor when I'm adding fine details. I often joke that the watercolor-stained paper towel I

used is the day's best work because it's always an abstract masterpiece when I'm done with it.

WORK SURFACE

To state the obvious, unlike oil or acrylic, which are often painted on an easel, watercolor requires a flat tabletop to avoid drippage.

OTHER GEAR

The following items will help expedite your creative process and allow you to share your creations.

- Hair dryer, for drying your watercolor quickly
- Drawing gum, a latex liquid that masks paper so it does not absorb paint
- Masking tape, to tape down the sides of watercolor paper so they don't warp. Tip: When you unroll your tape, tap the sticky side on your clothes a couple of times. It will add some fuzz and soften the adhesion. This will prevent the paper from getting roughed up when the tape is removed later.
- Photo-quality scanner, graphic tablet, and photo-editing software (like Photoshop) if you plan to share your work digitally
- Light box, for tracing

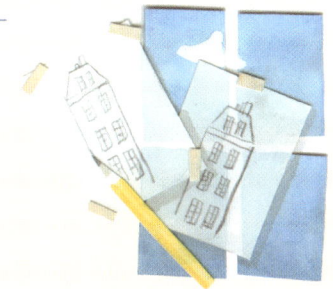

HOT TIP

CREATING YOUR OWN LIGHT BOX

In the interest of full transparency, I don't have a light box. I use a window and natural light for tracing instead. Here's how: Using masking tape, adhere the image you want to trace on a window during daylight hours.

Tape all four corners of the sheet of watercolor paper you would like to draw on directly on top of the image, ensuring it is completely flat. You should be able to see the image underneath to trace it.

WATERCOLOR 101

Painting with watercolor is like choreographing a dance between paper and paint: It's all about timing, execution, and a little bit of chance. In this section, you'll learn to tame watercolor into doing what you need it to do as I walk you through key principles to understanding the medium and a handful of techniques to obtain various effects. If you're a watercolor novice, use this section to start getting acquainted with watercolor and its particularities. If you're already a semipro, feel free to skim this section and move on to the daily exercises.

Activating Your Paint

Once you get your workstation set up, it's time to activate your watercolor paint. If using pan watercolors, you'll do this by wetting a brush and swirling it around until you can see a little color on the bristles. (You can also use a spray bottle filled with water to evenly dampen your paints.) If you're using tube colors, the consistency will be almost like mustard; squeeze out a pea-sized amount of paint onto a watercolor palette and dilute it with a wet paintbrush, adding more water until the consistency is loose like water. If not properly diluted, the thick tube paint can stick to the bristles of the brush and go on unevenly. If using tube paint, always blot off your paintbrush on a sheet of scrap paper or a paper towel to be sure that the paint is evenly coating the brush before applying it to the watercolor paper.

Q & A

WHAT'S THE DIFFERENCE BETWEEN WATERCOLOR AND GOUACHE?

Gouache is a quick-drying water-soluble paint. Because it provides fuller coverage than watercolor, you can achieve bolder colors. Watercolor is all about transparency, while gouache is all about opacity. Gouache is great to have if you want to create a matte, universal background on a watercolor, and it can also scratch the itch if your colors are looking dull.

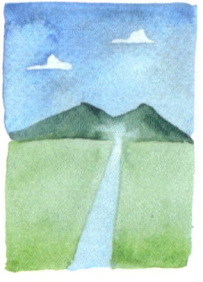
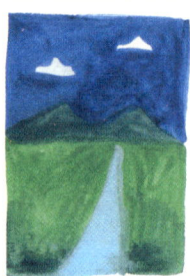

Watercolor   Gouache

Understanding Your Colors

Before you can start mixing colors, it is essential to understand the hues in your paint set.

INTENSITY

The *intensity* of color is its perceived amount of saturation. The first skill to develop in watercolor is adding enough water to adjust the overall brightness and transparency of the color.

1. Get out a sheet of watercolor paper and use an H pencil to lightly draw a few rectangles.

2. Activate a few colors from your watercolor set and check the intensity of the first color by dabbing your paintbrush on a piece of paper towel or scrap paper. Does it look like the color in the kit? If the color is too light, dab up some of the water from the pan with a paper towel. Once you've achieved the dark, pure color you're after, paint each rectangle with a color at 100% intensity. Rinse your paintbrush completely before moving on to the next rectangle.

3. Redraw and paint the same color chart—but this time, dilute each color with water on a palette until it is at 50% intensity. Verify the color by dabbing your paintbrush on a paper towel or scrap paper to see if you need to add more water or pigment before applying it to the watercolor paper.

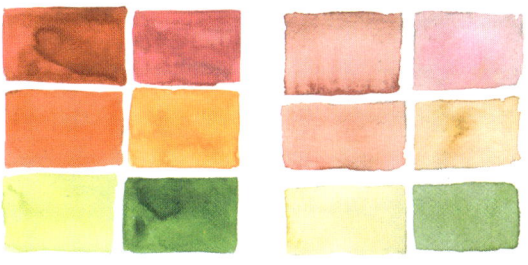

100% intensity   50% intensity

VALUE

The next watercolor skill to master is *value*, or the perceived lightness or darkness of a color. As we learned in the previous exercise, the more water you add, the lighter the color will be.

1. Using an H pencil, lightly draw seven rectangles on a piece of watercolor paper.

2. Activate your paint and fill in the leftmost rectangle with one color at 100% intensity.

3. Gently dip the paintbrush into water (without rinsing vigorously) to remove a little pigment from the brush and subtly dilute the color. Dab off on a paper towel, then check on scrap paper if the tone is lighter than the first. If so, you're ready to apply the next stripe.

4. Continue this process until you have seven progressively lighter shades of the color. Repeat this exercise until you are able to consistently achieve a progressive gradient.

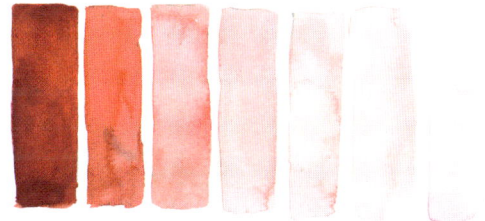

PUTTING IT ALL TOGETHER

Now it's time to take what you've learned about intensity and value and apply it to a watercolor.

1. Place an object, like a banana, on your worktable and sketch it out with an H pencil three times on a piece of watercolor paper.

2. Paint the first sketch not with the colors you see but with those directly from your palette. The result should look almost like pop art.

3. Paint the second still life using the same colors but with 50% intensity.

4. For the third still life, study the light and dark areas of the object and use different intensities to help create contrast between these areas. I use a blue at 50% intensity on the bottom and a red at 100% on the top to get variation. While the blue layer is still slightly wet, I load up my brush with a darker hue of blue and paint it under the bunch of bananas to render the shadow. I paint the bananas with yellow at 50% intensity. Then I go back with 100% yellow to add depth and differentiate the bananas in the bunch.

5. Look at all three paintings and ask yourself which is the most effective. Depending on what you are painting, it will be up to you to decide which intensity (or combination of intensities) you will use to achieve your desired look.

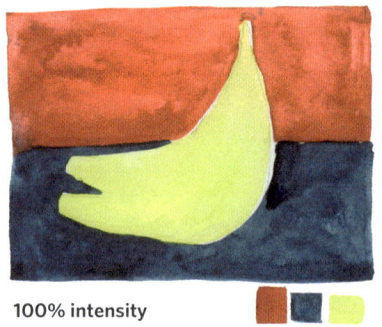

100% intensity

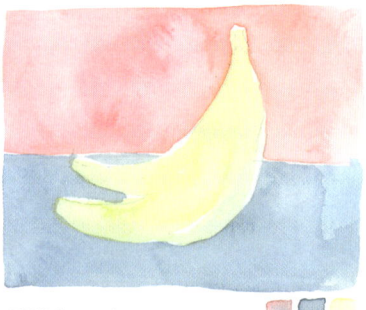

50% intensity

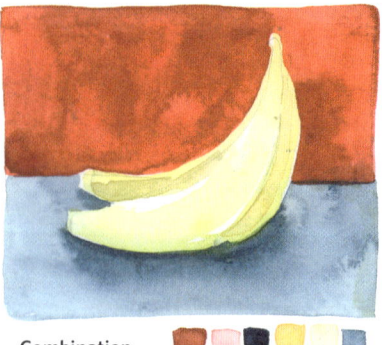

Combination

Manipulating Your Brush

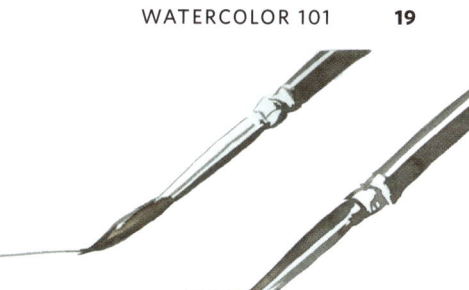

I highly recommend using a round brush when you are first starting out. This brush has the versatility to both create fine lines and fill in large areas of the page.

You will be able to create a very fine line with just the tip of the brush. If the bristles are applied flatter on the paper, they will create a thicker line.

All brushes are different, so experiment with the amount of pressure you apply when painting, twirling your brush around on the page to play with thickness and line weight (the width of the line on the paper). I have found that synthetic brushes keep their pointy tips much longer than their natural-fiber counterparts, so I often use a natural brush for better coverage and a synthetic brush for fine details.

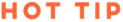

HOT TIP

THE CLOCK TRICK

If you are using a round brush, hold the brush as if it were a pencil, and imagine there is a clock beside your hand—if you were holding the brush with the tip at a 90-degree angle to the paper, it would be at six o'clock. Create fine detail by holding the brush at seven o'clock. More surface area can be covered if it's held at eight o'clock, where the bristles will be slightly flattened.

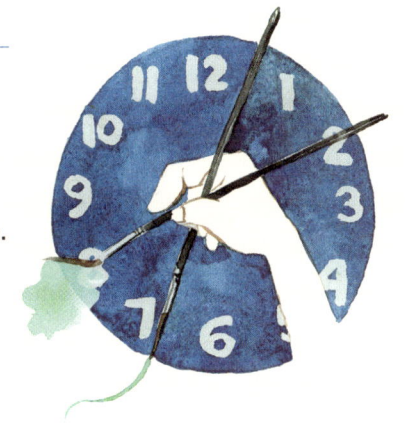

Essential Watercolor Techniques

It's time to learn a few techniques that play with the relationship between paint, water, and paper, to different effects.

TECHNIQUE 1: **WET ON DRY**

When applying wet paint to dry paper, you're in control. Once the paint is activated and mixed in the palette, the resulting color is painted directly on the paper. (This is what you did in the value exercise on page 17.)

After a color is applied using the wet-on-dry technique, it can still be manipulated by adding more water to the paper and pulling the color with a wet paintbrush to create transparency. This is an essential technique to render volume.

1. Using an H pencil, lightly draw seven rectangles on a piece of watercolor paper.

2. Paint the bottom half of the leftmost rectangle with the darkest version of a color.

3. Rinse your paintbrush clean and use the water on the brush to coax up the color you just applied until the rectangle is fully covered. If you have too much water on the paper, dab off the paintbrush on a paper towel.

4. Repeat this process, adding a little bit more water to the pigment on the brush before painting the next rectangle, until you have seven gradient rectangles.

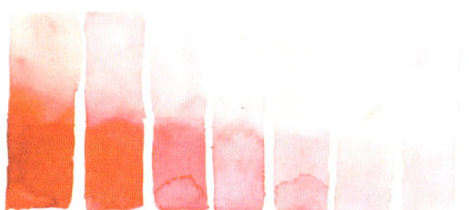

TECHNIQUE 2: **WET ON WET**

The water is in control when painting wet on wet. The surface of the paper is as wet as possible and the water takes the pigment on its own self-determined voyage. This technique is used in more abstract work and to create softer, irregular washes.

1. Using an H pencil, lightly draw seven rectangles on a piece of watercolor paper.

2. Use a large round brush to apply as much water as possible on the seven rectangles. If you hold up the paper vertically, the water should drip.

3. Load up the brush with as much paint as possible. Apply the color to the leftmost rectangle from the bottom up. Instead of rinsing your brush clean, add a little bit more water to the pigment on the brush by gently dipping your brush in your water jar before painting the next rectangle. You will see the color sit at the bottom where it's applied. As it dries, the pigment will continue to move on the dampened paper. It's got a mind of its own.

4. Continue dipping your paint-covered brush in the water before applying to the next rectangle.

TECHNIQUE 3: **50% FLOOD**

When using what I have dubbed the 50% flood technique, which is a more predictable version of wet on wet, the paint is in control. A designated area of the paper is lightly dampened before the color is applied, which encourages a more precise feathering on the paper. This is my go-to technique when I want to render something reflective or to represent volume.

1. Using an H pencil, lightly draw seven rectangles on a piece of watercolor paper.

2. Dip a brush in water and dab off on a paper towel so it is damp but not dripping wet.

3. Paint the surface area of the first rectangle with a light wash of water. If held to the light, the paper should reflect the light, but the water shouldn't drip off the page. Paint the leftmost rectangle with the darkest intensity of your color, applying the pigment at the bottom of the rectangle to see how it works its way up.

4. Paint the next rectangle, diluting the watercolor paint to mix a slightly lighter hue than you used in the first test. Repeat the process of dipping and painting until all seven rectangles are painted. You should see a transition from darkest to lightest.

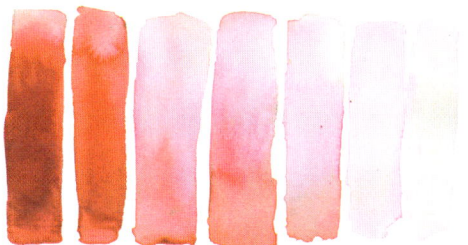

TECHNIQUE 4: **DRY BRUSH**

What's the opposite of a wash? A dry brush. This method results in a scratchy, irregular effect that is my go-to approach for tree trunks and other rougher textures, like hair.

1. Take a slightly wet paintbrush and dampen your paint until it is just barely activated.

2. Paint a line on a sheet of dry watercolor paper. The pigment just barely clings to the bristles of the brush, so what results is a scratchy effect.

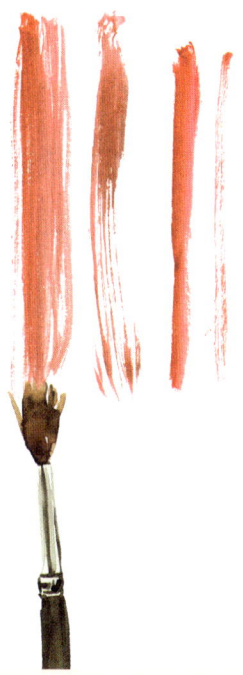

HOT TIP

TIMING IS EVERYTHING

Another particularity about watercolor is that it has a very limited active time because you are working within the moment or two before the water dries. Put your phone on silent and don't answer the door until you're done with your layer. It's watercolor go time.

Building Texture

You've already learned the first technique for texture, dry brushing, but texture can also be achieved by layering washes and mixing techniques.

TECHNIQUE 1: STIPPLING

One of my favorite techniques is *stippling*, evoking texture by building a pattern of dots. I use this technique to render the peel of an orange or to suggest the scales of a fish.

1. Using an H pencil, lightly draw four rectangles on a piece of watercolor paper.

2. Dip your brush in paint and dot the tip of the brush wet-on-dry in the leftmost rectangle until the surface area is completely covered.

3. Lightly dampen the surface area of the next rectangle with a clean, wet paintbrush to prepare for 50% flood. Load up your brush with more paint and dot the rectangle with the point of the brush, noticing how the water lightly diffuses each dot.

4. Paint a light wash in the next rectangle. While it is still wet, load up your brush with more color and dot the surface.

5. Paint a light wash in the final rectangle and let it dry. Load up your brush with more color and dot the dry painted background for a wet-on-dry approach.

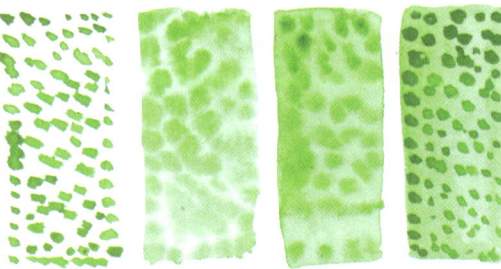

TECHNIQUE 2: HATCHING

Hatching is a pattern made up of parallel lines. I use this technique when I want to add stripes to a shirt or siding to an architectural structure.

1. Using an H pencil, lightly draw four rectangles on a piece of watercolor paper.

2. Dip your paintbrush in paint and draw parallel lines with the tip of your brush in the leftmost rectangle.

3. Lightly dampen the surface area of the next rectangle with a clean, wet paintbrush to prepare for 50% flood. Load up your brush with paint and draw parallel lines, noticing how the water lightly diffuses each stripe.

4. Paint a light wash on the next rectangle. While it is still wet, load up your brush with more color and paint parallel stripes.

5. Paint a light wash in the final rectangle and let it dry. Load up your brush with more color and add lines to the dry painted background for a wet-on-dry approach.

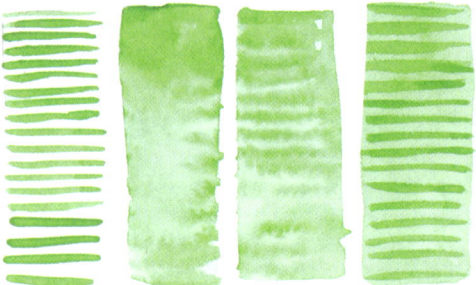

TECHNIQUE 3: **CROSS-HATCHING**

Cross-hatching builds on hatching, using a mix of horizontal and vertical lines. As with hatching, I use this technique most when rendering the texture of clothing—think a plaid or gingham shirt.

1. Using an H pencil, lightly draw four rectangles on a piece of watercolor paper.

2. Dip your paintbrush in paint and draw parallel lines with the tip of your brush in the leftmost rectangle. Turn the paper 90 degrees and paint perpendicular lines.

3. Lightly dampen the surface area of the next rectangle with a clean, wet paintbrush to prepare for 50% flood. Load up your brush with paint and draw parallel lines, noticing how the water lightly diffuses each stripe. Turn the paper 90 degrees and layer on perpendicular lines.

4. Paint a light wash in the next rectangle. While it is still wet, load up your brush with more color and paint parallel lines. Then turn the paper 90 degrees and layer on perpendicular lines.

5. Paint a light wash in the final rectangle and let it dry. Load up your brush with more color and add perpendicular lines to the dry painted background for a wet-on-dry approach.

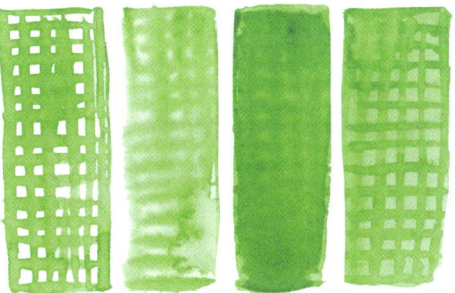

Q & A

THERE ARE SO MANY WATERCOLOR PRODUCTS. HOW DO YOU USE THEM?

I like carrying a few watercolor pencils around with me when I am sketching on vacation because they allow me to get the impact of watercolor without the excessive gear. They make marks like a regular pencil or pastel. However, if you add a stroke of a wet paintbrush, it activates the color to create a watercolor wash. They can also be used more pragmatically in your regular practice. I started sketching out my compositions using a sky-blue watercolor pencil because it blends into my paint once my paint is applied without making a harsh pencil line.

Refillable brush pens are great to have on hand when you need to paint a quick background wash on the go. To use, simply unscrew the top of the brush and fill it with water. The water is released from the bristles of the brush; squeeze it lightly and swirl on your paint to activate the color. If these brushes are not rinsed regularly, they can get muddy quickly, so be sure to clean them often. To do so, squeeze the brush to release some water while wiping it with a paper towel until clean.

COLOR THEORY

In this section, we will delve into color theory, or the science of perceiving and understanding color. The way you see color reflects your taste, your background, and how you perceive a hue optically. In the pages that follow, I'll walk you through the essential principles of color theory and a handful of exercises that will show you how to use color strategically, and how to troubleshoot any issues with color you may have as you approach your work. Although understanding color is a lifelong pursuit, by the end of this section you should at least know the colors in your palette better: how they can reinforce the overall emotion of your final piece, how to use complementary colors effectively, and how color wheels can often be revisited for inspiration and clarification. Now let's have some fun.

Color Wheels

The easiest way to understand color, and your paints, is by creating a series of color wheels. Like still life drawing, this isn't just a groan-worthy art class pastime. By re-creating these wheels with your watercolor paints, you will understand how to classify, mix, and select colors with confidence.

WHEEL 1: **PRIMARY COLORS**

All colors are derived from the holy trinity: red, yellow, and blue. You can't make these primary colors by mixing other colors, but you can make any other color by mixing a combination of these three.

1. Use an H pencil to sketch out a circle and divide it into three equal parts.

2. Paint each primary color at 100% intensity, letting each wedge dry completely before adding the next one.

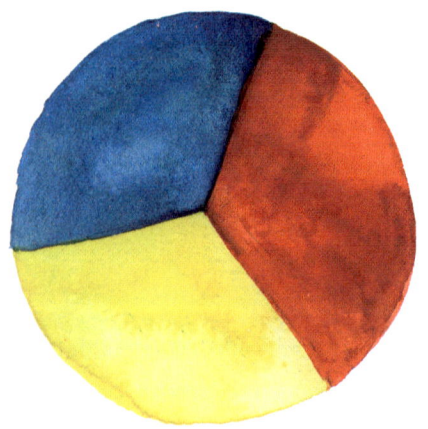

WHEEL 2: **SECONDARY COLORS**

The secondary colors—orange, purple, and green—are each created by mixing two primary colors. The colors on the opposite ends of the color wheel (blue/orange, red/green, and yellow/purple) are called *complementary colors*. Since they are the most contrasted pairs, these combinations really pop when put together (hence their use on many sports team uniforms). To make brown, mix two complementary colors together.

1. Use an H pencil to sketch out a circle and divide it into six parts.

2. Fill in the primary colors (red, yellow, and blue), leaving a space between each.

3. Once dry, fill in the wedges in between by combining the primary colors to the left and right, creating your secondary colors.

You may find that the secondary colors you create in this exercise aren't as saturated as those that come ready-made in your kit. The ones in your kit have been scientifically formulated to be intensely vibrant orange, purple, and green. When you're mixing with primary colors, they may not be entirely pure, meaning their pigments may not lead to the saturated color that you desire. Depending on the intensity of the color I am after, I may use the secondary color in my kit instead of mixing it myself.

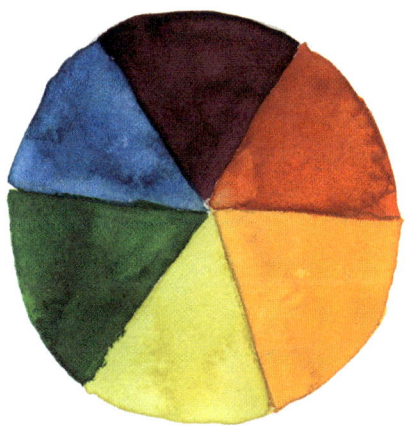

HOT TIP

RENDERING DEPTH WITH COMPLEMENTARY COLORS

Complementary colors are great tools for adding nuance to a watercolor. Once you understand how they are used, you'll regularly spot examples in other artists' work. In my mind, Edward Hopper's *Nighthawks* renders the contrast of fluorescent lighting in a café on a dark street corner. Studying the painting more closely, you'll notice it's a careful power play between red and green.

Because of the high contrast between complementary colors, adding a color's opposite to a painting can reinforce it. If I paint an orange, for example, I can add a little blue to its shadow to make it pop ever so slightly.

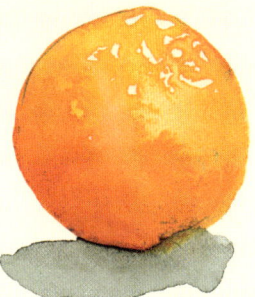

Black-and-white shadow

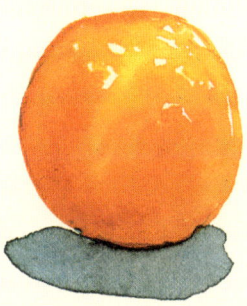

Complementary shadow

WHEEL 3: **TERTIARY COLORS**

Tertiary colors are variations of secondary colors. In the test below, you'll leave a blank wedge in between a primary and a secondary color to create a tertiary color: the mix of the two.

1. Use an H pencil to sketch out a circle and divide it into twelve equal parts.

2. Paint one primary color, move clockwise three sections, then paint the next, so the primary colors are equally spaced.

3. After these have dried completely, mix and paint the secondary colors in the center sections between the primary colors so each color is bordered by white spaces.

4. Once those are dry, fill in the wedges in between by combining the colors to the left and right, creating your tertiary colors: create yellow-green, green-yellow, yellow-orange, orange-red, and so on.

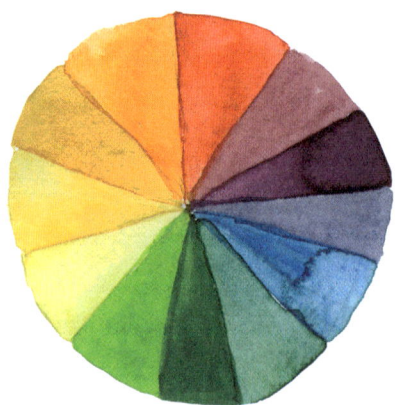

WHEEL 4: **BLACK AND WHITE**

Now it is time to delve into *value*, the relative lightness and darkness of black, white, and everything in between.

1. Use an H pencil to sketch out a circle, divide it into six parts, and fill in the first section with the darkest black you can mix. Let dry completely.

2. Dip your paintbrush in water and add to the black paint on your palette to dilute the color and make a lighter hue.

3. Test the color on scrap paper, then paint in the next section of the circle. Let dry completely.

4. Repeat until the circle is complete from darkest to lightest.

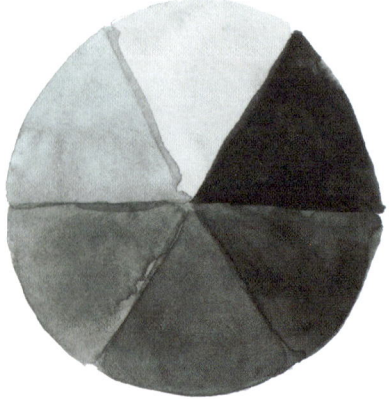

WHEEL 5: **HUE, TINT, TONE, AND SHADE**

Although my work permits me to live in a self-created fantasia, variety is the spice of life. The colors from the previous exercises need to be adapted for a greater range of needs and intensities. This can be done by manipulating hue, tint, tone, and shade.

1. Use an H pencil to sketch out a circle and divide it into twelve equal parts, drawing three concentric circles within.

2. Build your color wheel from the outside in, beginning with the pure colors or *hues*.

3. In the next ring, mix each color with white paint to create a *tint*. (Note, these will be less transparent than colors lightened with water alone.)

4. In the next ring, create a *tone* by adding gray to the pure color to create a dull hue.

5. In the innermost circle, create a *shade* or darker version of the color. There are two ways to do this: the first is to add black, which has the tendency to dull the vibrancy of the color. To achieve a richer, darker color, add a tiny bit of the complementary color instead.

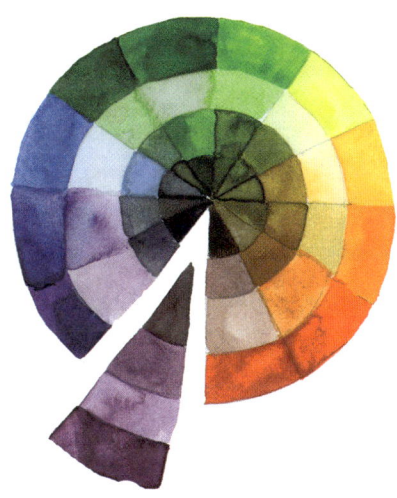

HOT TIP

HOW TO DRY A WATERCOLOR

- **USE A HAIR DRYER.** Lay out your watercolor on a flat surface. Turn on a hair dryer on low heat and hold it about 2 feet (30 cm) above the watercolor. I like to rotate the hair dryer in a circular motion to prevent the pigment from blowing around the paper.

- **ADD HEAT.** If you're lucky enough to have some sunshine, put your watercolor on a windowsill and it'll dry in a jiffy. Or set it on the radiator (I use this technique in my freezing vie bohème artist's studio, where I am already hugging the radiator with one arm and a pot of tea with the other.)

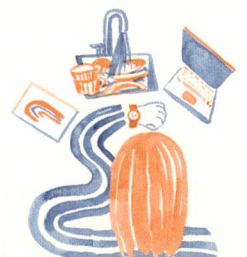

- **BE PATIENT.** Go walk the dog. Do the dishes. Check your email. Come back in 5 to 10 minutes.

Six Color Palettes

The color wheel is a good tool to help determine a color palette before you begin painting. Take inspiration from the following palettes, inspired by the color wheels we created on the previous pages and adapted to the fruit in my kitchen.

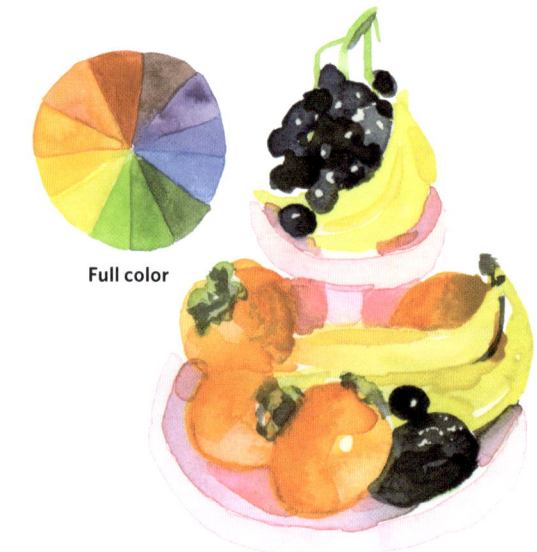

Full color

1. **Full color.** If you're new to watercolor, paint what you see as much as possible. My observational eye inspired this color palette, embracing the whole wheel.

2. **Monochrome.** Subdued and tranquil, this fruit plate uses just one color to a soft and restrained effect. Attention is not focused on any one portion of the fruit in particular.

3. **Complementary.** Choosing two colors on opposite sides of the color wheel yields a high-contrast final result. It draws even more attention to the fruit.

4. **Analogous.** This combination utilizes several neighboring colors on the color wheel. Think of a stunning view of the Atlantic Ocean, one blue merging into the next. This has a soft, calming effect.

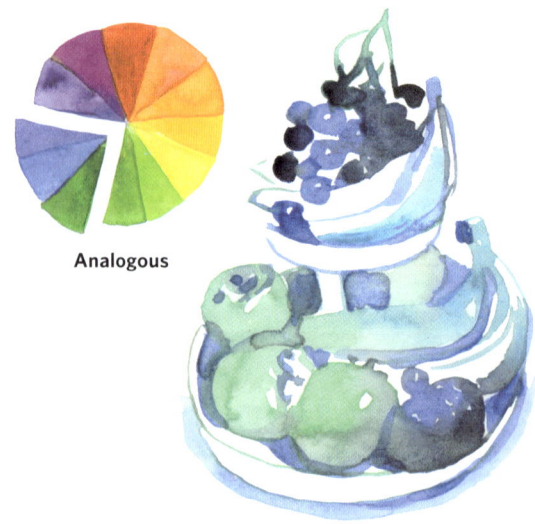

Analogous

5. **Triad.** This combination uses three colors, equally spaced on the color wheel (whether primary colors, as shown here, or secondary or tertiary hues). The palette exudes energy and balance.

6. **Tetradic.** These colors are created by drawing a rectangle on the color wheel to select four different colors. The effect is one of harmony and vibrancy, because there is no single dominant color.

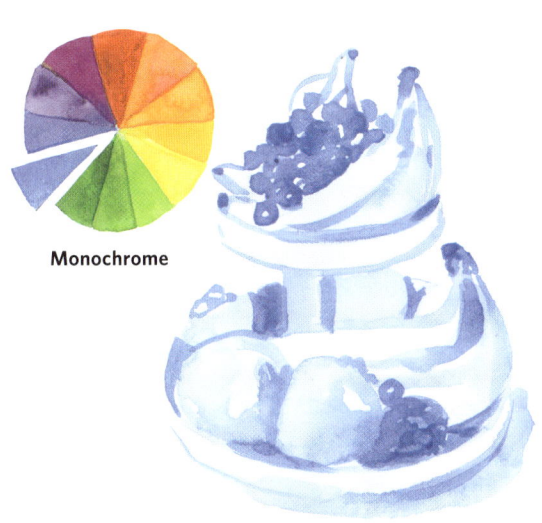

Monochrome

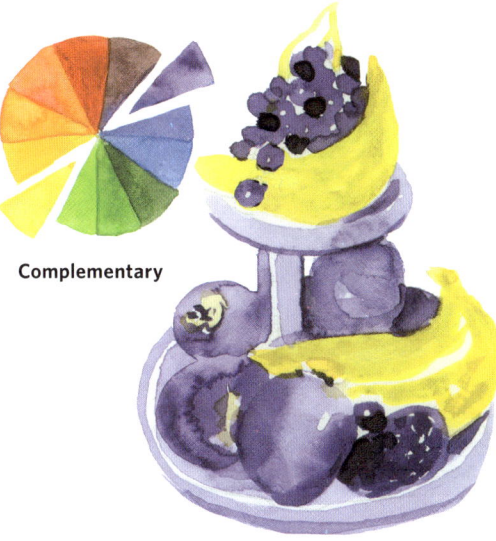

Complementary

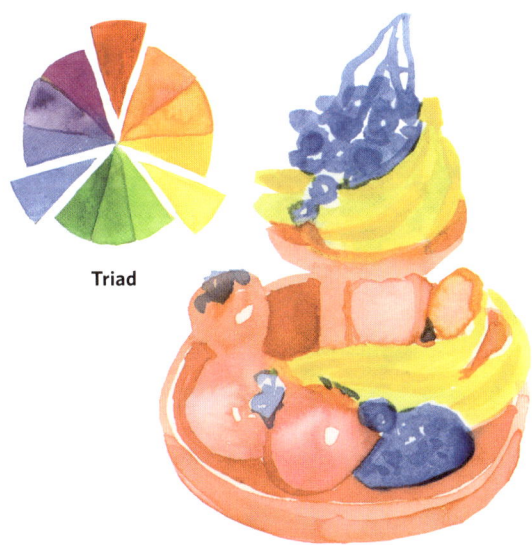

Triad

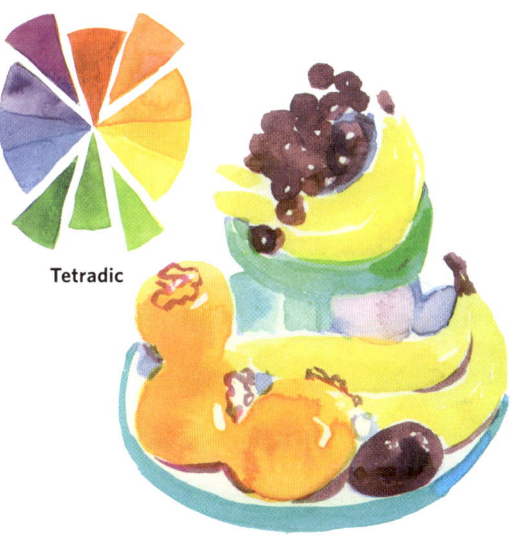

Tetradic

Mixing Colors

It's easy to just assume you know what your world looks like until you have to represent it on paper. Real progress happens when you begin painting what you really see instead of what you think something should look like. The same goes for color: You could easily just paint everything with the colors directly from your kit, but then your work won't be grounded in truth. To move beyond color-by-number-style paintings, really study the colors around you. Even if an orange is indeed orange, notice how it is more yellow the closer it is to the light source. Leaves on a tree aren't just green but are many overlapping shades of yellow, blue, and green in various shades, tints, and tones.

The greater control you have when mixing your colors, the better range your work will have. The following tests will help you understand how primary and secondary colors work and the various ways to manipulate them on paper. Each test begins with three rectangles. Work quickly, as you'll want everything to remain wet while you complete the tests.

In this first color test, you will be mixing primary colors directly on the paper.

1. **Divide each of your rectangles into three equal parts.**

2. **Quickly paint the top squares, from left, in yellow, red, and blue. Paint the bottom squares, from left, in blue, yellow, and red.**

3. **Using a clean, wet paintbrush, connect the top and bottom squares in each rectangle by making upward and downward strokes with your brush to mix the colors and fill in the empty square. You will see that there may be a prominent, dominant darker color.**

4. **Repeat this process for the other two rectangles, rinsing your paintbrush thoroughly between each.**

  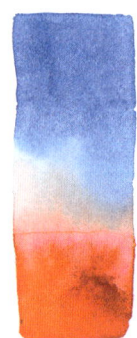

TEST 2: **MERGING PLANES**

This exercise merges two primary colors to mix the secondary colors directly on the paper.

1. Divide each rectangle into halves.

2. Paint the primary colors on the top halves of the rectangles, from left, in yellow, red, and blue.

3. While the colors on the top are still wet, paint the bottom halves, from left, in blue, yellow, and red. Using a clean, wet paintbrush, quickly blend the two primary colors together in the middle of the rectangles. Notice the bleeding that happens when the primary colors meet. Oftentimes the more vibrant color is the most dominant, bleeding into the lighter color. (You may notice water spots in the rightmost example below. This is because I added too much water to the paper—and it will surely happen to you, too. Avoid this by using a smaller brush and dabbing off any excess paint before applying.)

4. Your rectangles should now look like three tiny Rothko paintings.

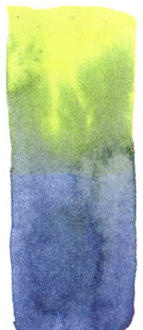 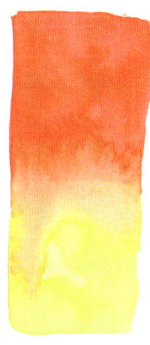 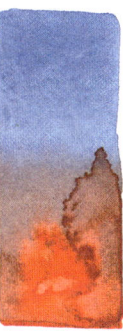

TEST 3: **MIXING & MERGING**

This exercise will challenge you to create a more harmonious transition between two primary colors by creating a secondary color on the palette before applying it.

1. Divide each of your rectangles into three equal parts.

2. Working quickly, paint the top squares, from left, in yellow, red, and blue. Paint the bottom squares, from left, in blue, yellow, and red.

3. Mix the three secondary colors on your palette and apply them in the relevant squares between the primary colors.

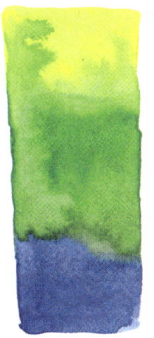  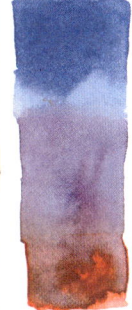

Choosing a Color Palette

Your color choices will influence the tone, energy, and composition of your watercolor. Once you're ready to move past painting from life, there are a few ways to get more intentional about using color to add another angle or emotion to your work.

The color wheel is divided into warm (red, orange, yellow) and cool (green, blue, purple) colors. Warm colors exude earthiness and energy, while cool colors are traditionally calming and serene. If you would like to render a certain emotion, choosing either a warm or cool color palette can reinforce your concept. A pairing of warm and cool tones can also be used to create drama or to highlight a focal point, the portion that draws your eye in at first glance.

Another complexity when it comes to understanding color is that colors have strong connotations, which differ from culture to culture. Is it merely by chance that stop signs and fire trucks are both red? Absolutely not. Red is the first color the human eye sees, so it is used as a warning and to alert you to action. But red has other associations, too. In China, red represents happiness and prosperity, and it is even worn by brides on their wedding days. Understanding the impact of colors can add greater emotion to your watercolors, especially if you are telling emotional stories.

So how do you decide which colors to use in the end? Creating art is all about the micro decisions you make along the way. Assume that nothing happens by chance. Once my sketch is fleshed out, I like to make a few photocopies of it and loosely paint on top to get an idea of how the use of color will impact the overall concept.

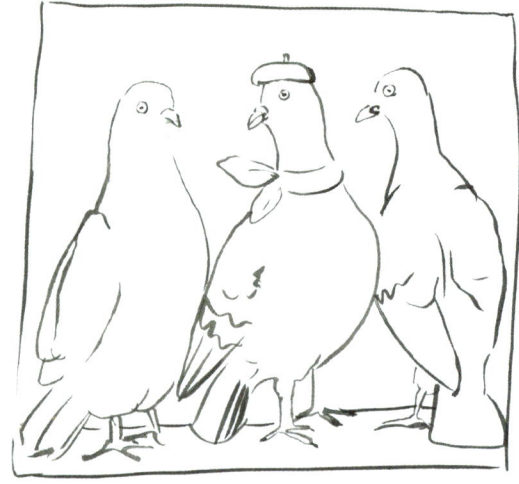

My original sketch.

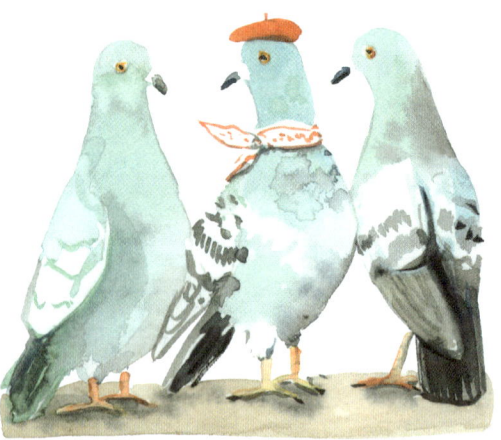

In this version, the red beret and scarf contrast with the cool colors of the pigeon's body, drawing attention first to our "hero" pigeon's face.

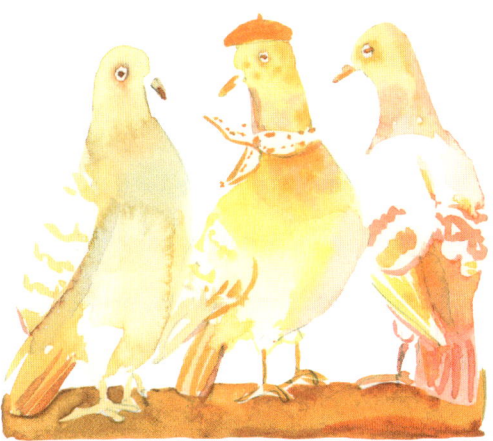

The pigeons painted in warm colors are dynamic and punchy.

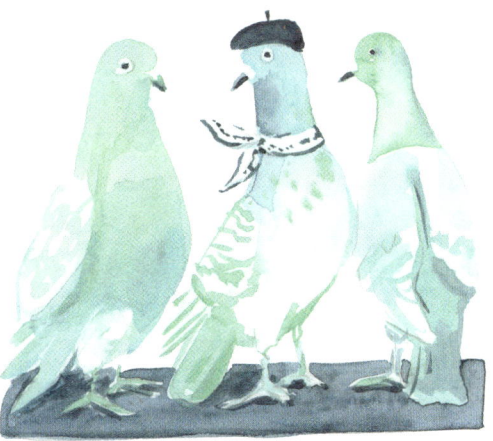

The cooler pigeons are more sober and calm.

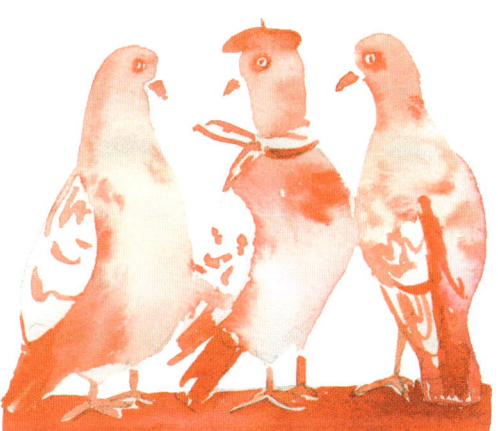

The same scene painted in red is alarming and almost apocalyptic.

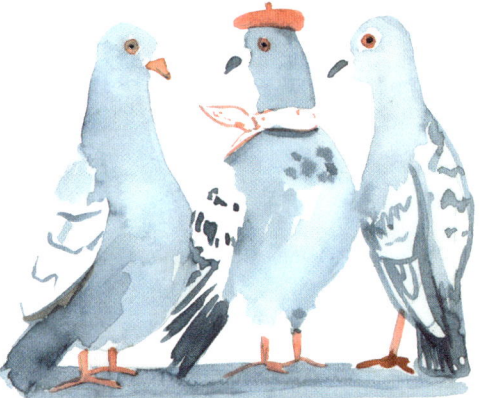

Through this process, I discovered that a combination of red and blue is a perfect choice to reinforce the idea of Parisian pigeons.

WATERCOLOR HOTLINE, HOW MAY I HELP YOU?

Feel like you've got the hang of watercolor? I didn't think so. Here are some common problems and how to troubleshoot them.

Painting Pitfalls

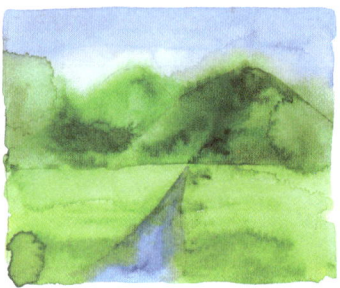

Blurred lines. Are your planes of color merging into a blurry mess? To avoid this, you must wait for each layer to dry before building the next one. When sketching, determine different isolated areas that you can attack individually to expedite the process. Feel free to use a hair dryer on each layer before building the next (see more tips for quickly drying your watercolor on page 27). Dose out color from lightest to darkest to avoid any unsightly color bleeding.

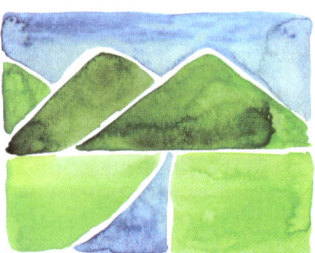

Halo. What's the opposite of blurred lines? Instead of waiting for a layer to dry before adding the next one, you avoid connecting them. What

results is a white outline around each section, which can flatten the composition.

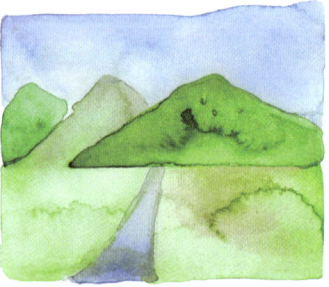

Waterlogging. This is the curse of any novice watercolorist. The colors are dim. The paper is warped. Everything fades into a nondescript softness. Use a smaller brush to eliminate excess water. Invest in better-quality watercolors that have richer pigments. And use heavier paper to give yourself more control.

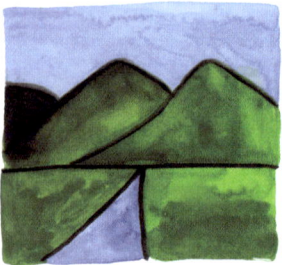

Outline outlaw. If you are new to watercolor, you may be tempted to outline everything in dark black. This is counterproductive to one of watercolor's greatest qualities: its ability to render volume. Instead, create a light pencil outline before putting pigment to paper, and then build up the color, portion by portion. Think about creating the shadow of an object instead of its outline.

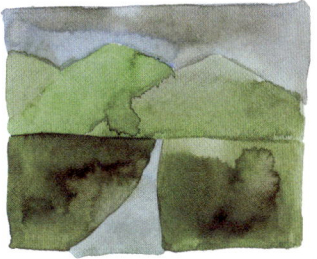

Mud puddle. Remember that all the colors mixed together make brown. Always start with a clean palette and watercolor paints, and clean, transparent water. Systematically rinse your brush clean before moving on to the next color.

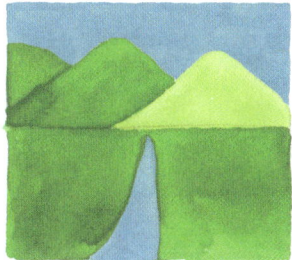

Paint by number. Applying unmixed color directly from the watercolor kit leads to hyper-saturated, obvious color choices, which completely avoids the beauty of watercolor's transparency. Mix, mix, mix (beginning with the exercises on pages 30–31).

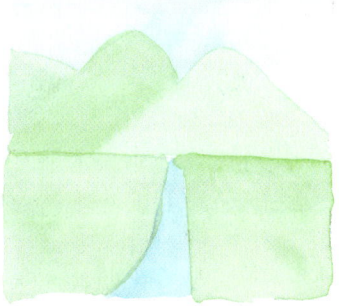

Contrasting opinion. Just because watercolor is a game of transparency doesn't mean you should forget about building contrast. Before you begin, always identify the lightest and darkest portions of the composition and do your best to build depth to avoid a flat and washed-out watercolor.

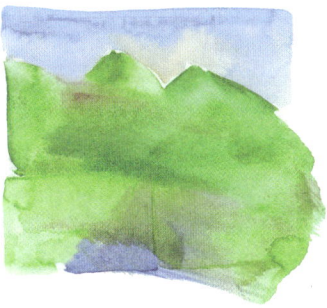

Smear campaign. If you're struggling with ruining your painting with a false stroke of a hand or an unnecessary watercolor splash, tape down your watercolor paper with masking tape or buy a pad of watercolor paper with glued sides (a block). Feel free to frame the white space with paper towels to protect the watercolor paper. Always let each layer dry before applying the next. Fold a paper towel in half and use it to rest your hand on while working to avoid smearing.

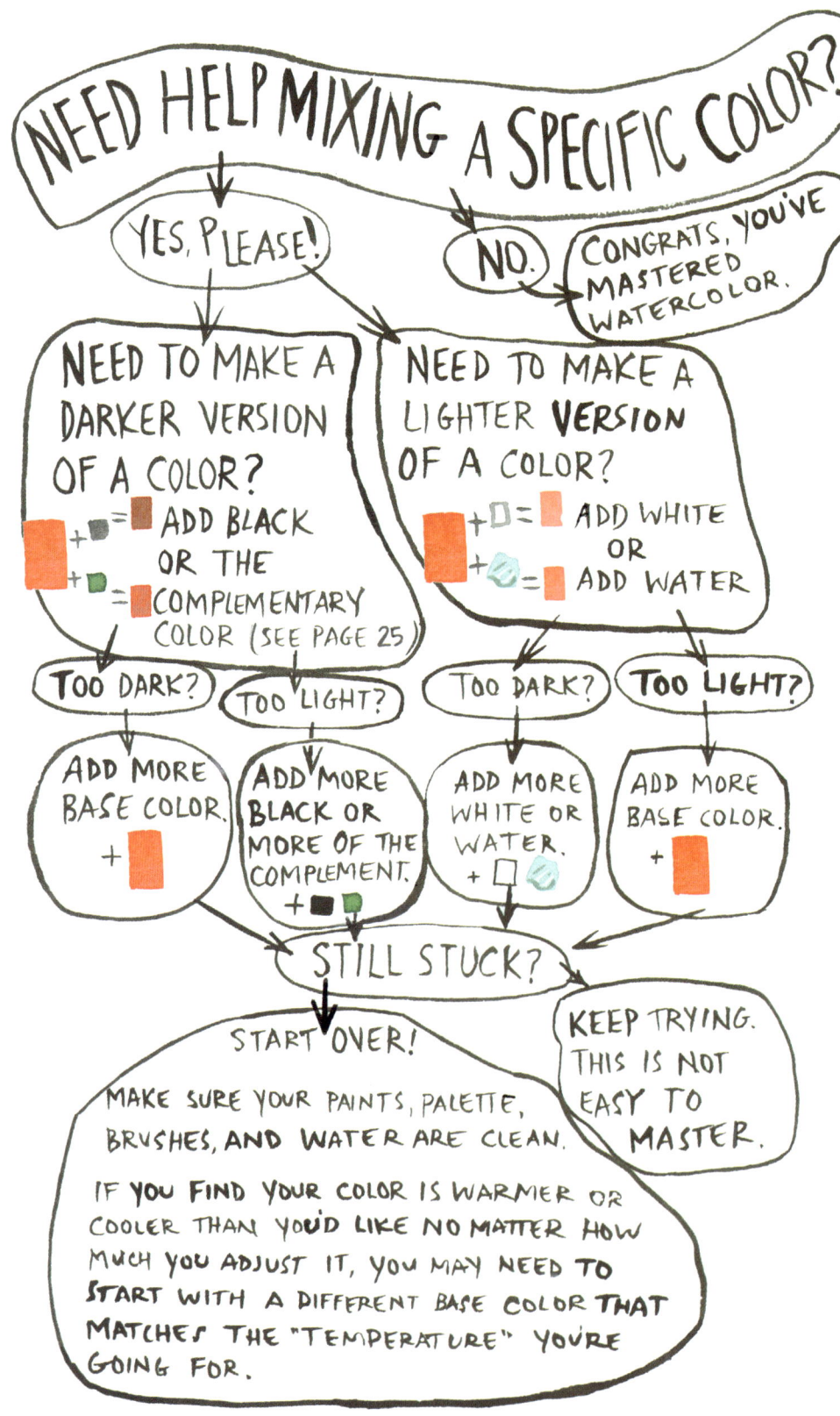

Supplies SOS

Brushes. Is your watercolor brush looking like it's having a bad hair day? Does its fine tip not work like it used to? After cleaning it gently with brush cleaner or a gentle shampoo, swirl it between your pointer and middle fingers to redefine the tip before leaving it to dry either flat on a table or bristle-side up in a cup. If it is not doing what you need it to do, you may need to replace it.

Paint. Is your watercolor painting looking muddy? To get the colors looking like new, use a big wet brush to wet the surface of each hue. Use a paper towel to wipe up any excess pigment until it looks like the color it is supposed to be. Remember that the cleaner the colors are, the easier it will be to mix the hues you want.

Palette. Is your palette caked with fifty nuances of brown? Congrats, you're a true watercolorist. Systematically clean it before it gets to this point. To get out of this brown zone, clean your palette with warm soapy water and a sponge until it is a clean slate.

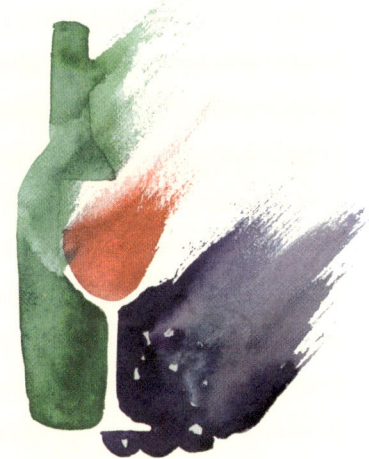

HOT TIP

HOW TO SALVAGE A WATERCOLOR

We've all been there. Nervous jitters take your cup of coffee to the wrong place. The sweep of a hand swipes away hours of meticulous details. Watercolor can't be undone, but here are a few tips to save (or accept) your watercolor.

- **DAB IT.** If your paintbrush accidentally drips on your paper, dab it up as soon as possible with a clean paper towel. It will remove some of the pigment before it permanently stains the paper.

- **WORK IT OUT.** Since watercolor is water soluble, buff it out. Swirl a clean, wet soft brush around the stain to loosen up the pigment. Dab up the water with a clean paper towel and repeat until the stain gets lighter. Use a light touch, as extra friction may rough up the surface of the paper.

- **COLLAGE IT.** This is an easy way to save the pristine portions of your watercolor. If I can salvage what I've done, I'll cut out the good parts and start a new composition on a clean sheet of paper. You may be surprised at how rewarding it can be to move and shift around different components. You can even add a new layer of watercolor on top.

- **SCRAP IT.** It's not easy typing this, but art is inherently wasteful. If a watercolor is not working, you're not going to change your mind about it later.

Brush it off as an experiment and put it aside. Since I paint with heavy-duty 140 lb (300 gsm) watercolor paper, I often reuse paper and paint on its reverse side or use it when I'm doing preliminary tests for a new watercolor technique.

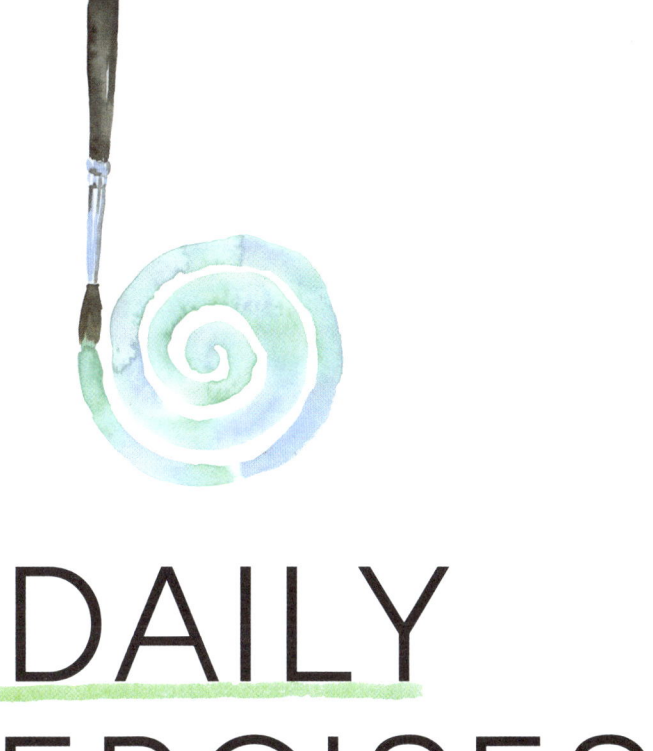

DAILY
EXERCISES

The exercises that follow have been adapted from
my own personal practice and vocabulary. This is
not a prescriptive book with rights and wrongs, and
I don't want you to copy what I do, but to instead
begin where you are. I hope this nonacademic
approach will help you avoid the roadblocks that can
get in the way of creation. I will walk you through
how I understand watercolor, how to conceptualize
complex ideas and digest them into impactful
imagery, and how to share your own story.

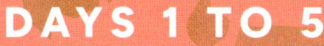

DAYS 1 TO 5

WASHES 101

These first five exercises will reinforce the concepts fleshed out in the Getting Started section and help you to continue refining the interplay between observation and building washes. What's a wash, anyway? It's a transparent layer of watercolor that covers the surface of the paper. This chapter is dedicated to the many nuances of washes: saving the white space, defining textures, identifying colors that speak to you, and building layers.

DAY 1

SAVE THE WHITE SPACE

Since watercolor paint is inherently transparent, it is always in collaboration with the paper itself. The secret to watercolor and one of the most difficult things to achieve is understanding the relationship between preserving the white space of the paper and controlling the transparency of the paint you apply on top. This exercise is adapted from a classic art school assignment (typically done in charcoal): rendering a still life beginning with just three tones (white, black, and gray). The goal here is to identify and reserve the white space of the paper and build a three-tone watercolor. Other skills this exercise will fine-tune are applying washes evenly and identifying water-control issues.

BRAINSTORM

To begin, set up a few objects on a tabletop, arranging them artfully together so there is an interesting balance of positive and negative space.

Ask yourself where the light is coming from: a window? An overhead lamp? Or is light coming in from many directions? Look for the highlights, or where the surface of the object is reflecting the light. How does each object reflect or absorb the light differently?

STEP 2
SKETCH

Sketch out the composition lightly with an H pencil. Outline the white space with a pencil line (shown in red in the image at right). This is what will stay white once the paper is painted. If you're using drawing gum (see page 15), dip your paintbrush into the product and paint the surface area that you want to mask from the watercolor paint. Let the drawing gum dry completely before applying the first watercolor layer.

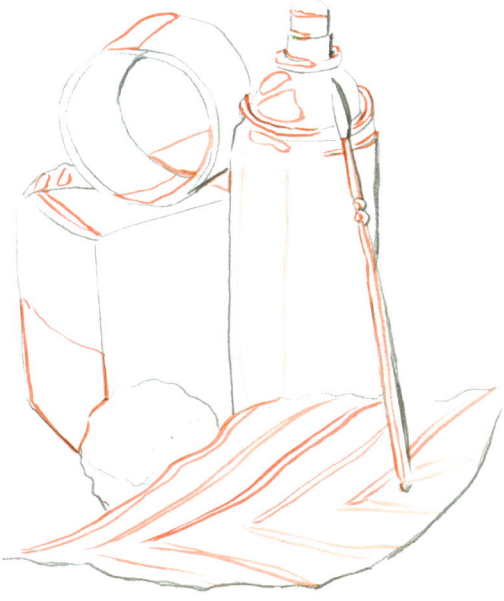

PAINT LAYER 1

Using a large round brush to cover greater surface area, dilute black watercolor to create a wash of what I'll call a 50% gray, halfway between black and white. Dab off your paintbrush lightly on a paper towel before applying it to the paper. Paint everything that is not the white space marked off in the previous step, diligently adding more paint to the paintbrush as needed and creating a uniform layer of wash. If your paint has a scratchy effect, try using a larger brush and applying more paint. If the surface of the paper is pooling with water, try using a slightly smaller brush and lightly dab off the paint on a paper towel before applying. Let this layer dry completely. If using drawing gum, gently rub it off with your fingertips until you can see the white paper underneath.

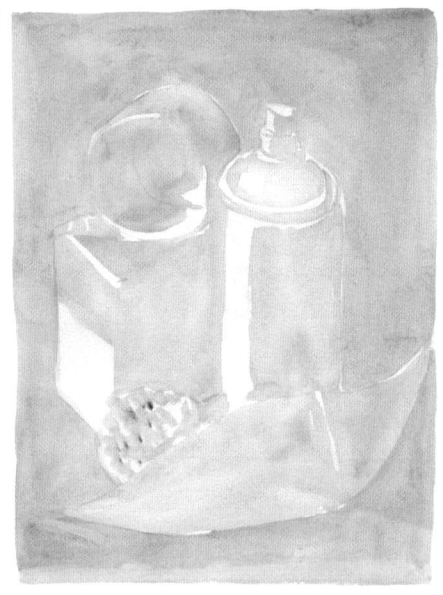

PAINT LAYER 2

Now identify the darkest portions of the composition, painting them with black paint using a small round brush for more controlled application. Can you already see how you get such a sense of volume with three simple tones? Congratulations! You've managed to execute one of the most difficult first steps of understanding watercolor: saving the white space.

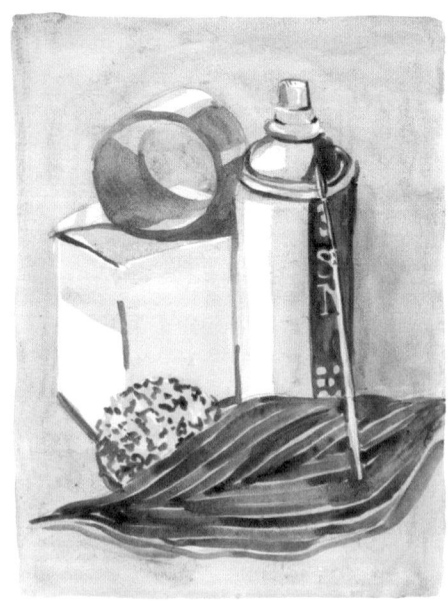

STEP 5

REFLECT

Were you able to preserve the white space on the paper? If not, be diligent about identifying and sketching those areas before painting or mask them off with drawing gum. How do your washes look? Are they even in texture, or do they have water marks? If you have uneven coverage or water marks, you may need to consider using a smaller paintbrush to avoid waterlogging your watercolor. If your wash is still looking opaque and scratchy in texture, add some more water to your paint. Repeat this exercise as needed until you feel confident you've mastered these techniques.

HOT TIP

HOW TO KNOW WHEN TO STOP PAINTING

Masterful watercolorists make their work look effortless. A master's work isn't just about the application and manipulation of color—it's also knowing when to stop. If you're unsure whether you've taken your painting to the dark side, here are a few tips to help you decide if you should stop, add more, or scrap it completely.

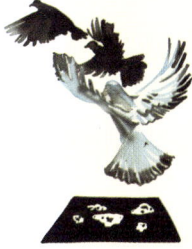

Step away. If you're deep in the creative process, your eyes may stop seeing. Step away for a short time. Check your email. Water the plants. Let a few days go by. Take your painting outside to look at it in natural light. Ask yourself what it's missing. Is the focal point obvious enough? Is the action or concept understandable?

This one is a little bit kooky, but look at the painting upside down. Is it still visually appealing removed from its original context? Are the colors vibrant enough?

Although you may not have the intention of sharing your watercolor on social media, snap a pic or scan it. Then observe it as a thumbnail on your phone. Can you still "read" the concept even if it's tiny? Does it need to be more graphic or colorful to be impactful?

Ask a friend what they think of your painting. Is the concept distinguishable to the untrained eye?

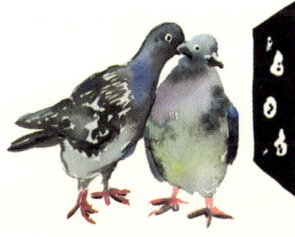

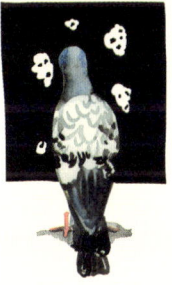

If your painting is overdone and muddy, there's only so much an extra watercolor wash or a Photoshop facelift can do. You may need to recycle it and call it a day. Not every master's work makes it into a museum. Write it off as a learning experience and move on to what's next. Could you cut out the strongest elements and regroup them together as a collage?

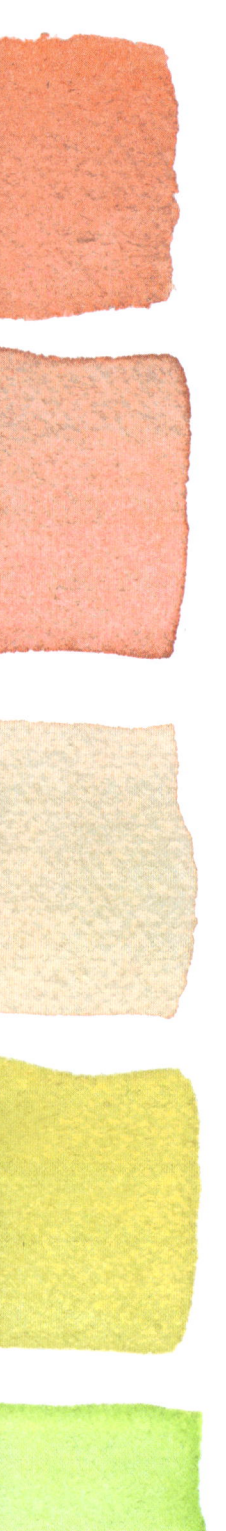

DAY 2

DRAWING FROM LIFE

Much like with any long-term art practice, before you can break the rules for watercolor, you need to learn the basics. There's a reason art students are bombarded with still life observational assignments: Working from real life, rather than a reference photo, requires greater engagement with what you're painting. You have to adapt to the nuances of what's in front of you, rather than relying on what you *think* something looks like. I like to say that when you are painting from life, you have the luxury of having the primary reference in front of you. All the information is there, but you have to be intentional about really seeing it. This exercise maps out how to pragmatically analyze your subject matter and break it down into actionable steps. You'll also learn how to re-create texture using watercolor.

STEP 1

BRAINSTORM

Go into your fridge and pull out a fruit or vegetable. Set it on a table in a room with natural light and study it for 2 to 3 minutes, asking yourself the following questions:

- Where is the light coming from? What are the lightest and darkest spots? Where will you save the white space, if anywhere?
- If you squint, how do you see it differently?
- Study the transition of color from where the fruit or vegetable touches the table to where it reflects the light. Do the colors change when closer to the light source? For example, if you are painting an apple like the one below, is it simply red or does it transition from red to yellow to green? How does it either reflect or absorb the light?

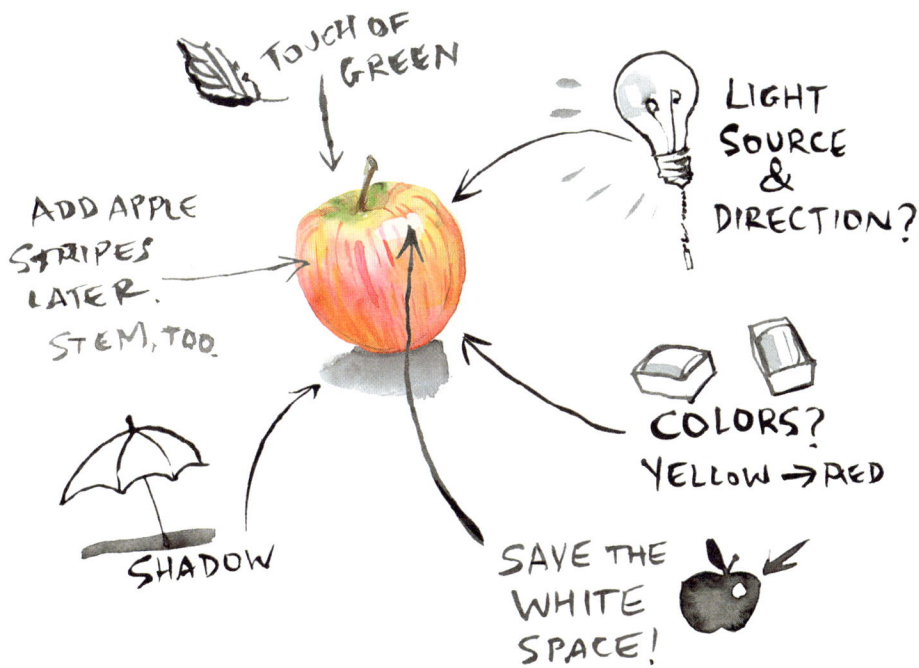

TOUCH OF GREEN

LIGHT SOURCE & DIRECTION?

ADD APPLE STRIPES LATER. STEM, TOO.

COLORS? YELLOW → RED

SHADOW

SAVE THE WHITE SPACE!

STEP 2
SKETCH

Sketch out the fruit or vegetable lightly in H pencil on watercolor paper, mapping out the white space to avoid when painting later.

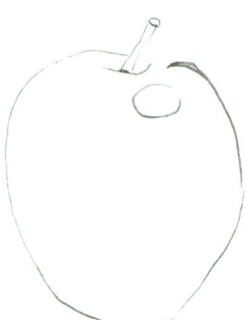

STEP 3
PAINT LAYER 1

Take out your paint and activate your watercolors. Dip your paintbrush in water and dab it off lightly on a paper towel before applying it to the paper to lightly dampen the surface area within the sketch. (This is what I call the 50% flood—see page 21 for more on this technique.) Notice in **(A)** how I wet everything except the circle in the upper-right-hand corner, which is the reflection of the light.

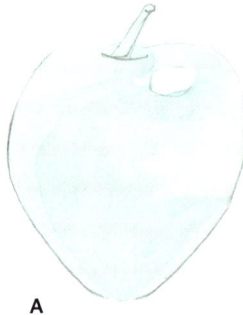

A

When the paper is activated or wet, it's time to start building the colors **(B)**. To paint my apple, I mix a yellow-green wash and apply it to the top, noticing how the wet surface automatically pulls the color downward and taking care to save the white space. I mix a red wash and apply it to the bottom of the apple, working the color upward with the side of my brush until the two colors merge.

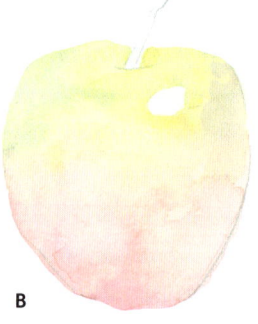

B

While the surface of the apple is wet, I create a greater sense of volume **(C)**. I add darker red stripes on the bottom of the apple. Notice how the wetness of the paper will diffuse the color. I mix a green wash to layer on the upper portion of the apple to represent the concave top and paint a darker brown for the stem.

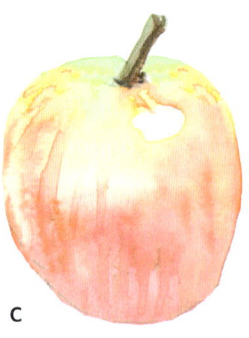

C

STEP 4

PAINT LAYER 2

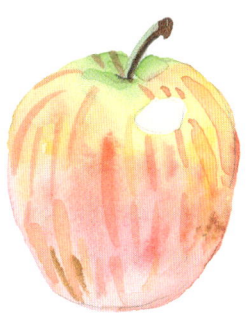

After the base layer has dried completely, I go back and add more confident red stripes, applying the paint dry on dry to suggest the texture of the apple's skin. I add a darker green around the stem to create contrast.

STEP 5

REFLECT

Did you save enough white space? Are your colors as vibrant as you want them to be? Were you too impatient to let each layer dry completely before adding the next? Are you obtaining a good range, comparing washes and darker, more saturated colors? Are you able to authentically represent your subject matter? These early exercises are just to document your evolving understanding of watercolor. If your paintings aren't frameable yet, give yourself the grace to know you are simply doing the work to fine-tune your skills. And that is enough.

The Elements of Design

The elements of design below are the building blocks of constructing a composition in a piece of artwork. Developing a visual vocabulary is not only an entry point into understanding what you see but also a tool to assess whether you are communicating effectively. If you are evaluating the success of a watercolor, go down this list and ask yourself how you did with each element and what you can do to improve. The better you can articulate the structure of your watercolor, the stronger your work will be.

- **Line** is what connects two points and identifies a form by outlining it.

- **Shape** is a two-dimensional geometric or non-geometric form (think circles, squares, triangles, diamonds, trapezoids, etc.).

- **Form** is the three-dimensional perception of a shape (e.g., cube, cylinder, sphere, cone), which is usually achieved using shading or a suggestion of variation between light and dark.

- **Space** is the relationship between different shapes or forms. This can also include the relationship between positive and negative space. For example, if you look at yourself in the mirror and put your hands on your hips, the space between your arms is the negative space. The rest of your body is the positive space.

- **Color** is the perceived hue of something, depending on how the light is reflected or absorbed.

- **Value** is the measure of lightness or darkness when the hue is constant.

- **Texture** is the apparent roughness or smoothness on the surface of a form or shape.

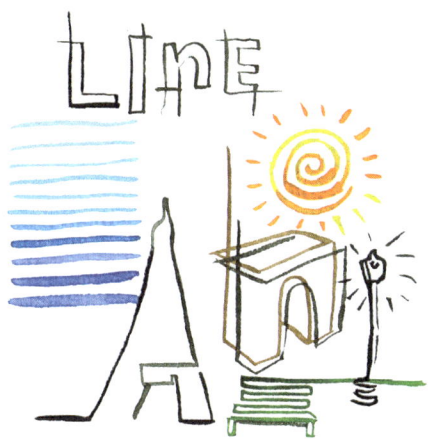

LINE

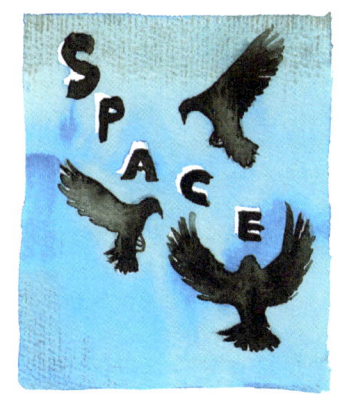

SPACE

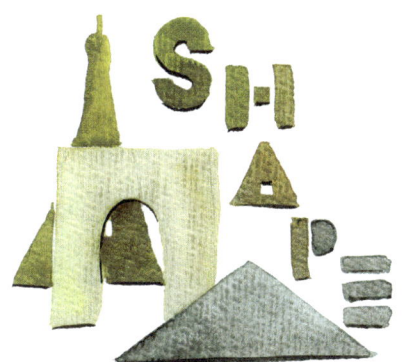

SHAPE

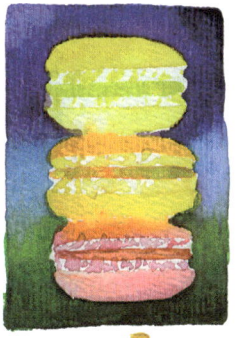

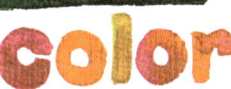

color

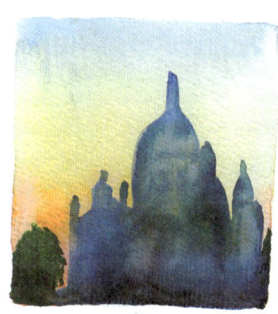

value

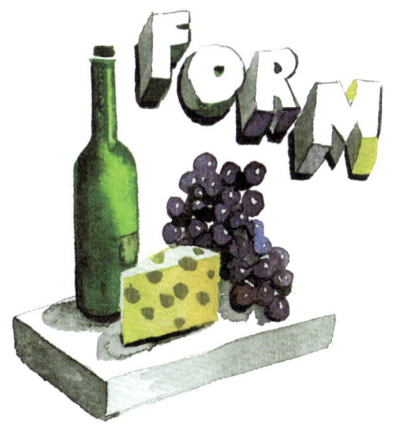

FORM

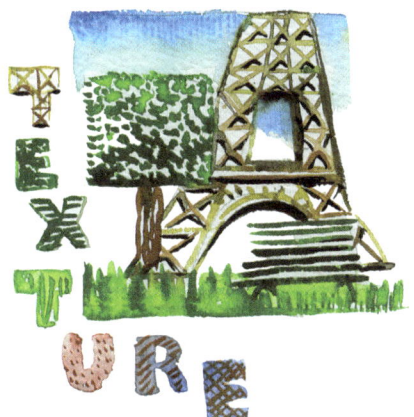

TEXTURE

DAY 3

STILL LIFE LAYERS

There is no one-size-fits-all technique for building layers and achieving color in watercolor painting. This exercise will have you layering various techniques to render and differentiate three unique objects. Always take a moment to strategically break down what you see before you commit to putting your paintbrush to paper.

BRAINSTORM

Find three items in your home and arrange them on your worktable. Ideally they should be different materials and textures to create the greatest possible contrast. Here I assembled a shiny black pepper mill, a ceramic pitcher, and half of an apple. Before I begin, I always look at my subject through squinted eyes to understand the lightest and darkest portions of the still life. The darkest part of this still life is the pepper mill. And the lightest portions are the upper-right-hand corners of each object, where they reflect the light.

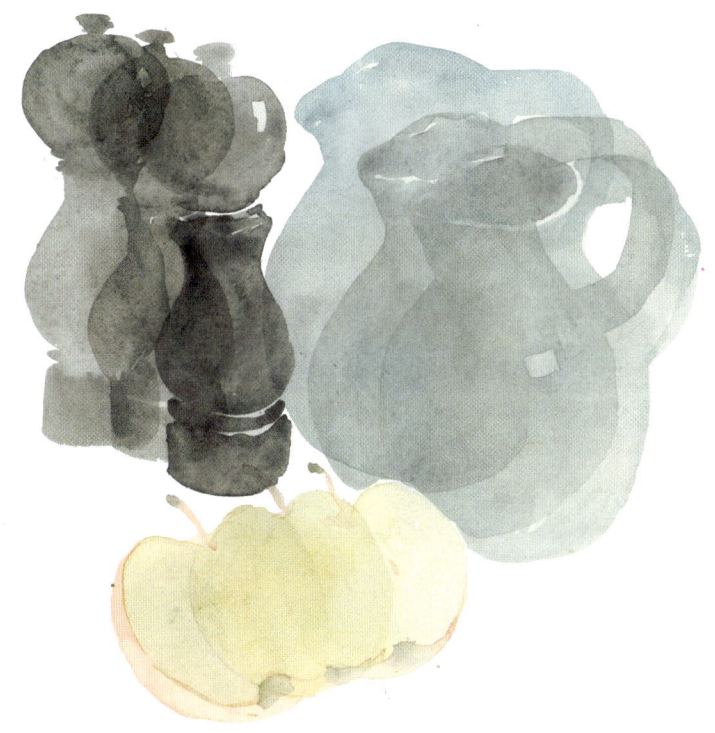

SKETCH

Sketch out the items lightly with an H pencil on watercolor paper. To save the white space, be sure to draw a line around the highlights that you will avoid painting later or paint the desired surface area with drawing gum.

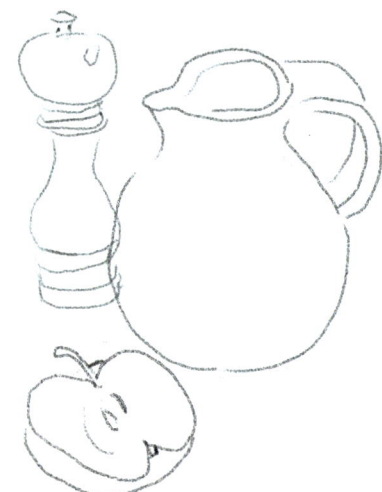

PAINT LAYER 1

Because each object is different, each one will get a different treatment to develop texture and create contrast. Since the pepper mill is black, I commit to going straight ahead with the darkest black I can mix. Using the wet-on-dry technique, I apply the paint to the top sphere of the pepper mill, being sure to save the white space. While the layer is still wet, I add more black paint to my brush and paint the right side of the sphere to create volume. I work my way downward on the pepper mill, rendering out section by section, form by form. If I need more shadow, I add less water to the black of my watercolor kit to obtain a darker hue.

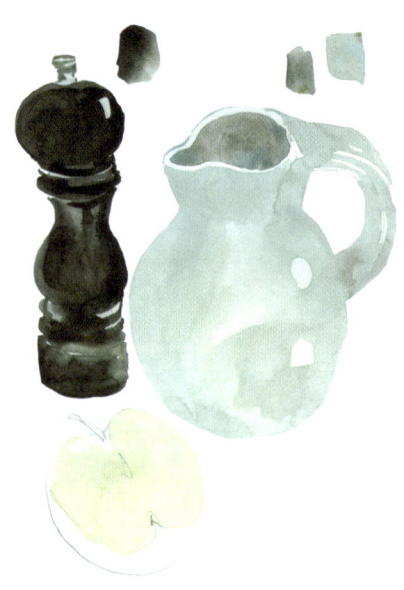

To paint the pitcher, I activate the surface area to prepare for 50% flood, being sure not to wet the area I am saving as white space. I mix a blue-gray paint and apply it where I notice shadows, on the bottom half and on the handle (the wet paper pulls the color). While the first layer is still wet, I darken the blue-gray by adding a little bit of black paint, and then I paint inside the pitcher and on the top and bottom of the handle.

I mix a light yellow wash and apply it to the surface of the apple's flesh using the wet-on-dry technique.

STEP 4
PAINT LAYER 2

Once the first layer is dry, I build a second layer of washes to create a better sense of depth and volume on the pepper mill.

On the pitcher, I do another layer of 50% flood and paint on another wash of blue-gray, working the pigment upward. I also define the lip of the handle and the upper spout portion with a darker wash.

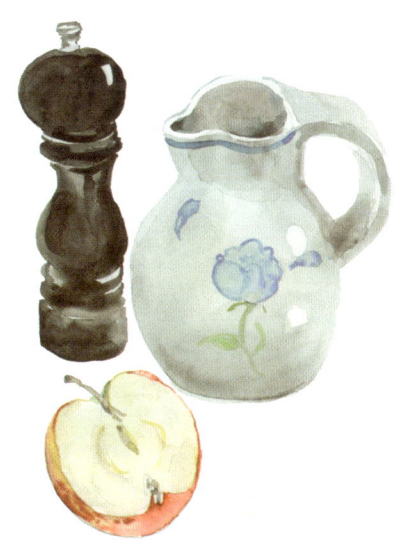

I paint the area of the apple skin with a yellow wash wet on dry. I apply red watercolor to the tip of my brush and build it from the bottom right up to mix itself up the page until it reaches the yellow wash to merge the colors. I let it dry slightly until it is barely wet. Applying a dark, concentrated red on the tip of my paintbrush, I dot it along the surface of the apple skin to create the stippled texture (see page 22). To suggest the core and seeds of the apple, I mix a light brown wash and apply it wet on dry.

STEP 5
PAINT LAYER 3

I add all the fine details, like the floral motif on the vase and some contrasting, darker colors on the stem of the apple, dry on dry, until I am happy with the final result.

STEP 6
REFLECT

Can you see how dosing out the layers and being intentional about transparency and building details can lead to some beautiful, nuanced watercolor painting?

DAY 4

A LAYERED LANDSCAPE

Painting a landscape is an interesting experiment in creating depth, perspective, variety, and texture by building layers of different levels of transparency. Whenever I sit down to paint a landscape, I am intimidated by how many details I *could* paint. If you were to attempt to render every leaf and branch, you might as well not even begin. Instead of getting lost in the infinite amount of information you could paint, concentrate on shape and texture, rather than detail. Realism isn't the ultimate goal. If you cannot say it all, think about how you can *suggest* it instead.

BRAINSTORM

Find a photo of a landscape that you love (if you have a stunning view from the comfort of your own home, even better). Since this is a study in layers, your landscape should include sky, water, some vegetation, and an identifiable horizon line (where the sky meets the ground).

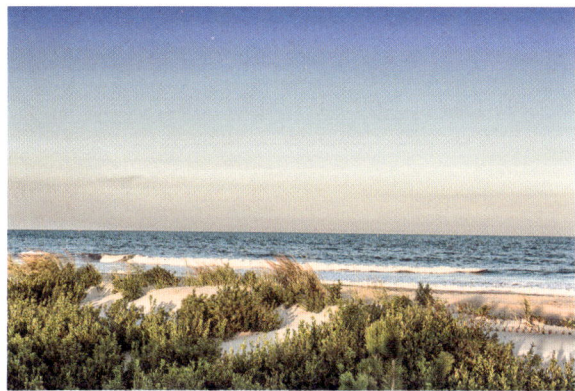

STEP 2
SKETCH

Observe your landscape and ask yourself how you will break it down into individual layers. Sketch them out lightly in pencil. I also sketch where I want to save the white space, to re-create where the waves hit the beach.

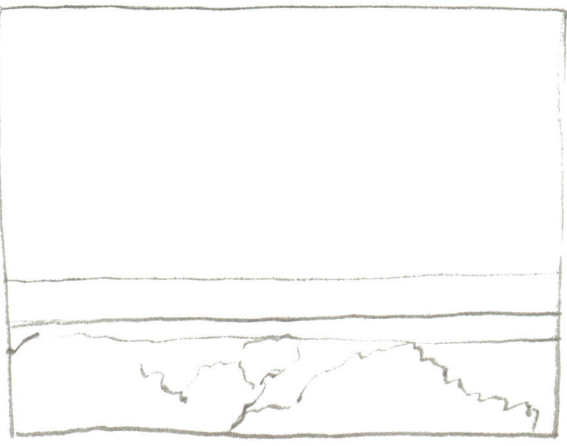

PAINT

Consider which technique to use for each section. Think about creating contrast in texture; for example, compare a dry brush to a 50% flood wash. Can the colors in your landscape be re-created with the existing hues in your watercolor set, or do they need to be customized and mixed?

Apply the first layer in the technique of your choosing. While the first layer of wash is still wet, consider adding pigment on top before it dries completely, to take advantage of how the colors can merge and blend on the paper while still damp; this is when a lot of interesting spreading and pulling can happen.

In my coastal scene, I begin with the sky layer **(A)**, lightly dampening the surface area (50% flood), loading up my round brush with blue, and painting a stripe on the top third of the rectangle with the side of the brush. You will see how the pigment travels downward. While the layer is still lightly damp, I paint the very bottom with a pink-beige.

For the water layer **(B)**, I paint the surface with a blue wash and build some texture on top by adding darker blue horizontal lines.

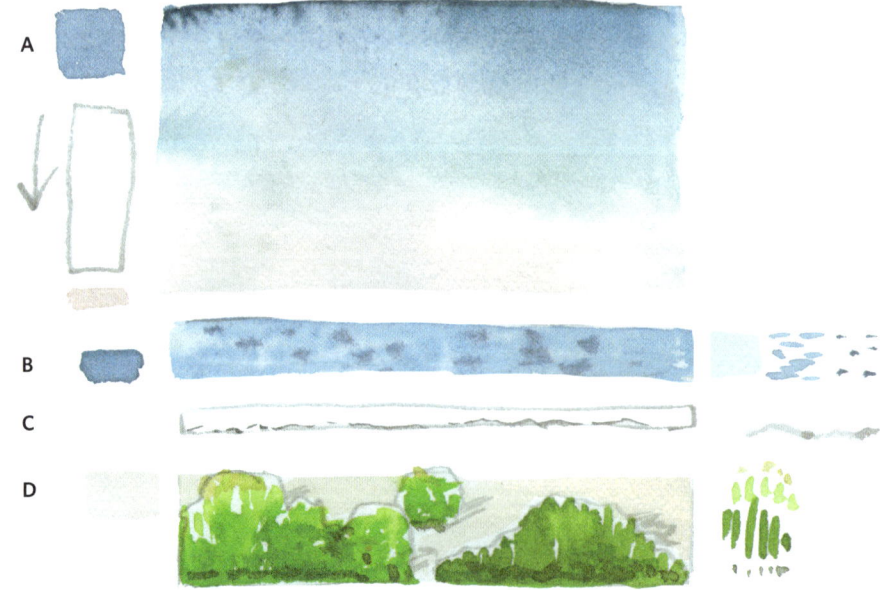

I keep the white of the paper to represent the waves **(C)**, but add an irregular gray line to create contrast between the sea and shore.

The beach **(D)** gets a warm beige wash. Once it dries completely, I build a stippled pattern with yellow and several hues of green to represent the vegetation closest to us.

Once the landscape has completely dried, ask yourself if it needs any contrast or shadow. In this case, I add some shadows on the beach and some dark green stipples at the bottom of the plants.

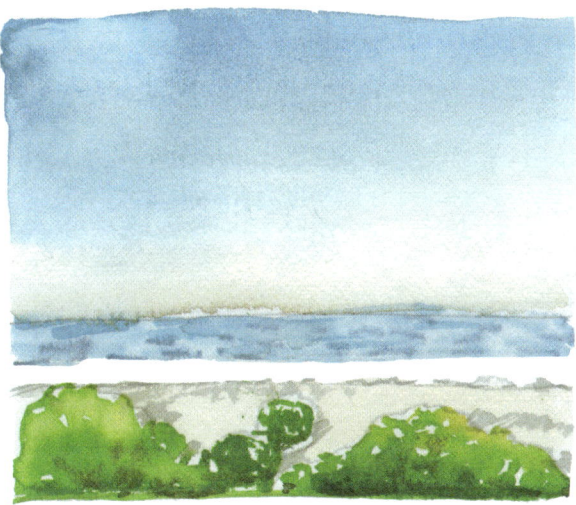

STEP 4
REFLECT

One of things I still find difficult when painting landscapes is breaking down the perspective and rendering each section accordingly (for more on perspective, see page 66). If you can't tell which layer is closest to you and which is farthest away, you may need to continue building the contrast by adding darker colors or more detailed renderings for whatever is closest.

(for more on perspective, see page 66)

HOT TIP

PAINTING BACKGROUNDS

It took me many years to figure out how to avoid uneven, spotty, or too-tame background washes. Here are a few tips on how to get an even background that doesn't compete with what is front and center.

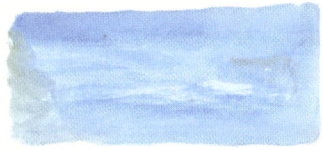

- If your background looks scratchy, you are probably using the wrong brush. Opt for a large round brush to ensure a smooth, even application.

- If you are using cheaper, wood-based paper, water won't absorb quickly and instead will pool on the surface, which can lead to water spots and blooms.

- Be sure to mix more color than you think you will need before applying so you don't run out and need to mix more from scratch. It could lead to inconsistencies in color and texture.

DAY 5

IN ALL TRANSPARENCY

I am always on the hunt to see watercolor paintings in museums and galleries because they are exceedingly rare, siloed more into the preparatory sketch phase before an artist starts painting in oil or acrylic. I was strolling through the Drawing Now Art Fair in Paris when I stumbled upon a watercolor, *Black Watercolor (ref.607) 2014*, by German sculptor and artist Joachim Bandau. At first glance, it looked almost like an X-ray of overlapping silk chiffon scarves. Taking a closer look, I realized that it was overlapping watercolor rectangles, meticulously layered until they morphed into a black hole that brought my eye into the center of the composition.

Painting things as you see them is a wonderful way to learn, but today we are going to try out something a little bit more abstract by overlapping layers of the same shape. The goals of this exercise are to build layers in a less literal way to develop a visual concept and approach color by layering transparency.

BRAINSTORM

What I love about Bandau's painting is the watercolor edge that is almost like a soft outline of the form. Find a shape or a symbol that you would like to overlap and repeat. It could be a geometric shape, a house—whatever comes to mind. Ask yourself how the overlapping will create depth in layering the color. I'm going to draw a loosely inspired silhouette of my head with an empty window to my mind.

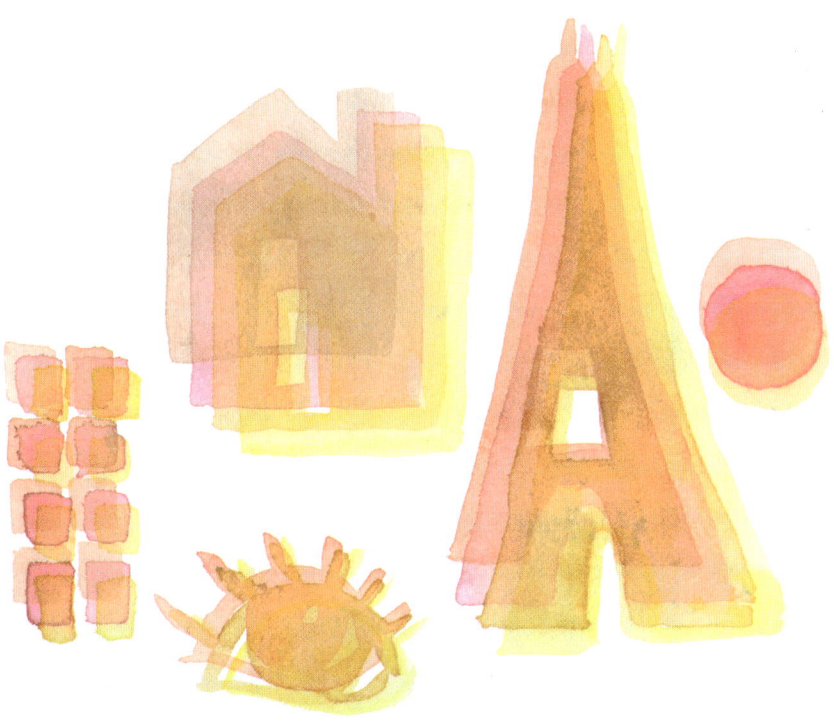

SKETCH

Lightly sketch out the shape, asking yourself how you will overlap it to create interest in your watercolor. Maybe you'll arrange the shapes in a row, group them in some other fashion, or even create ever-smaller versions, one on top of the other.

Ask yourself how you can use color to create transitions. Do your layers go from lightest to darkest? I overlapped similar pink/orange hues, but feel free to use some of the principles of color theory described on pages 24–33 to play around with different combinations.

In the spirit of Joachim Bandau's watercolor, it's essential to keep the form as regular as possible to create harmony in the final painting. This test revealed that my heads don't look consistent enough to be the same person, so I decided to sketch out my silhouette on paper and cut it out to create a template. I also decided that while I like that my sketch looks like I could thread a needle to connect the four heads, in my final watercolor, I want to overlap the head shape to draw attention to the window of my mind. I begin again, lightly tracing the first layer on watercolor paper and marking off the white space to create the window.

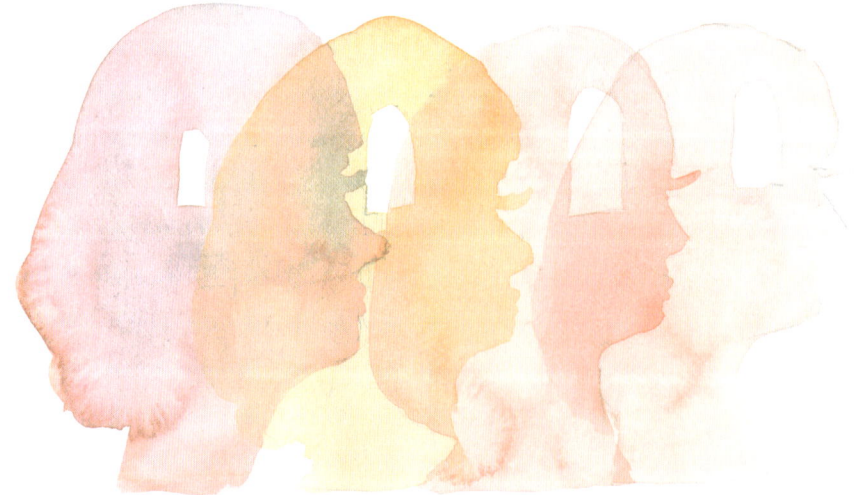

STEP 3
PAINT

I mix a light pink wash and apply it to the surface of the first silhouette using a large round brush. You can see that when the pigment dries, it leaves a light line around the first silhouette. This is the ultimate game of patience, letting each layer dry completely before building the next, but I expedite the process with a hair dryer (see page 27).

I lightly sketch out the next layer using the template, mix a slightly darker shade of pink, and continue layering. I let each layer dry before adding the next, making sure not to paint the window shape, which will remain white.

You'll be surprised by how much nuance can be created by using a variety of washes and one simple shape—I add more yellow to some of the layers to add visual interest.

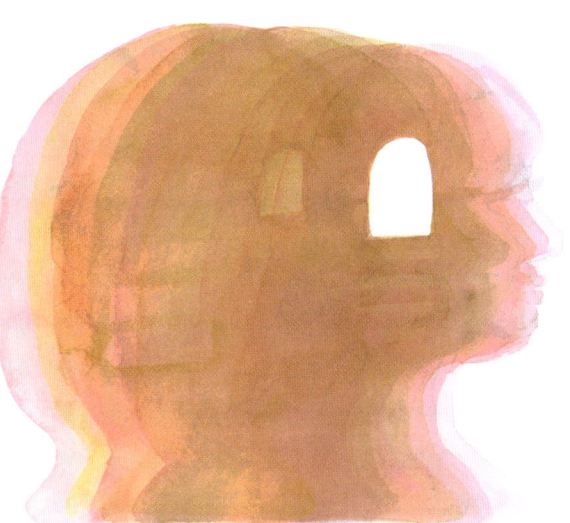

STEP 4
REFLECT

This exercise helps you understand how layers of transparency can be used to create a form, with enough time and patience. Were you able to create distinct objects while also creating a harmony with the colors?

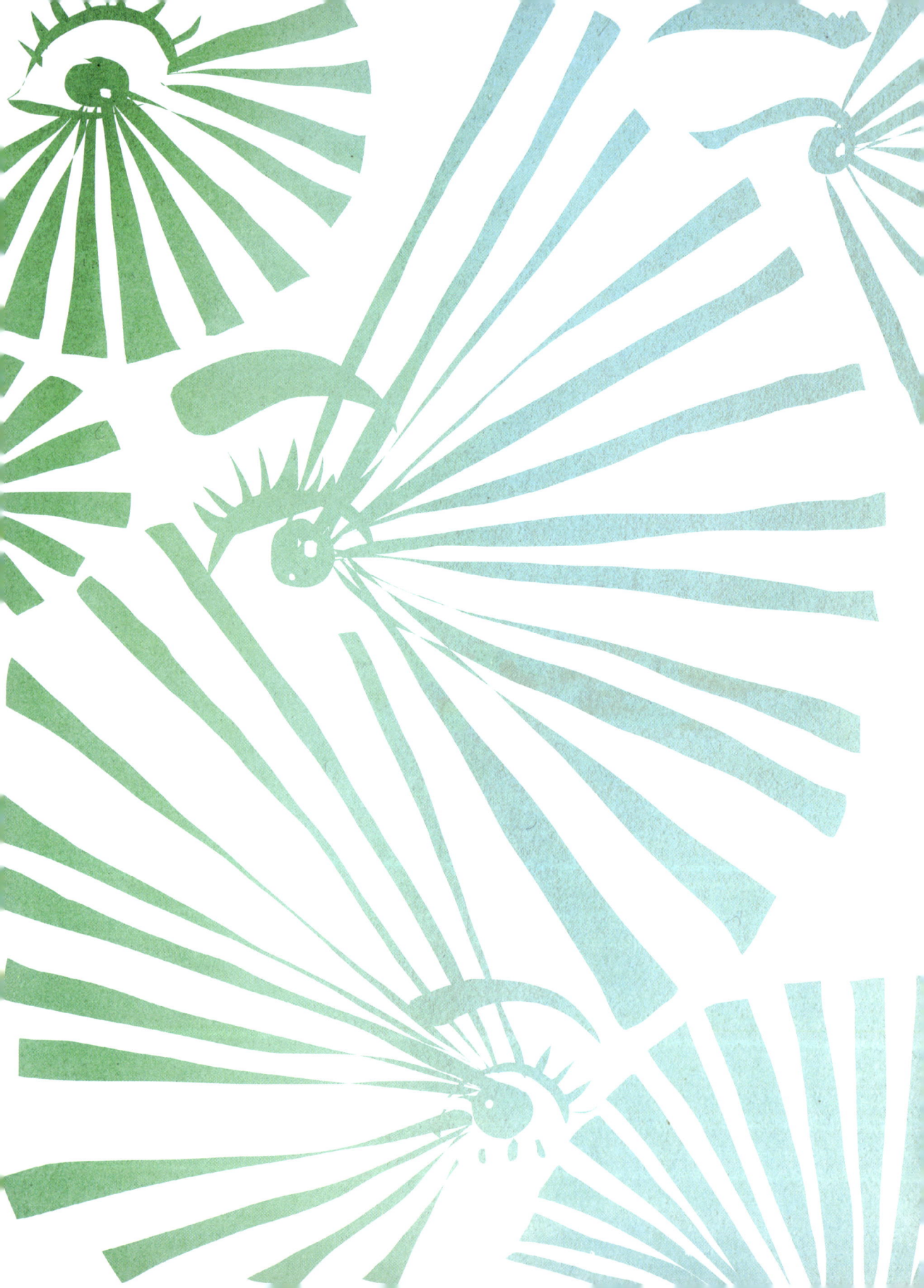

DRAWING IS SEEING, SEEING IS PAINTING

Drawing with ease is the foundation of any art practice and important to master before moving on to more conceptual work. In fact, I often use the words *drawing* and *painting* interchangeably. These next five days of exercises will loosen up your technique and acquaint you with the many possibilities that drawing with a paintbrush can reveal. We will also touch on essential concepts like perspective, line weight, and how to capture likeness.

Perspective 101

To get the most out of the drawing exercises on the following pages, you'll want to know the basics of perspective. Understanding and implementing a few rules will take your watercolor from flat and cartoonish to something dimensional and true to life.

ONE-POINT PERSPECTIVE

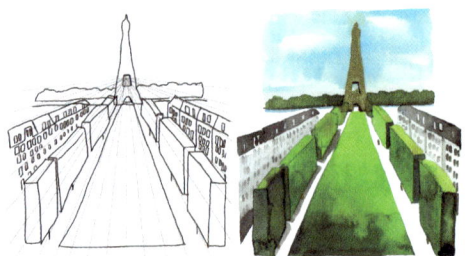

TWO-POINT PERSPECTIVE

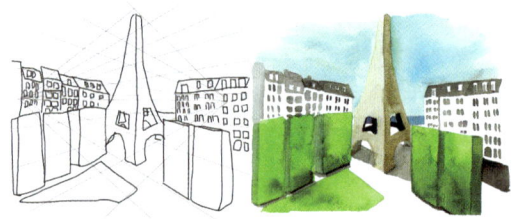

This is the simplest form of perspective. Imagine you are walking straight down the middle of a highway, looking into the horizon. Everything looks smaller the closer it gets to the vanishing point (a designated point on the horizon line). To re-create one-point perspective like in the illustration above, draw a horizontal line on a piece of paper. Mark a dot on the horizon line. Imagine that dot is the sun. Now draw the sun's rays extending out of the dot in all directions below the horizontal line; this will create the grid you'll use to establish the perspective. When you begin adding trees and buildings, follow the sunlike lines to make sure that each element gets smaller as it gets closer to the vanishing point. The trees' and buildings' vertical lines should stay parallel to one another, while the composition shrinks into the horizon.

Alas, life isn't as simple as walking straight down a one-lane highway. If you are looking at the corner of the room you are currently in, notice how the walls are being pulled outward. This is an example of two-point perspective. This more complex form of perspective relies on two perspective points that pull the subject matter in two directions.

Draw a horizonal line and add a dot on each end. Now imagine that each dot is the sun, and draw its rays inward. If the vertical lines of the walls of the buildings and trees stay parallel to one another and their top and bottom angles follow the sun lines, it will be in correct perspective. As you can see in the rendering of the Eiffel Tower above, it looks as if it's getting pulled from the two vanishing points.

THREE-POINT PERSPECTIVE

The elements in this type of composition are pulled in three different directions. You encounter three-point perspective in the real world when you are looking down at other buildings from a rooftop or looking up at skyscrapers from the sidewalk. As with two-point perspective, start by drawing a horizontal line and adding two points, one on each end. Find the middle between the two points and draw a vertical line going upward from the horizon. Add a point on this line so you have three vanishing points. Create the sunlike rays going inward from each dot, and build your composition within the structure of the three perspective points. As seen in the sketch below, whatever you are drawing should have an exaggerated way of getting smaller or larger in the distance.

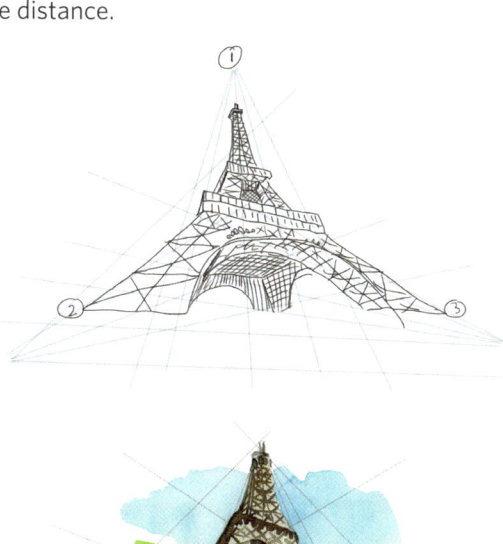

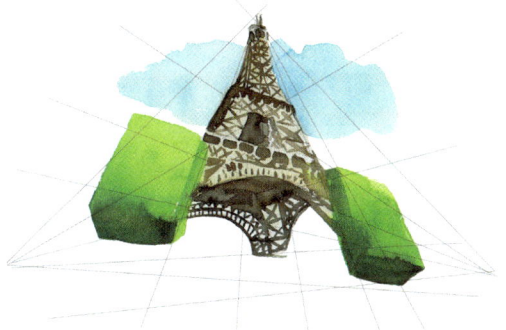

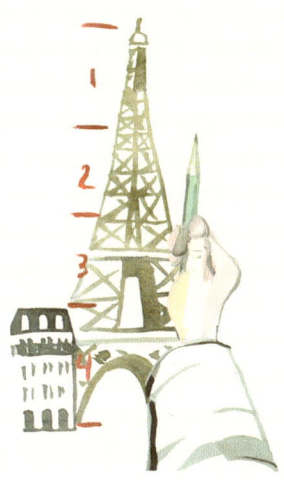

DAY 6

STILL LIFE CITY

Inspiration isn't always a rapturous eureka or a lightning-strike moment. Sometimes the mountain-high pile of dirty dishes takes up too much mental space for me to find "real" inspiration. Because my life's work requires me to stay inspired, I don't go to lofty heights to find the "right" or "wrong" inspiration. Sometimes it comes from just starting to sketch and waiting for the ideas to reveal themselves.

If you love to paint but still feel like you don't know *what* to paint, this is a wonderful exercise. Start with the banal and let your imagination run wild. Even if you are drawing a still life, you can still apply the principles of perspective. Feel free to revisit this exercise from time to time, because the options are endless and it'll snap you out of your thinking brain.

FIND INSPIRATION

Choose three to five objects from your home; be sure to select a variety of shapes, textures, transparencies, and heights to get your imagination flowing. When observing, ask yourself to identify if the still life is one-, two-, or three-point perspective. Here I use a banana, a bowl, a drinking glass, some teacups, and a roll of tape. Stack your objects and play around with their balance and the use of positive and negative space until you are happy with the composition. Can you identify the perspective lines?

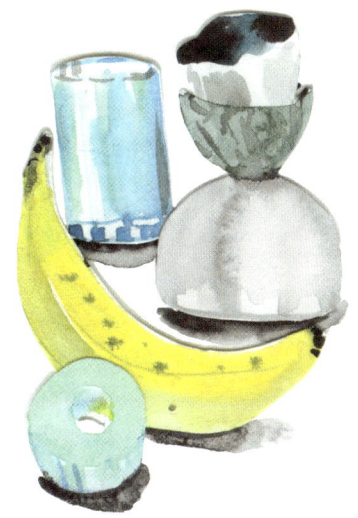

SKETCH

Closely observe what is in front of you for a full minute before sketching. (This may seem painfully long!) Identify each object and where they touch one another. Study the negative space around them. Where is the light coming from? How does it reflect differently on each object? What does that tell you about the texture of each object? And how can this fact help you render the details more accurately? With an H pencil, lightly sketch the still life on watercolor paper.

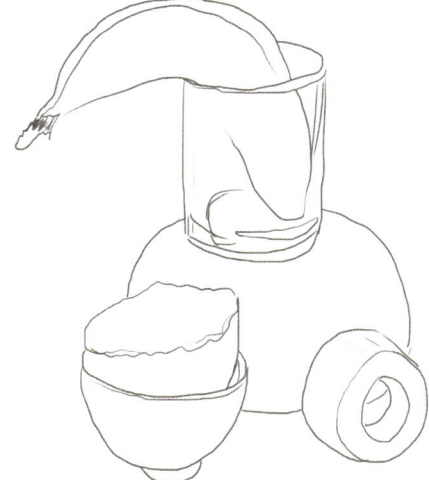

BRAINSTORM

Once you have the foundation of the still life as inspiration, it's time to transform it into the city of your dreams. To begin, ask yourself a few questions:

- What makes a city a city? Windows? Chimneys? The lack of a horizon?
- Do you want this city to be inspired by where you live or by some metropolis far, far away? Mumbai? The moon?
- Research several cities. How could their architectural elements be adapted to the objects in the still life?
- How can you emphasize the volume and form of each object to create variety in the composition?

Update your preliminary sketch. Draw the horizon line and take a moment to study the perspective. Then adapt the architectural details to the form of each object accordingly. Let your imagination run wild. In my final sketch, note how the doors and windows wrap around the objects.

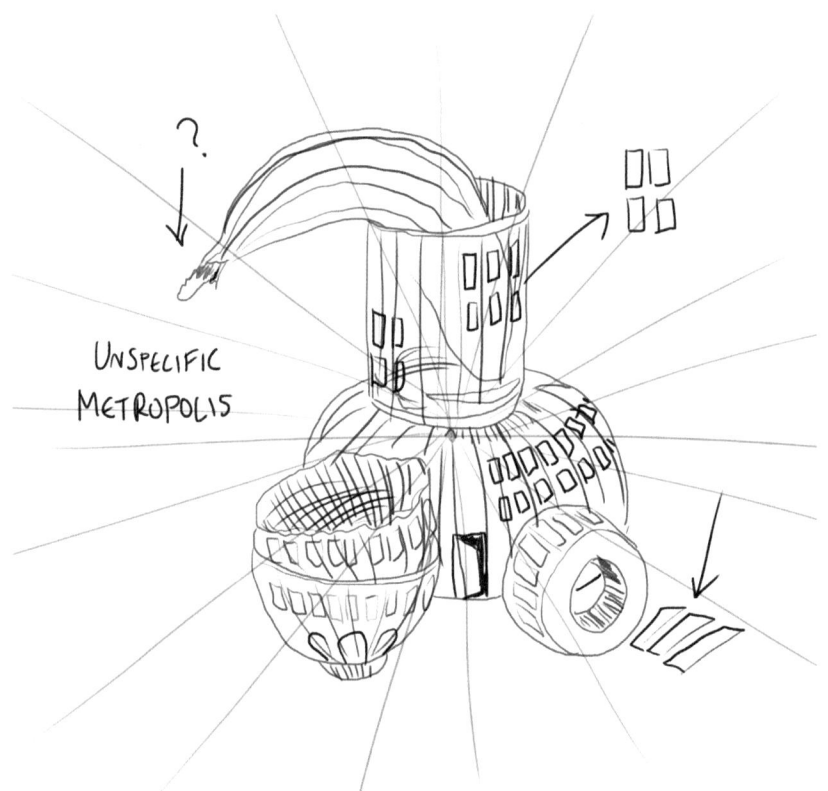

STEP 4

PAINT

Your choice of color palette can make your watercolor more conceptual by removing it further from reality. Here, I use only black watercolor, so at first glance, the image looks like a city. It's only upon closer inspection that a viewer sees the volume of the still life. To create some contrast, I use gray tones to suggest the transparency of the glass cups.

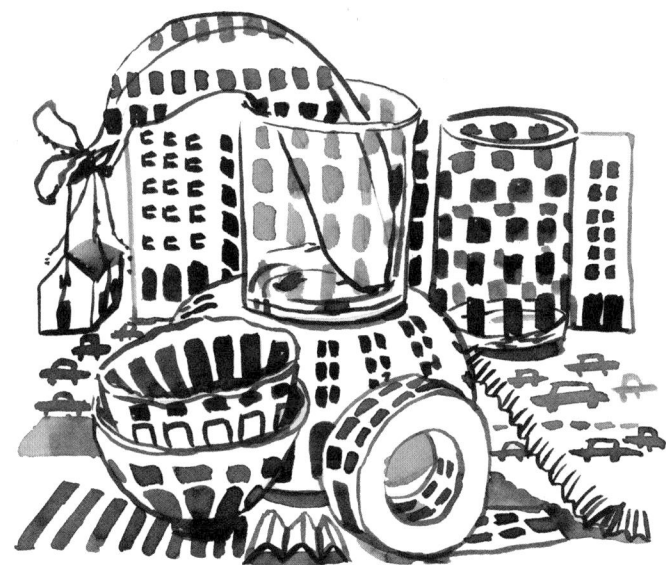

STEP 5

REFLECT

Did this exercise help you infuse more imagination into your watercolor? Would you push it further or scale it back if you were to do it again? Were you able to successfully implement the principles of perspective?

Drawing a Portrait

Since the days of grade-school stick figures, you may have learned the "correct" or "academic" way to draw a person. I could walk you through the method of measuring the body in mathematical proportions, but the human body is not a one-size-fits-all formula. My best advice is to shake off the preconceived ideas you have of what noses, eyes, and frown lines look like. Instead of drawing features, draw the shapes that you see. Here are a few other pointers for rendering portraits grounded in observation and truth.

HEAD AND NECK

You're not drawing a face, you're drawing a head. Always draw the head first and then fill in the face with features, or else something will always seem a little off. And note that the neck is indeed the same width as the face.

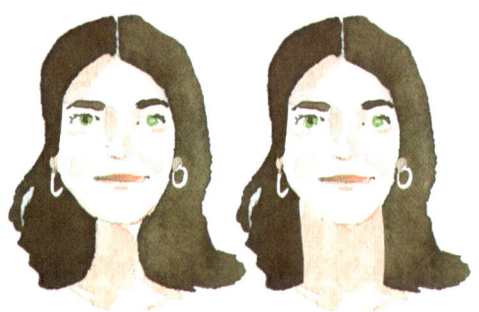

SHADOWS

Think about drawing a face like you would a still life: Begin by identifying the light source, the highlights, and the shadows. The highlight on the tip of the nose and the shadow under it suggest that it is protruding from the face. The shadows under the eyes suggest that they are sunken within the skull (more on this below). And contrary to popular belief, the whites of the eyes and teeth are not completely white. Eyes are shadowed by the lids. Teeth are between two protruding lips. They have shadows.

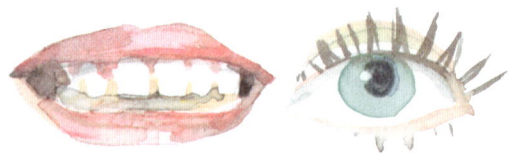

EYES

When drawing eyes, always remember that the eye is a sphere set deep into the socket of the skull. What you see of the eye is just a small portion of the sphere, so avoid drawing a *Clockwork Orange* homage or a deer in the headlights. The iris may be partially covered by the eyelids.

EYELASHES

Eyelashes grow out of the eyelid and often stick together in clumps of two or three lashes, much like individual false eyelashes. Draw them in sections of two or three to avoid cartoonlike lashes.

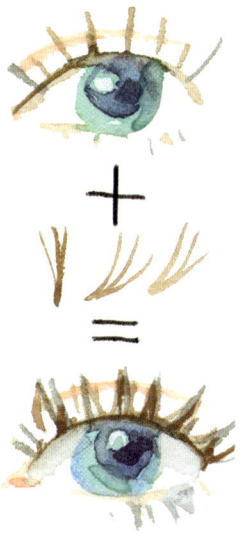

LIPS

Don't outline the lips (leave that back in the 1990s). Instead, closely observe the hue of the top and bottom lips. Draw the line between the lips first. Notice how the lips are darkest at the corners. If the teeth are visible, avoid outlining each one (which will lead to a look of orthodontia gone terribly wrong). Instead, draw the top lip and work some of the pigment down to suggest where the gums separate the teeth.

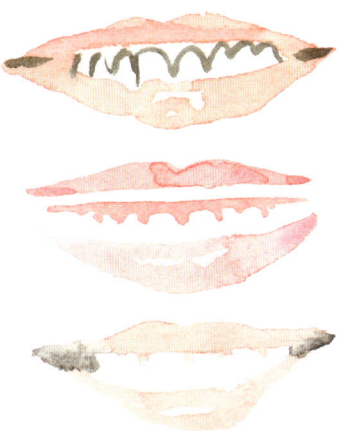

EYEBROWS

To sketch the eyebrows, I like to paint dots to mark the beginning and end and to understand the arch. Then I make small strokes to connect the dots. Next I add a wash layer on top, wet on dry. Then I go back and add a few hairs with a dry brush.

DAY 7

SELFIE SESSION

Capturing likeness is still one of the most difficult challenges for me. The artist's technical skills and the strong opinions of the sketchee need to align. I was feeling very proud that I nailed a self-portrait of myself for this very exercise. A friend of mine broke out in a chuckle when she saw it lying on my desk. "Who is this?" she asked. "The earrings look like yours!" Ego lightly bruised, I went back to the literal drawing board. Perhaps I jinxed myself, but I redid my self-portrait at least ten times until I made one that I thought resembled me.

In this exercise, you will take a stab at drawing yourself in a mirror. This is all about observation in the present, synchronizing your hand and eye in a several-step process. Because your body may be in motion, you also need to make executive decisions about what to capture and what to leave out. By the end of this exercise, you should have a loose, gestural representation of yourself. Whether it looks like you is in the eye of the beholder.

_____
STEP 1
BRAINSTORM

Find a pose you can comfortably hold for 5 to 10 minutes (save the toothy grin
for another time; it isn't easy to draw and will be too difficult to hold). Keep it
natural. Take a good look at yourself. Imagine you are meeting yourself for the
first time. What draws you in? What's unique about what you see?

_____
STEP 2
WARM UP

Take out a few sheets of scrap paper and a pencil. Set your timer for 10 seconds.
Draw yourself as quickly as you can. Redo this exercise with 20 seconds on
the clock. Then 30 seconds, and then 1 minute. These sketches may look like
chicken scratches, but you may be surprised that there is real truth in them, too.
They help you snap out of your thinking mind and capture what you see. Feel
free to repeat as many times as necessary until you feel warmed up.

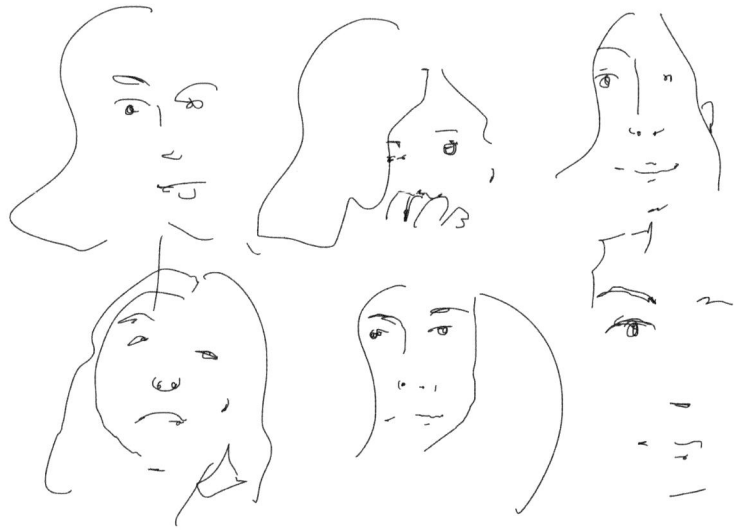

SKETCH

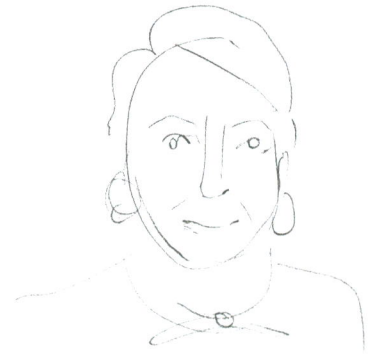

Take out a sheet of watercolor paper and your supplies. Set your timer for 30 seconds. Quickly sketch yourself in pencil on the watercolor paper, getting down as much information as possible. It may not look anything like you. But this is the "truth blueprint" for your drawing. Lightly erase the pencil until the lines are as faint as possible. I usually know in the sketch phase whether I see any resemblance or not. This comes with practice, but if you don't see any fragments of resemblance, keep sketching or start over.

PAINT LAYER 1

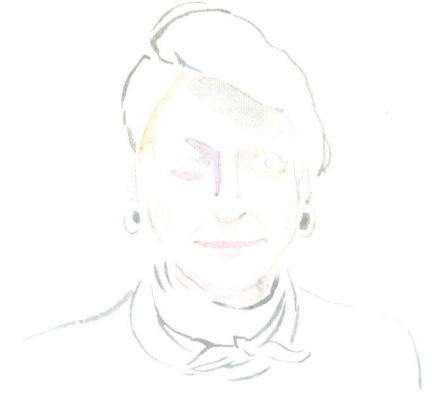

Think of this first layer of watercolor as sketch 2.0. You are going back to your rough sketch to clarify any necessary information related to the placement of the features. Activate your watercolors and mix a skin tone that resembles your own. I mixed one that is more pink and another that has a more yellow tone, which I can use interchangeably to create variety. I can also use these two layered together to build the shadows on my face. The yellower tone can be used to suggest a middle tone between the pink and the white space from the paper. I mix the lightest pink wash I can and begin defining the features of the face by identifying the shadow under the nose, the corners of the eyes, the jawline, and so forth.

Depending on the light source, the tip of the nose, the highlight on the pupil, the lower forehead, and the chin are the lightest parts of the face. I'll be sure to keep those parts of the paper white and avoid applying color there to create volume.

STEP 5

PAINT LAYER 2

Now that all my features are in the right places, I'm ready to start building bold colors and darker hues to add contrast between the face and neck. I paint the hair dark brown using wet on dry, saving a few spots of white to suggest the reflection of the light and the side part. While the layer is still wet, I add a redder brown on the right side of the hair to create more depth in the hue. To create a rougher texture for the hair, I swirl my paintbrush in brown paint and flatten down the bristles between my fingers until the brush fans out. This is essentially dry on dry and gives me an irregular texture.

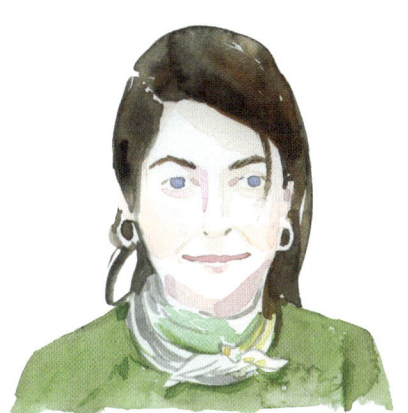

STEP 6

PAINT LAYER 3

With a dark gray watercolor, use the tip of a small round brush to start building depth. Avoid overdoing this step. It's just to define where the hair frames the face, identify the part in the hair, mark the corners of the eyes and mouth, add texture to the scarf and sweater, the frown lines, and place the pupils.

Is there a good range of contrast between the darkest and lightest parts of your painting? If not, continue building layers of wash.

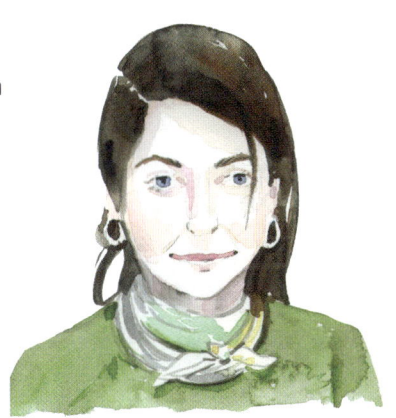

STEP 7

REFLECT

If you hold up your final watercolor next to your face and look in the mirror, do you see any resemblance? If not, continue sketching yourself with watercolor from time to time when you have a few moments to kill.

DAY 8

OBJECT INCARNATE

Today's exercise is inspired by what I call my *mental health barometer*. It's how I respond when I pull my earphones out of my jacket pocket, depending on how tangled they are: "I'm a mess." "WTF." "Urghhhh." In this exercise, you will project emotions onto an object, whether they are positive, negative, or anything in between. You'll also explore line weight (the thickness of how a line is drawn) using only black watercolor. The greater the variety of line weights in a piece, the more interesting and nuanced the final drawing.

BRAINSTORM

Find an object onto which you can project your emotions. Position it in four to six poses, manipulating it as needed to find the greatest range of emotion. Can you cut it? Distort it? Manipulate it? Twist it? In this case, I am going to project onto an everyday kitchen sponge because I have the tendency to absorb the energy of everything around me.

SKETCH

To flesh out your concept, quickly sketch out a few options before committing to watercolor. I often overproduce so that I can eliminate any weak images that don't work well with the overall concept. Since we will be painting only with black watercolor today, I'm going to scrap sketch four because I imagined it being a sponge covered in colorful watercolor spots. It won't read well in black and white. Do you need to add text to make your visual metaphors more understandable? In my case, the copy reinforces the humor in the visual.

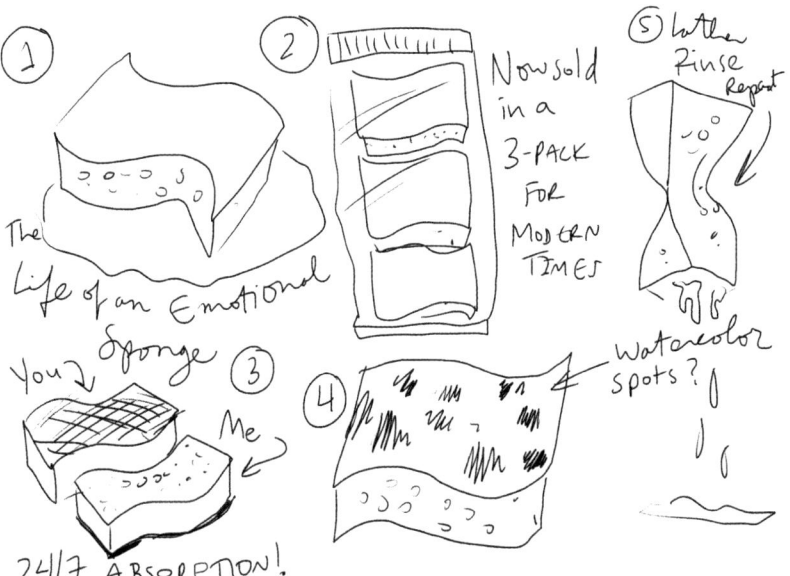

PAINT

Once you are feeling confident in your concept, it's time to paint. The challenge will be to play around with how much pressure to apply to the paintbrush to achieve a variety of line widths (see tip below for more on this).

You may feel constrained in what you can do just painting with line and one color, but restrictions often lead to the most creative breakthroughs because you have to be quick on your feet to find variety in a limited range of possibilities.

REFLECT

Being an artist is all about straddling the line between your comfort zone and full-blown discomfort. Creating art isn't all reward. A moment of breakthrough comes when you are completely lost and ready to give up, but remaining confident in the process and being rooted in your technique pulls you to the other side. As you are making your way through these daily exercises, try to understand what you like while you're working. Is it when you're painting fast and furious? Slow and controlled? How did you feel working with restrictions? Do you prefer the painting or the idea development? Was it easier to execute this exercise using just lines and not layers and layers of watercolor? Are you ever surprised with the result when you must push yourself to try something new? You may need to lean into that more.

HOT TIP

LINE WEIGHT 101

Here are two versions of the same sponge. The sponge on the left was drawn with a black pen using the same consistent line width. The version on the right was drawn with watercolor, playing with the pressure applied to the paintbrush. The version on the right looks more nuanced and three-dimensional because the thicker line weight suggests the porous surface and shadows.

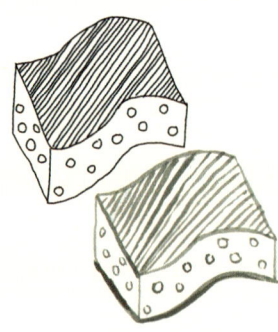

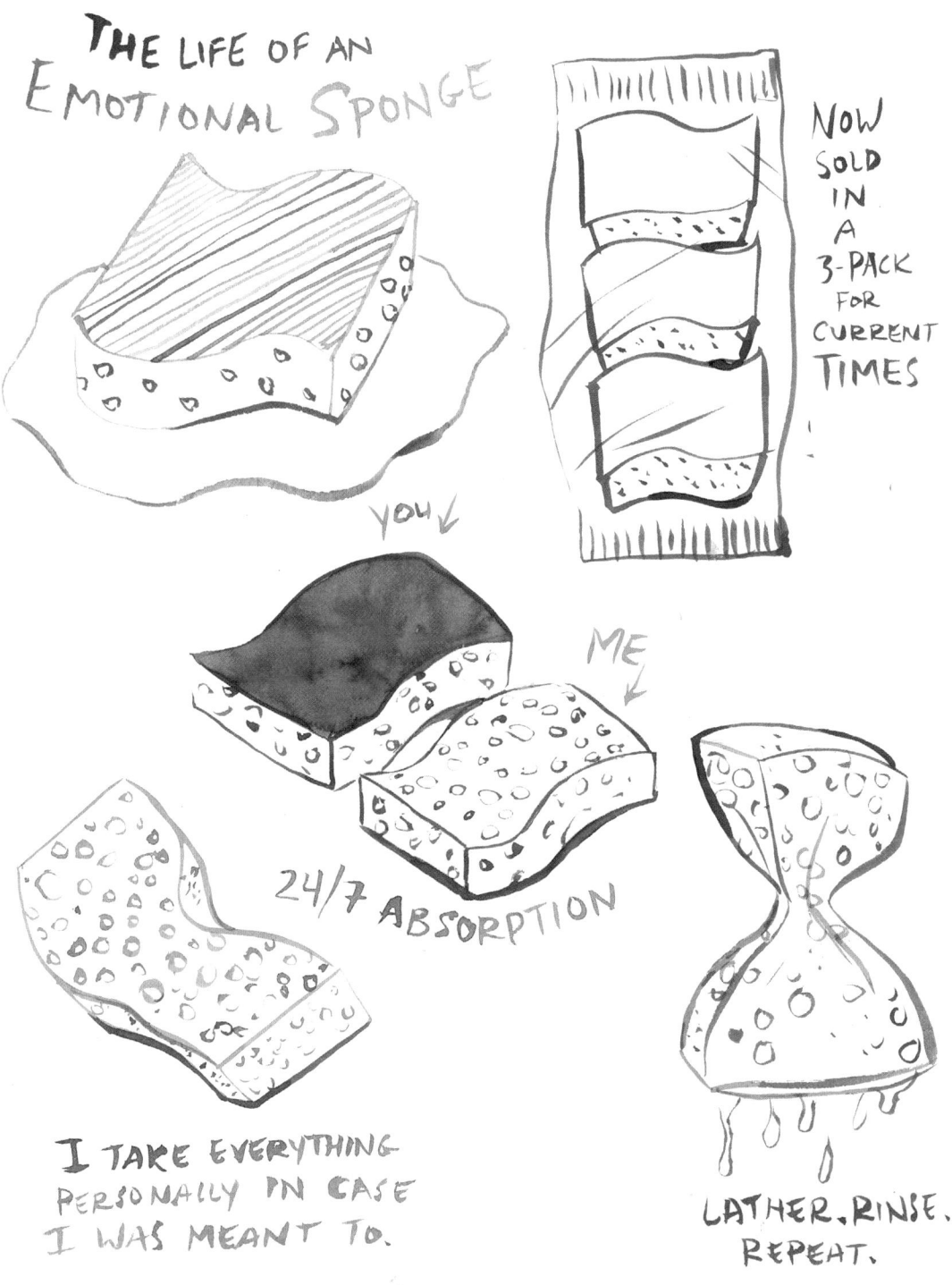

THE LIFE OF AN EMOTIONAL SPONGE

NOW SOLD IN A 3-PACK FOR CURRENT TIMES

YOU ↓

ME ↓

24/7 ABSORPTION

I TAKE EVERYTHING PERSONALLY IN CASE I WAS MEANT TO.

LATHER. RINSE. REPEAT.

DAY 9

GIMME SUPERPOWERS!

For today's prompt, you will visualize a comic book superpower
that will enable you to transform your greatest weakness into
a superstrength. One of the minor casualties of being an artist
is hypersensitivity (as you can tell from the object I chose in
yesterday's exercise). After more than fifteen years in France,
where being frank is a national pastime, I would love to be
able to care less about what other people think of me, so my
superpower would be deflecting criticism like water rolling off
a duck's back.

STEP 1

BRAINSTORM

What kind of superpower would you love to have? How would you use it—to help yourself, or others? What gear would you need? What would be in your utility belt?

STEP 2

SKETCH

Sketch yourself wearing your superhero costume. Does wearing a costume make you stand a little taller or more confidently?

Next, write three to five sentences about how your powers will be applied to your life. Since my superpower is *water off a duck's back*, I think "impenetrable to unsolicited parenting advice from little old ladies." "Deflects all commentary from my mother-in-law about my weight!" "Quack, don't crack!" I sketch the duck costume in profile to reinforce the gesture of the water rolling down the back and have the phrase *water off a duck's back* flow off the duck itself. Ask yourself if the text complements or takes away from the image itself. Continue sketching until you feel like you have a harmonious composition.

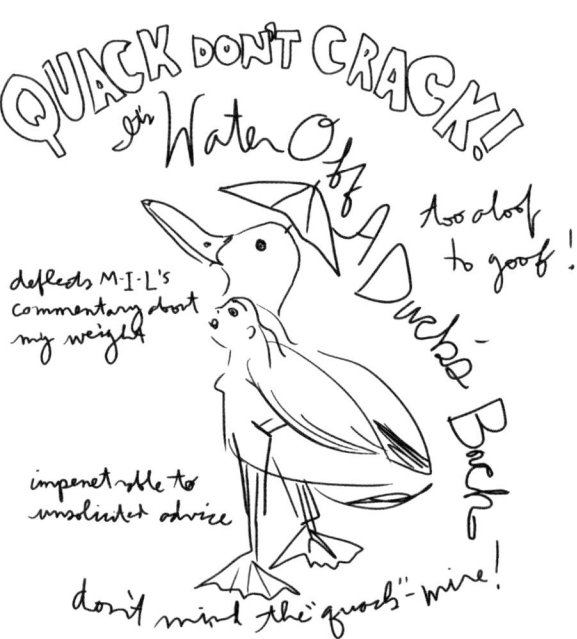

PAINT

Because we're approaching this like a comic book, you want to draw the reader in with graphic text and bright colors. If you don't have a strong point of reference for this, study the work of comic artists to understand how they balance color and copy. I recently saw an exhibition of Daniel Clowes, a lauded cartoonist of the second generation of American underground comic artists. He is one of the last comic artists to do everything by hand. I usually avoid a black pen line in my personal work because it has the tendency to flatten the volume of watercolor, but Clowes uses it masterfully to bring focus to certain areas of his composition and create balance and harmony. I closely observed his line work and adapted it to my final drawing.

I choose to draw a Rouen duck because of its colorful hunter-green head, orange feet, and yellow beak. Looping back to yesterday's exercise, how can you apply pressure to your paintbrush to achieve a variety of line thickness in building details and contrast?

REFLECT

I am a devoted *RuPaul's Drag Race* fan. One of the moments that gets me watery in the eyes is when Mother RuPaul tells contestants that the power and invincibility they feel in drag can be adapted to real life as well. How does it feel seeing your superpower visualized? It may be ambitious, but how can this be adapted to your real life?

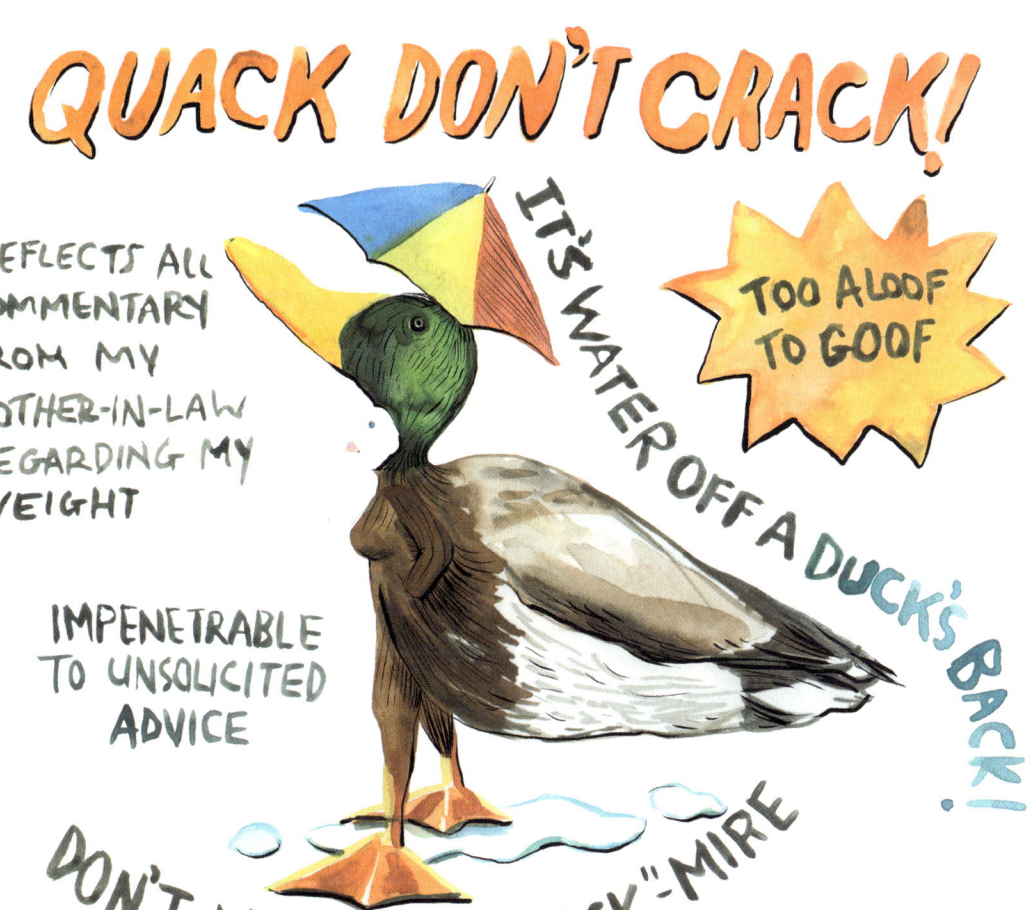

DAY 10

DRAW ME SOMETHING TO EAT

A few years back, I came across the very first cookbook
I wrote, *Jessie's Book of Fabulous Recipes*. If this was an
omen to what my life had in store, it was a hilarious face-
palm moment: "An alive pigeon with honey Dijon mustard.
A caramel apple gyro." Not bad for a seven-year-old—and
practically French molecular gastronomy, for what it's worth.
This is all to say that my career as a food-forward illustrator
was written in the stars, but it took me twenty or so years to see
the crumbs left along the winding road.

Food is a wonderful entry point into creating editorial
watercolors because it is deeply nostalgic and personal. In
today's prompt, I will walk you through my process of bringing
a recipe to life, visualizing the process of preparing said recipe
and telling a tightly rendered story in just one watercolor.

BRAINSTORM

Think of a dish you love. Jot down all the details required to make it—not just the ingredient list and recipe instructions but the utensils you use, any gestures you make while preparing it, the specific way you like to eat it. If you're not culinarily inclined, it could be a peanut butter and jelly sandwich or a cup of coffee and a cigarette—just be as specific as possible regarding the process.

Today I'll be drawing a Dutch baby pancake, which grows in the oven into a golden-topped blob. This used to be a brunch-time pièce de résistance that my mom would ceremoniously plop on the table when I was a kid. Now that my son is old enough to appreciate a little flair for the dramatic, I've added it to my repertoire. Looking at the recipe, I loosely sketch out the process and ingredients required for making this pancake.

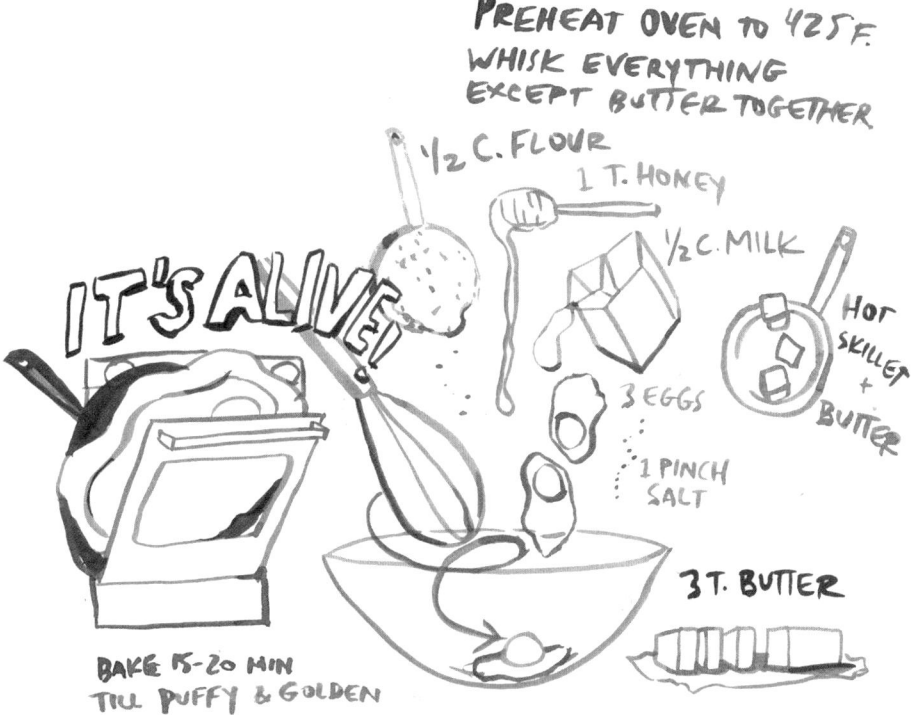

SKETCH

Looking at your notes from the brainstorming session, quickly sketch out everything that comes to your mind when you think about this recipe. When I think of a Dutch baby, I imagine the drama of a crêpe being taken to the third dimension. I look up 1960s horror movie posters for some *It's Alive!* inspiration and pay special attention to their typography and color combinations. I'm drawn to one in particular that shows King Kong playing dominoes with skyscrapers in the streets of New York City. What if the pancake is a metastatic mass that takes over Parisian streets? Of course, I'm dreaming big here. But feel free to keep it as simple as you need it to be.

Next, I need to make the watercolor as descriptive as possible, ensuring that the ingredients are visible and the steps of the recipe are comprehensible. Whether you incorporate written text is up to you. Ask yourself if the image really needs it.

HOT TIP

HOW TO GET UNSTUCK

When you're committed to learning and growing in an art practice, it's incredibly frustrating and uncomfortable. Your skills may not match your taste level yet. You may not know why you are doing what you're doing. What's the value of even trying?

While going through one of these bouts of self-doubt myself, I happily stumbled upon my friend and fellow illustrator Kendyll Hillegas's podcast, *Art Lab*, which features invaluable pragmatic advice surrounding the creative process and how to get unstuck.

Kendyll encouraged me to think like a scientist. If the experiment doesn't work, change the variables and formula. "To get better, you need to do less and more often" is the main takeaway from the podcast. By lowering my expectations for my final product (I'm not aiming for a photorealistic representation, but more of a suggestion of what I'm painting), and doing it more quickly, I can work away at fine-tuning my muscle memory by capturing only the essentials.

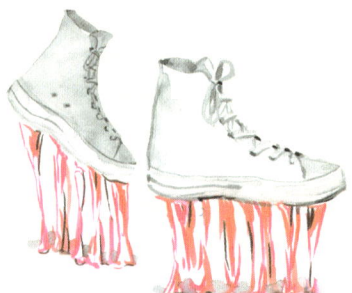

IT'S NOT A CRÊPE. IT'S ALIIIIVE!

INGREDIENTS: 3 EGGS · ½ C. FLOUR · ½ C. MILK
1 T. HONEY · 1 PINCH SALT · 3 T. BUTTER

PREHEAT OVEN TO 425°F.
MIX EVERYTHING EXCEPT
BUTTER TOGETHER.
PLACE PAN IN OVEN
AND MELT BUTTER

BAKE 15-20 MIN
TILL PUFFY AND
GOLDEN

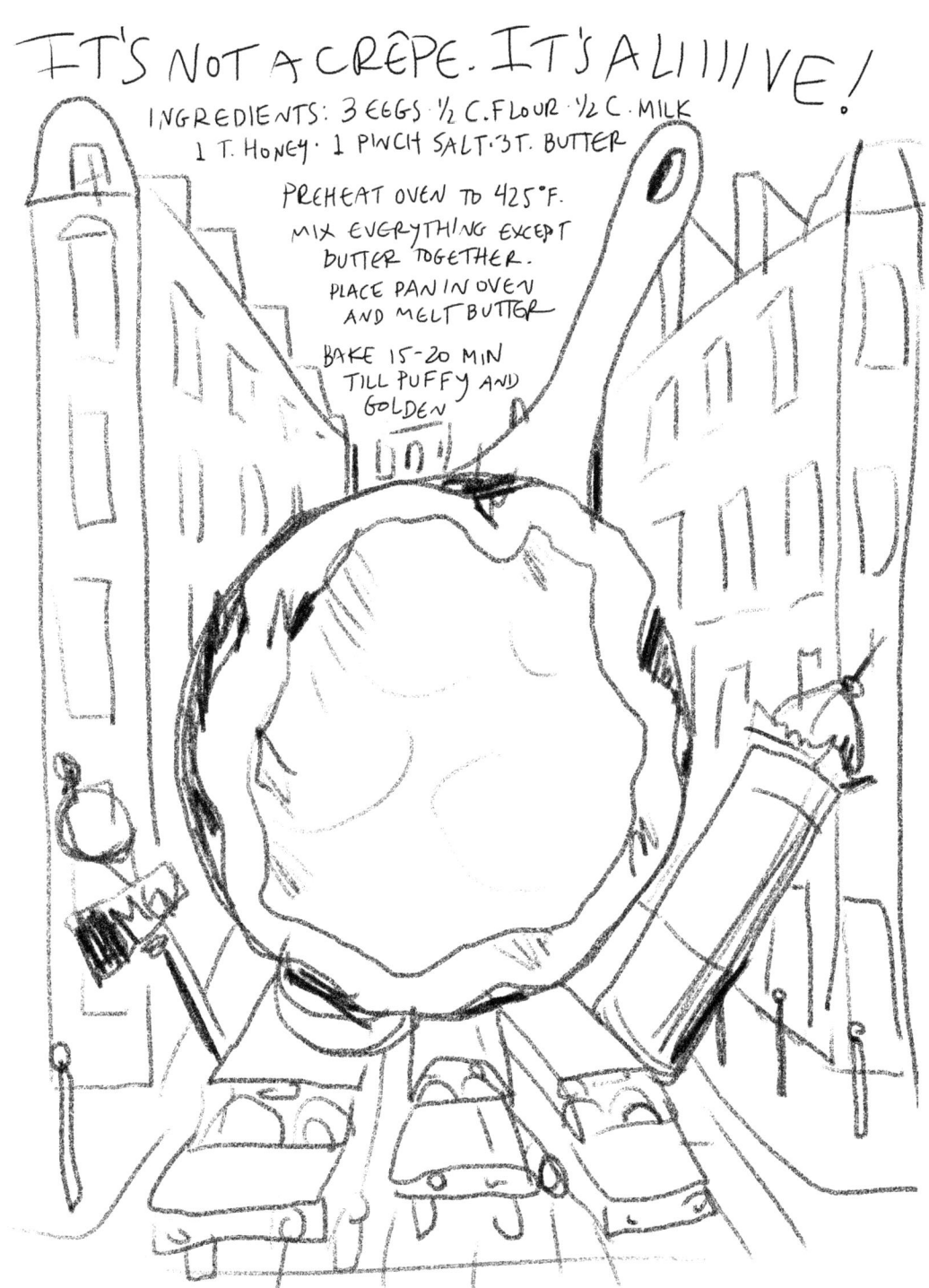

PAINT

As I approach building color, I think about how to draw attention to the pancake. Circling back to the lessons I've learned on color theory (see pages 24–33), I remember that the complement of the orange-brown of the pancake is blue. I decide to paint the Parisian cityscape in cooler tones of blue and gray to maximize the impact of the bulging pancake. To further draw attention to the dish, I render the pancake in a lot of detail and everything else surrounding it in less-defined washes.

Now that I've defined the colors and filled in the surface area of the paper with washes, it's time to build the depth by adding a layer of contrast and shadow. Notice the dark shadow on the right of the skillet handle and how I add a dark reddish brown to exaggerate the scale of the puffy pancake. I paint the ground black to give the pancake an exaggerated sense of weight.

REFLECT

If you were to compare your illustration to the picture of a final recipe in a cookbook, does it offer more insight into the process of making the dish? I like to say that illustration is like a superpower; it can say even more than photography can. Did this illustrated version of a recipe say more than a photo could? If you included text, does it work in equilibrium with the rest of the image? Would someone be able to make your chosen dish from looking at this image alone?

INGREDIENTS: 3 EGGS   ½ C. FLOUR   ½ C. MILK   1 T. HONEY   1 PINCH OF SALT   3 T. BUTTER

IT'S NOT A CRÊPE. IT'S ALIVE!

PREHEAT OVEN TO 425 F.
WHISK EVERYTHING
EXCEPT BUTTER TOGETHER

HEAT PAN IN OVEN UNTIL HOT.
ADD BUTTER AND MELT.
POUR BATTER INTO HOT SKILLET.

BAKE 15-20 MIN
TILL PUFFY
& GOLDEN

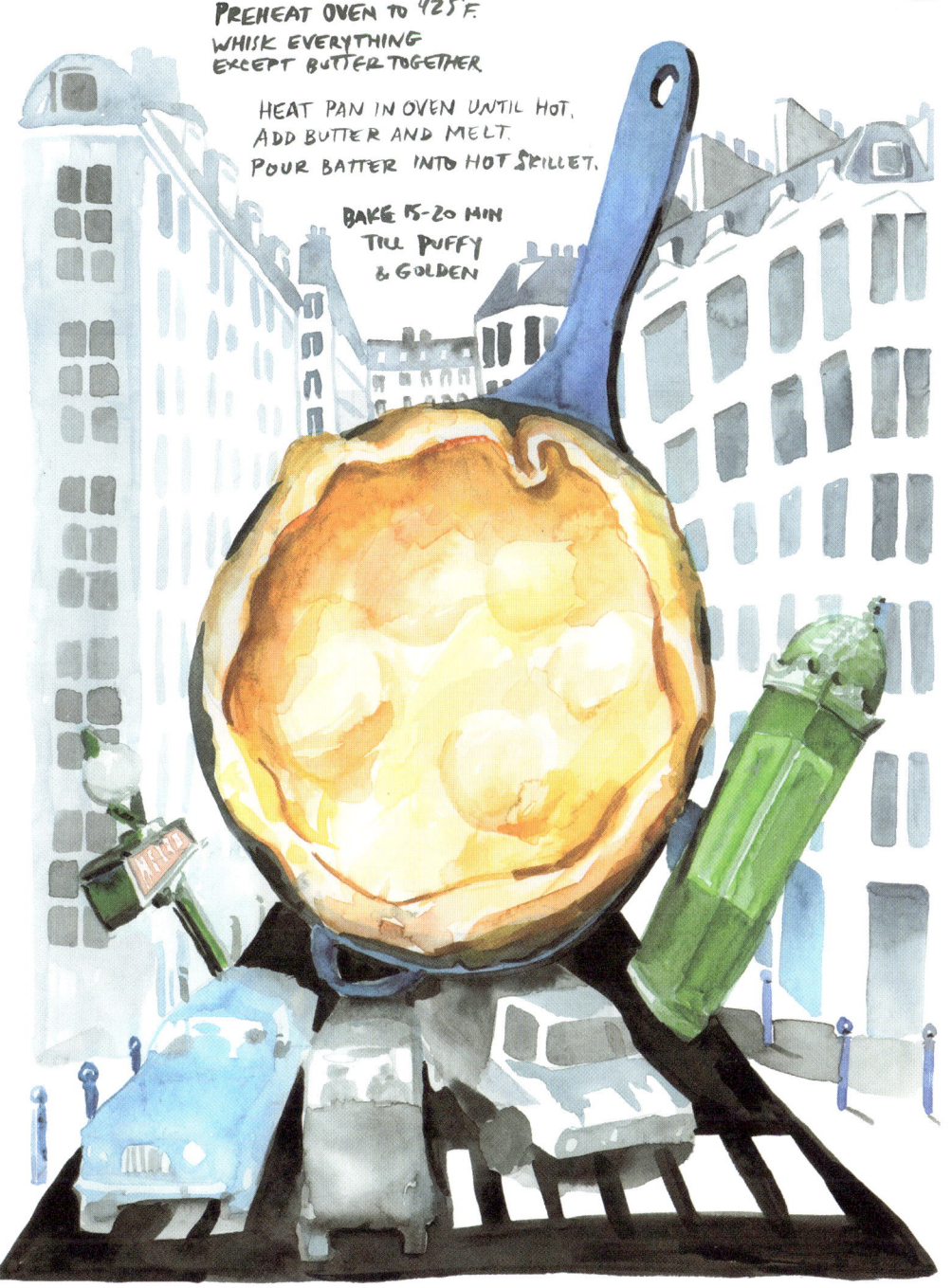

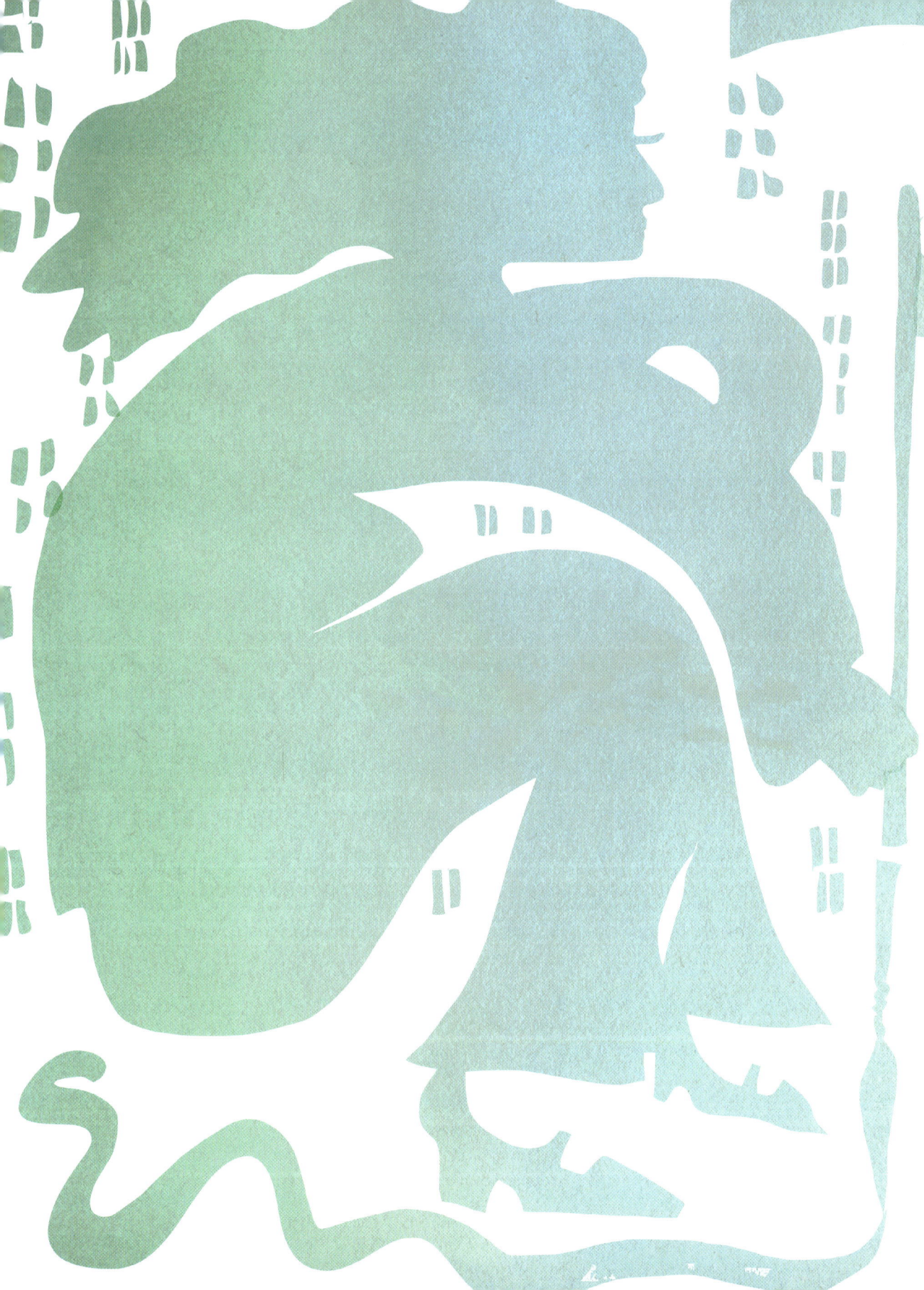

OBSERVATION STATION

Drawing your own world, wherever that may be, is the secret to finding your voice. These five prompts will encourage you to start applying the techniques you've developed to your surroundings. You may think that you need to have an overactive imagination to fuel a drawing. But the easiest entry point is you.

DAY 11

PEOPLE IN PLACES

In my early au pair days, I would often get bored with how slowly my pencil would travel along my paper while sketching ornate metalwork and other Parisian architectural intricacies. When I started sketching the forms I saw rather than the infinite details, I could focus more on building depth and perspective.

In this exercise, you will divide a composition into several sections and render them with washes. Painting watercolor in distinct actionable steps makes it easier to understand and execute a complex scene without getting overwhelmed by the details. If you need to brush up on perspective, turn to page 66.

BRAINSTORM

Find a photo you love of people in a place, or commit to finding a spot in a park and painting from life (see page 107 for more about how to set yourself up for success). I love the perspective of this image of a Parisian park and can already envision it broken down into interesting layers of grass, people, buildings, and greenery.

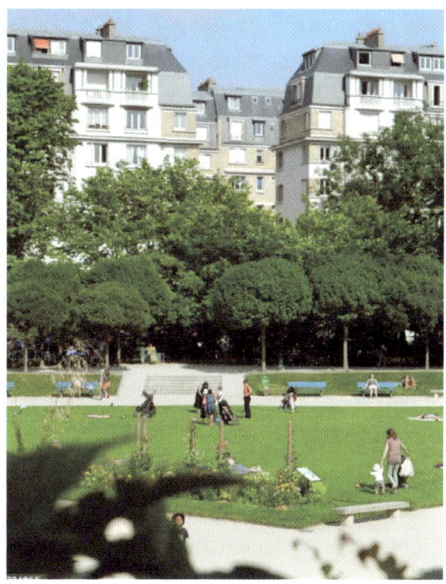

SKETCH

Before beginning your sketch, ask yourself a few questions: What layers can you separate this into? What are the lightest and darkest parts of the composition? How will you play with painting in perspective? Will you paint the colors you see or find another palette? What techniques will you use to add variety and texture to the piece?

Looking at my reference image, I lightly sketch out the essentials of the composition and break it down into seven layers so I can work on separate planes to avoid merging colors. This includes the following, in the order in which I'll paint them: **(1)** grass, **(2)** round trees, **(3)** rooftops, **(4)** people, **(5)** under the trees, **(6)** leafy trees, and **(7)** buildings.

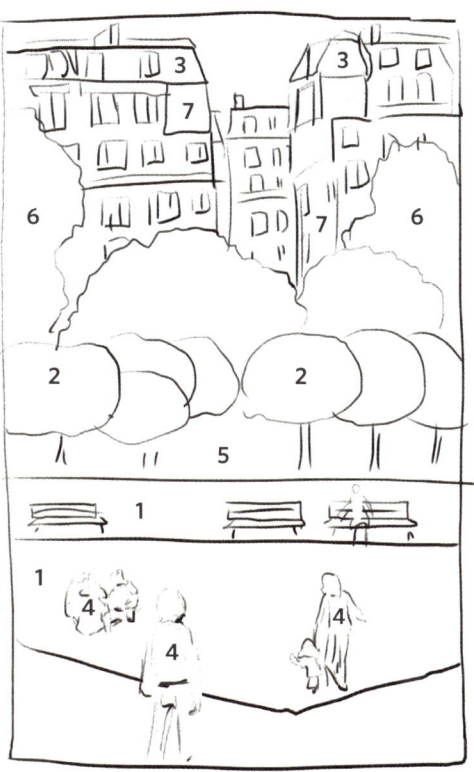

PAINT LAYERS 1 TO 3

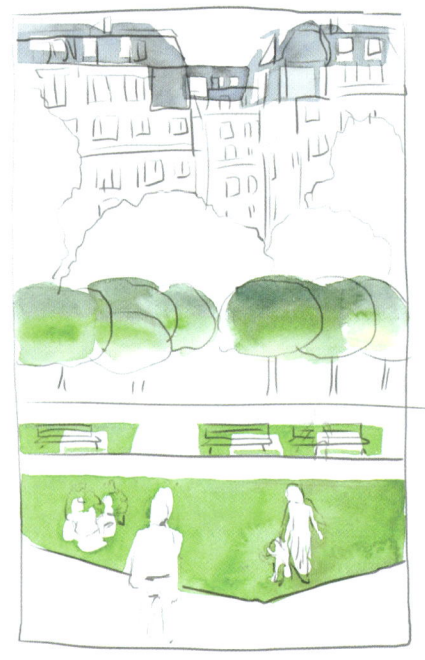

In layer 1, I paint the grass green using wet on dry, saving the white space of the silhouettes of the people to fill in later.

To render the round trees of layer 2, I lightly dampen the paper to apply two greens using the 50% flood technique. I apply a dark forest green on top by moving my brush from side to side and a grassy green on the bottom, letting the paper pull the color on its wet surface.

To paint the Parisian rooftops in layer 3, I mix several hues of blue-gray and start filling in the roofs wet on dry.

I let these layers dry completely.

PAINT LAYERS 4 AND 5

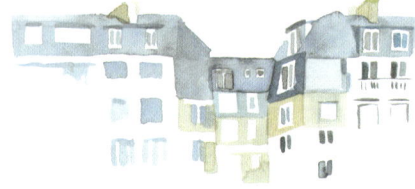

Because this image is all about the harmony of the overall composition, I am not going to torture myself by making the people in layer 4 hyperdetailed. Instead, I dampen the paper where their silhouettes are and drop in color with the tip of my paintbrush, suggesting where the arm meets the body or where the feet touch the ground.

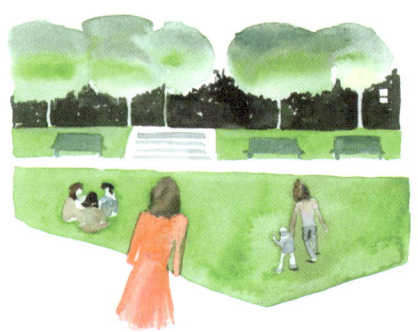

For the stripe of shadows underneath the line of trees, I mix black with dark green and paint layer 5 using the wet-on-dry technique. I don't cover the whole surface with a matte color; rather, I randomly add dots of black with the tip of my brush and leave small dots of white space to create texture.

STEP 5

PAINT LAYERS 6 AND 7

I have the distinct challenge of rendering two types of trees with different textures. Instead of creating a matte painted surface like in layer 2, for layer 6 I mix together several shades of green and start stippling, or building a pattern by dotting the tip of my brush onto the paper. Where there is more light in the trees, I add more yellow to my paint. Remember that you don't need to paint every leaf on the tree; it's more about looking at the photo and rendering the shapes and how they reflect light.

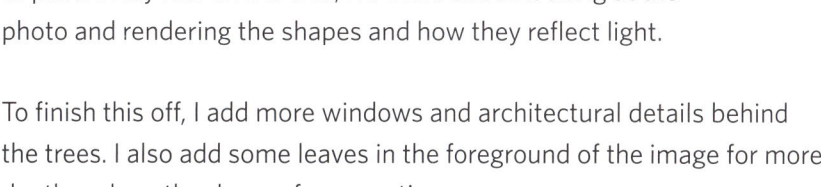

To finish this off, I add more windows and architectural details behind the trees. I also add some leaves in the foreground of the image for more depth and another layer of perspective.

STEP 6

REFLECT

Was it helpful working in distinct layers? How would you describe your personal watercolor technique in this final piece? Washy or scratchy? Were you able to use different techniques to render different types of textures? Were you able to build depth and perspective in this exercise?

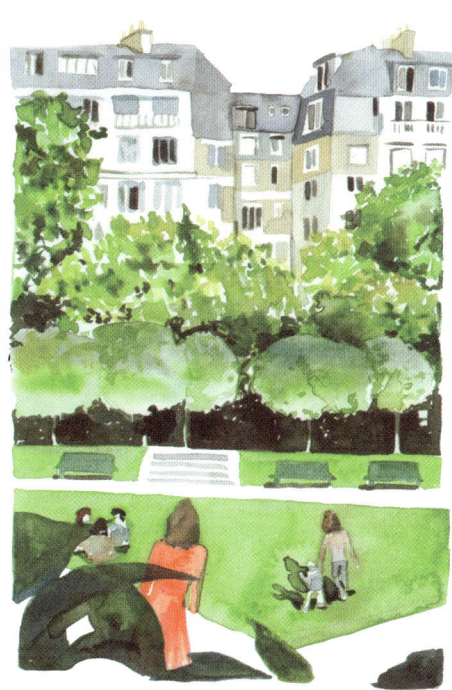

DAY 12

COVER STAR

Getting one's work on the cover of *The New Yorker* is the ultimate goal for illustrators. I've yet to land one, but believe me, I am always trying!

One of the reasons why the cover of *The New Yorker* is so iconic is because it is a stand-alone image. It usually has nothing to do with what is inside the glossy pages of the magazine—it speaks of a moment in time. I am always on the lookout for the latest cosmopolitan food trends, social movements, and sartorial eyesores to mine for a cover idea. If I'm inspired, I put together a sketch and email it off into the abyss.

Today you will create a *New Yorker*–style cover inspired by the place where you live. The goal is to identify what makes your city or town unique and re-create the essence of it. Your painting must have a point of view. The more specific and personal, the better.

STEP 1

BRAINSTORM

Whenever I begin a new project, I refer to my illustration holy trinity: imagery, conflict, and client. Once you have a vague idea of what you'd like to do, these considerations will help frame further brainstorming and give your final drawing more intention. The *imagery* includes the places, things, and characters in the place where you live. The *conflict* captures the action of what is happening in the place (culture wars, election-sign one-upmanship, a pigeon eyeing a hot dog, etc.). The *client* is the intended audience for the illustration. If it's readers of *The New Yorker*, the theme needs to be more universal to be understood. If you are illustrating an inside joke as a gift for a friend, it can be much more personal.

For this exercise, take a moment to ponder what's going on out and about where you live. What's on the lips of everyone in town? What do you find funny or curious? Is there a cat-infested haunted house on the corner or a local diner filled with a gray-haired clientele? If you're stumped, take a walk around your neighborhood and get firsthand inspiration.

I have a vague notion to render the circuitous streets of Paris filled with friendly corner cafés. I like the idea, but it still doesn't have a specific point of view. If this is a cover for *The New Yorker*, perhaps it is all seen through the eyes of a French bulldog looking out a window? Perhaps he just caught the red-eye from New York City and is dying to engage with his native culture? Reframing my concept with the holy trinity, here's how I broke it down:

- **Imagery:** People walking around Le Marais in Paris, Parisian café, French bulldog, French windows
- **Conflict:** French bulldog looking out the window at a Parisian street and longing to be taken out
- **Client:** *The New Yorker*, well-read, urbane readers

SKETCH

I start sketching to meld together the elements of my concept. My composition is divided into the six squares of a Parisian window frame. I could just draw the back of a French bulldog's head, but I give him a slight head tilt to suggest his yearning to engage with the outside world. Since the pup is looking out onto a sunny day, I imagine that he will be backlit and we will see only his silhouette, so the focus is on the world outside.

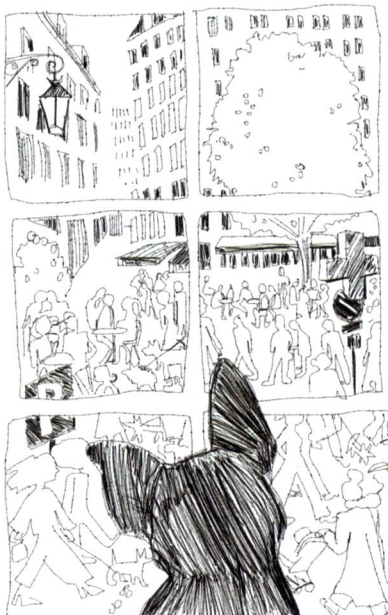

PAINT LAYERS 1 AND 2

Now that my composition is fleshed out, it is time to think about color. I am reminded that dogs perceive hues differently than humans do, seeing mostly cool colors. Why not use only a dog-identifying color palette?

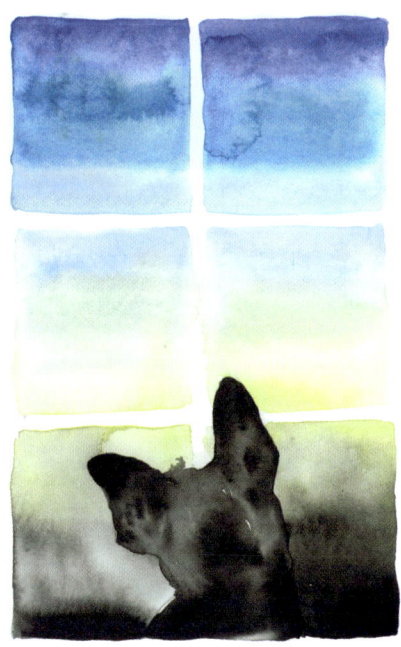

I execute the first layer using the 50% flood technique. With a wet paintbrush, I lightly dampen the surface of the six squares with water. Optimizing the time the paper is wet, I start building the color from top to bottom: navy blue, sky blue, yellow, and gray. Once this layer is completely dry, I build the silhouette of the French bulldog using 50% flood, applying more black pigment to the ears and the back of the head to suggest volume.

STEP 4

PAINT LAYER 3

I begin work on my Parisian cityscape. If I've learned anything while drawing in Paris, it's all about suggesting identifiable architectural elements without getting lost in centuries of detail (e.g., two parallel rectangles to represent windowpanes, the cross of the pharmacy sign, etc.). What would the dog be focusing on? He's probably looking at people walking other dogs. I commit to using yellow for vegetation and blues and grays for everything else.

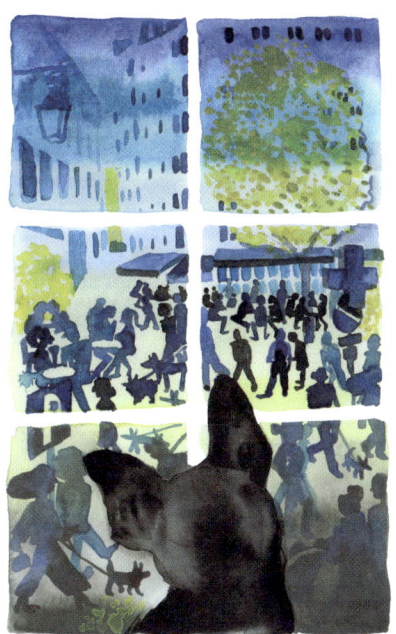

STEP 5

REFLECT

A good *New Yorker* cover is complex. It's graphic enough for the often-nuanced subject matter to be instantly understood. How did you do? At first glance, can you identify your neighborhood? How does color reinforce your concept or emotional intentions? Since a good magazine cover needs to be graphic and effective in communicating a strong message, what are the strengths and weaknesses of your final watercolor?

Q & A

WHAT IS ILLUSTRATION, ANYWAY?

Unlike a piece of artwork, an illustration serves a greater purpose than just hanging on a wall. It could reinforce an idea in an article, add a pattern to an object, or visualize a concept in a book. And an illustration involves collaboration between the artist and the person who commissions the work.

DAY 13

EAT, PONDER, PAINT

I recently treated my drawing students to croissants from the best local boulangerie. These weren't your run-of-the-mill anemic pastries from my students' far-off home countries—those wannabes that need to be stuffed with ham and cheese to up the appeal factor. One of the first American in Paris 101 lessons is the difference between a good and a bad croissant. I am generous enough to educate the next generation so they don't have to gain the Parisian 15 (or moveable feast, as I like to say) to learn for themselves. I told the students they could have one of these beauties, but they would have to tell the story of eating it in four to six quick sketches. What resulted was a handful of very different interpretations, from a how-to-eat-a-croissant diagram to a comic strip starring a bug-eyed croissant avatar.

When you feel stumped and can't access inspiration, reignite your senses. Take a walk around the block, reduce all distractions, sketch away, and let the ideas flow. Today's exercise was created to help you do just that.

STEP 1

BRAINSTORM

Treat yourself to something delicious, and ask yourself why it's so special. Is it because it's rare? Is it super indulgent? Is it something that reminds you of your childhood? To help clarify what you want to communicate, refer back to the illustration holy trinity (see page 99): imagery, conflict, and client. Before you begin, ask yourself a few questions to find your point of view: Who is this illustration for? You? A friend who isn't familiar with this treat? Will you draw the treat before devouring it? Will you draw yourself in the process of eating it and capture your response? Do you want to demolish it and wear the evidence?

If you're not yet inspired, take a first bite of the treat. How does it make you feel? Are you transformed into someone else when tasting this thing? How can you describe the process of eating it?

I want to make a chart of what to look for in a good croissant for my students: It reflects the light from a generous egg wash. It makes a thumping sound when tapped with a finger. When you pull it apart by the knobby ends, the yellow middle bit reveals itself before choosing the right or left side. This is how you know you've got the real deal.

HOT TIP

A WORD ON THE MUSE

The muse often hits me like an unexpected bolt of lightning. When it strikes, there's a small buffer period before the electric shock leaves my body. At that point I can either write down the idea or bang out the illustration immediately, or, just like that, the storm clouds will clear and it will be like nothing ever happened.

I like to say, "I don't get inspired, I stay inspired," meaning I know the exact conditions under which I am intellectually and physically stimulated enough that those bolts will strike when I need them to. Sometimes this is as simple as reading the newspaper every morning and taking a walk in nature. Brainstorming regularly with other creative friends helps to flex that muscle, too.

And though I'm not a committed keeper of a sketchbook, I do jot down chicken-scratch sketches on loose sheets of paper that I stock away for when inspiration *doesn't* strike on its own.

SKETCH

Start sketching until you have four to six different frames. Include a few sentences of added information. Ask yourself if anything can be scrapped and how it will impact the overall progression of the images.

I like my initial sketch, but the written descriptions aren't specific enough, so I'm going to steer away from a text-heavy interpretation and draw some visual cues in the next step.

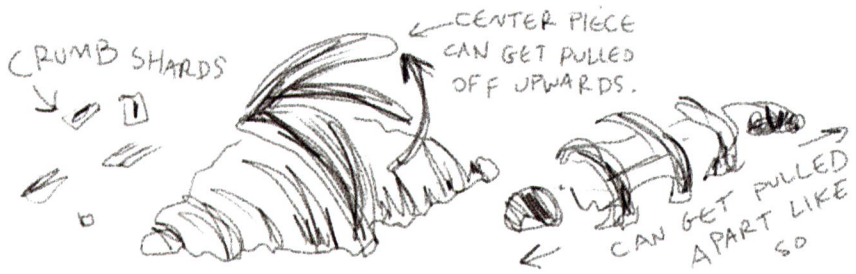

PAINT

Choose your palette. If this is a matter-of-fact how-to, you might opt for minimal colors. If this is a food-crazed fever dream, is there a playful, fantastical way to use color? How can color reinforce your concept? If your concept is more instructional, look at how-to illustrations as inspiration. Since my guide is more matter-of-fact, I keep the focus on re-creating the elements of the croissant and add simple black handwriting.

This is not the first time I have painted a croissant. Instead of wasting time building washes to add volume to each section of the croissant, I mix several techniques by adding a preliminary yellow wash to define the volume of each section, being sure to identify where the light source is coming from. While the layer

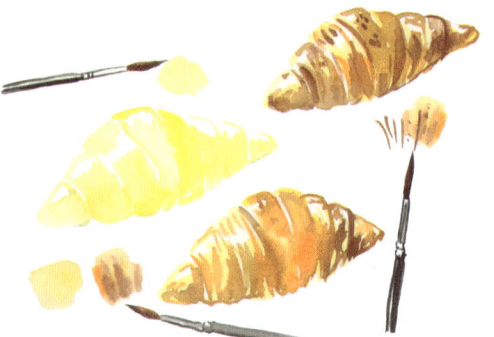

is still slightly wet, I add extra pigment or thicker paint to the tip of the brush and start dotting the brush and making stripes to begin rendering the scraggly texture. Once this first layer is completely dry, I continue building wet-on-dry lines and dots.

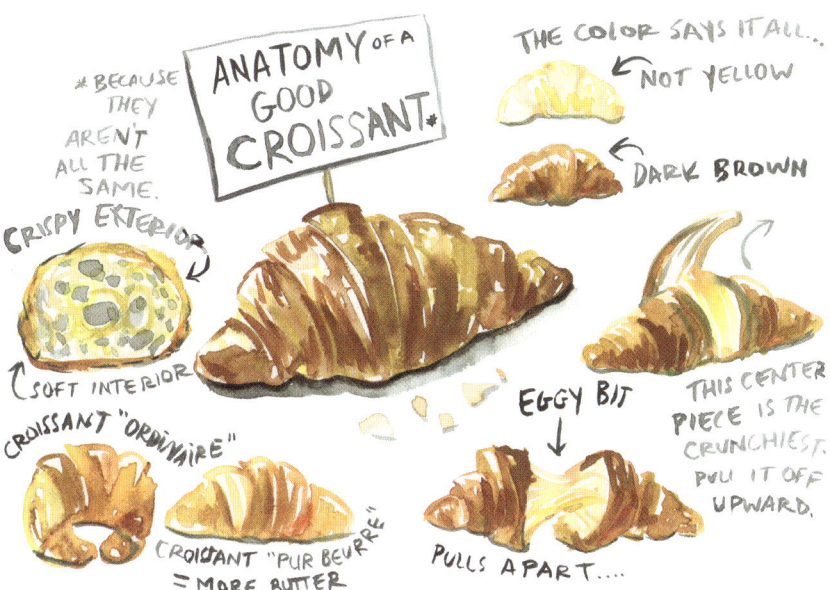

STEP 4
REFLECT

If you appreciated this exercise in particular, then make a mental note to lean into your senses when the ideas aren't flowing. If you are ever stuck and get sucked into the vortex of swiping and scrolling on your phone, get out of the house. Walk the dog. Make a cup of tea. Recommit to finding a primary reference in your own world.

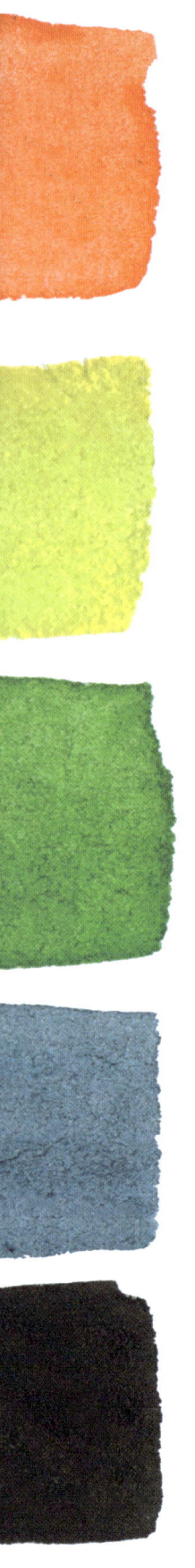

DAY 14

SCAVENGER HUNT

Today, you will examine a place and record it in your sketchbook. Imagine yourself as a visual journalist, documenting all the tiny bits and pieces that make the place unique and capturing the energy of a distinct moment.

This exercise will take you out of the comfort of your studio and put you directly into the trenches of inspiration. You don't have time to hem and haw over the what-ifs—you have to commit to capturing as much of the living world as possible within a short amount of time. Two things that are different about today's exercise are that you will sketch directly with watercolor and that you will be working with a limited palette of one to four colors. You will be surprised at how your own personal sense of humor and style will be revealed in this exercise; it's a favorite of my drawing students'.

STEP 1

BRAINSTORM

Where can you go to immerse yourself in your visual research? It could be a museum, a gallery, a shop, Walmart, or another easy place to access. I courageously took my son on an early-morning jaunt to the Centre Pompidou. How would we fare in this funhouse of an art museum? (The building, with its visible interior structures, is a living organism and is just as much a part of the museum as the art collection.) I braced myself and my watercolor paints for what would reveal itself.

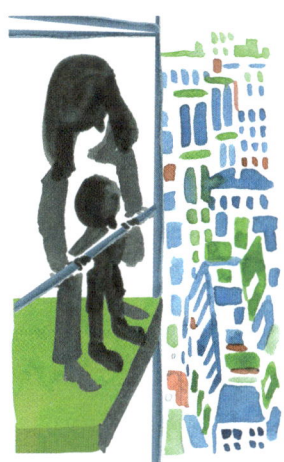

HOT TIP

LIVE WATERCOLOR ESSENTIALS

For obvious reasons, most museums discourage you from walking around with giant vessels of watercolor water among their world-class collection, and many have specific rules around what kinds of art supplies are permitted. But drawing and painting from life is a thrilling exercise of engaging in capturing the present. Here is what you need to facilitate painting in the flesh without breaking your back or getting kicked out of the Louvre.

WHAT TO BRING

- Two or three H pencils
- A watercolor-compatible sketchbook

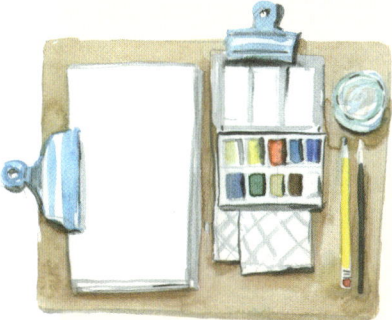

- A travel watercolor set (like the Raphaël Watercolor Travel Pan Set)
- Paintbrushes or refillable watercolor brush pens (like Pentel Aquash Water Brushes; for more on brush pens, see page 23).
- A roll-up brush carrier
- A plastic cup or a collapsible watercolor cup
- Paper towels. If you don't have time to let the watercolor in your sketchbook dry completely, cover

it with a clean paper towel and hope for the best.

- A 15-by-16-inch (38 by 41 cm) sketchboard or clipboard
- Adhesive. My friend, illustrator and live artist Francesco Lo Iacono, attaches his essentials on his clipboard with Velcro so everything stays where it belongs. You can also use giant rubber bands, drawing clips, or adhesive putty to keep paper and other gear in place.
- A portable stool, if necessary

PAINT

There's no sketching today. This exercise is scavenger hunt style, meaning you'll need to quickly jot down a watercolor sketch using a limited palette of four colors maximum, inspired by each of the prompts below. I take inspiration from the Centre Pompidou's façade and use its primary color palette: red, blue, green, and yellow. Paint as many of the following prompts as you can.

1. Paint yourself.
2. Paint something that speaks of the current moment.
3. Paint someone's shoes.
4. Paint a portrait of someone.
5. Paint someone looking at something.
6. Create a "focused transcription" of something noteworthy (see page 110).
7. Paint an architectural detail.
8. Paint something you think is perfect.
9. Paint someone who works at this place.
10. Paint something you find annoying.
11. Paint something strange.
12. Paint something you consider funny.
13. Paint yourself at the end of your visit.

REFLECT

How did it feel working through a long list of to-dos in a short amount of time? Did you feel destabilized or extremely present? Did you learn anything about working with watercolor paint in this new way? If you feel tense and restrained in your watercolor practice, give this exercise a go from time to time. You may be surprised at how much you'll like what you put together in such a short period and when you can't edit yourself into oblivion.

A DAY (OR HOUR) AT THE MUSEUM

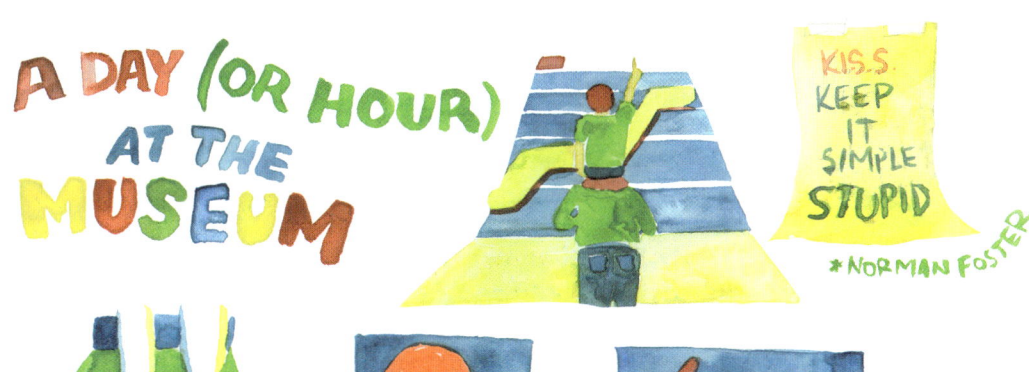

K.I.S.S.
KEEP
IT
SIMPLE
STUPID

*NORMAN FOSTER

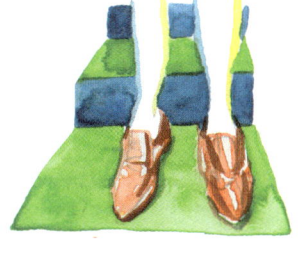

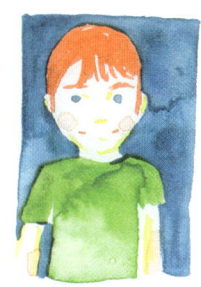

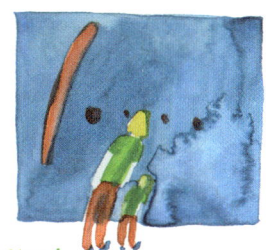

MIRÓ "BLEU II"

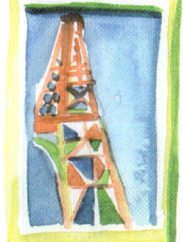
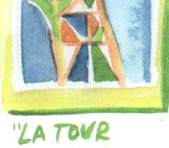

"LA TOUR EIFFEL" DELAUNAY

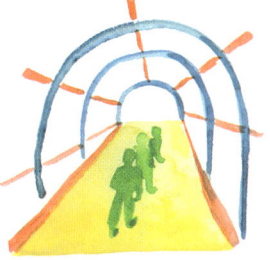

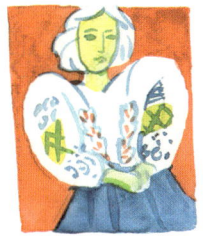
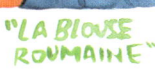

"LA BLOUSE ROUMAINE"

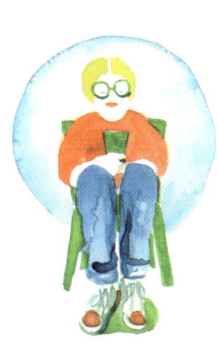

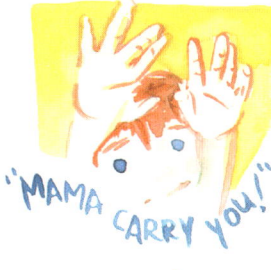

"MAMA CARRY YOU!"

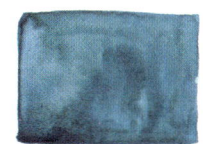

SOULAGES

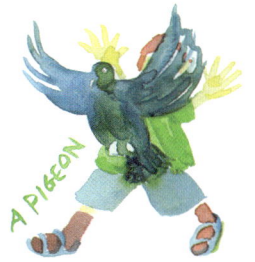

A PIGEON

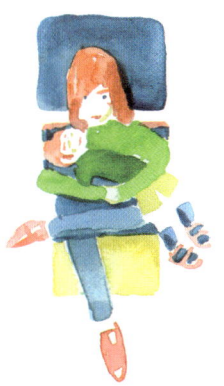

Focused Transcriptions

One of the joys of teaching students in Paris is sketching at all the major art museums. There's nothing like drawing in the presence of a masterpiece. It's a combination of the lighting, the energy in the room, and the unsolicited comments of American passersby ("Gooooood," a Baby Boomer once whispered over my shoulder in a perfect Midwestern accent).

If you can, pack up your drawing supplies and camp out at a museum for an hour or so (for tips on live painting, see page 107). Not all museums permit painting, so always check ahead of time for any specific rules around which supplies you can bring along. If you can't get out of the house, you are more than welcome to sketch from a reproduction of a painting, but just note that it is not the same experience.

I took inspiration for this practice from Jake Spicer's book *How to Draw: Sketch and Draw Anything, Anywhere*, a wonderful resource for fine-tuning your observational drawing skills. Spicer insists that studying great paintings will challenge you to question all the micro choices made by the artist, including color intensity, composition, scale, emotion, depth, and harmony, and understand why those choices are successful. Find a painting that you gravitate toward and ask yourself the following questions to start dissecting the composition:

- Where is the light coming from?

- Where is the focal point?

- Can you identify the horizon line?

- What colors were used? How were complementary colors used, if at all?

- How is the composition formed? If you draw a line to connect the elements, does it create a geometric shape?

- How was texture used, if at all?

Sketch out the composition, building up shadow little by little by layering longer strokes with the side of your pencil. For this exercise, feel free to use a softer pencil (2B, 4B, 6B, etc.) to obtain more range in value. Squint occasionally to understand the use of tone to differentiate the different elements. Continue building your monochrome sketch until it suggests the darkest and lightest parts of your inspiration painting. If you draw a line to connect the predominant elements, do you see any shapes form? Can you see visible brushstrokes in the artwork? If so, how can you translate those with a pencil line?

When you're ready to move to watercolor, you're not aiming for a perfect replica of the painting. Taking the principles and techniques you've developed already, paint the piece to the best of your ability. What is the focal point of the painting, and how did the artist direct your attention to this portion of the composition? How did the artist use color to either emphasize the focal point or draw attention around the composition? How will you adapt the white in the painting to saving the white space in your watercolor?

Try out this exercise from time to time to continue challenging your color-mixing skills and to fine-tune your critical eye on the great masters. It will completely transform the way you visit museums.

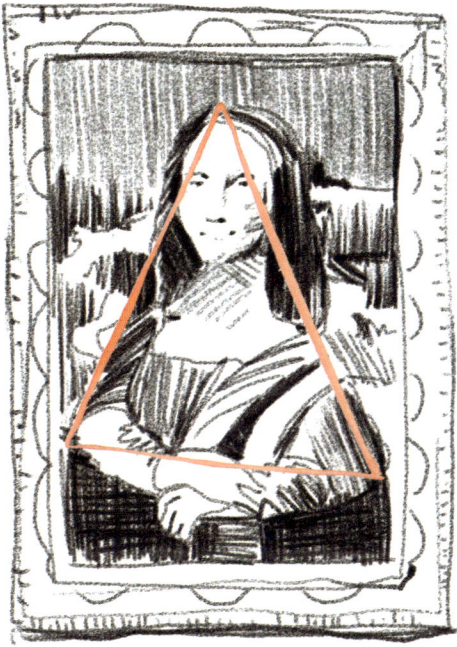

In approaching this transcription of the *Mona Lisa*, I look for a dominant shape in the composition: a triangle connecting the head with the hands.

DAY 15

PAST, PRESENT, FUTURE PAPER DOLLS

Long before I picked up a paintbrush, I used fashion for my daily dose of self-expression. When I got off the plane at Charles de Gaulle, I was boldly armored in my favorite ruffled red Chiquita Banana–inspired dress. And I was rudely awakened to what I had become . . . a brazen foreigner. I passed some impeccably chic French women on the street, with their gently styled bedhead, invisible makeup, and sober silhouettes. In one of my first attempts to assimilate in France, I adapted the local fashion to my own style. Since then, I've found a happy medium between the two sartorial extremes. In today's prompt, you will visualize your past, present, and future personal style by making paper dolls. I'll walk you through how to develop your concept, the secrets to drawing clothes worn on a human body, and also how to render texture and detail in watercolor. Let's start dreaming up your paper self.

STEP 1
BRAINSTORM

To jump-start the creative process, identify a sartorial chapter of your life to draw inspiration from. Your coming-of-age? The style evolution of your adult life? Fashion faux pas from each decade you've lived? Can you find a sartorial thread connecting each outfit? Can you make each one representative of a certain moment in time by adding pop culture references or other details from the era? I'll be recapping my style evolution from my early au pair days to the present.

STEP 2
SKETCH

When you buy a book of paper dolls, you always have the base doll in their skivvies, ready to get dressed. Sketch out a representation of yourself and three to five outfits. Don't forget the accessories.

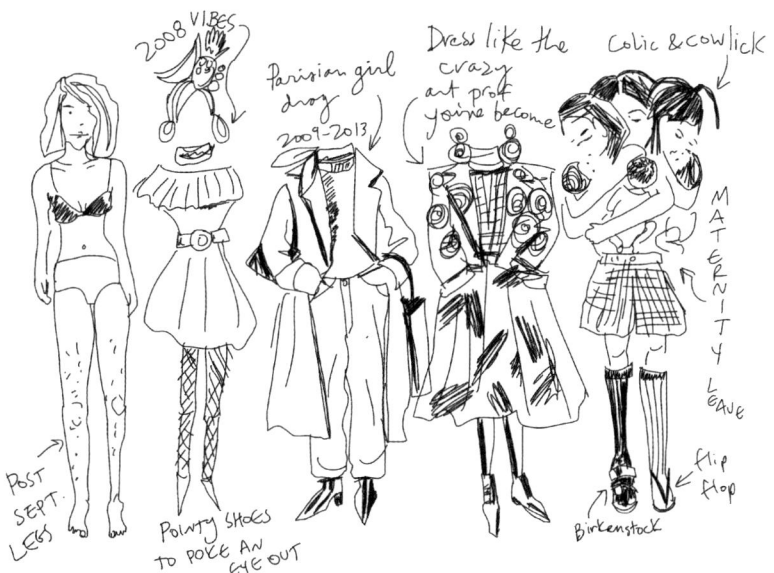

In my sketch above, I draw my doll, my Chiquita Banana arrival look, my French-girl years, my current commitment to prints on prints, and a visual recap of the scary early days of my maternity leave.

STEP 3
CREATE YOUR DOLLS

Once you sketch the *you* doll, cut it out. To ensure that the outfits will seamlessly cover your avatar's unmentionables, trace the outline of the body on your clothing sketches.

As you sketch out each outfit on watercolor paper, add rectangular tabs so the outfits can be attached to the avatar and are understood to be paper doll clothing.

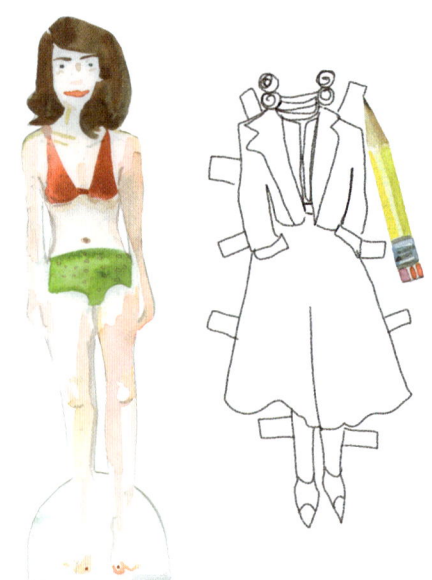

STEP 4
PAINT

Before you start painting the clothing, ask yourself if the garment is exaggerating, highlighting, or hiding the human form. Think about how patterns can be rendered in perspective in relationship to the human body. Observe the two red dresses at right. The first one hugs the body to reveal the silhouette of the form underneath. The second has a ruffled neckline and a full, flouncy skirt, which exaggerates the form. Closely observing the highlights in the ruffled dress, I suggest the excess fabric by saving some white space in the skirt.

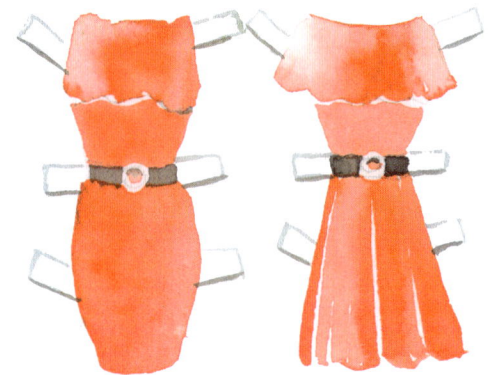

Think about the kind of texture that you would like to render and which technique is best adapted to it. Do you want a softer, diffused texture to evoke cotton? Paint with 50% flood. If you want something like plaid or stripes, go directly with wet on dry to get precise details.

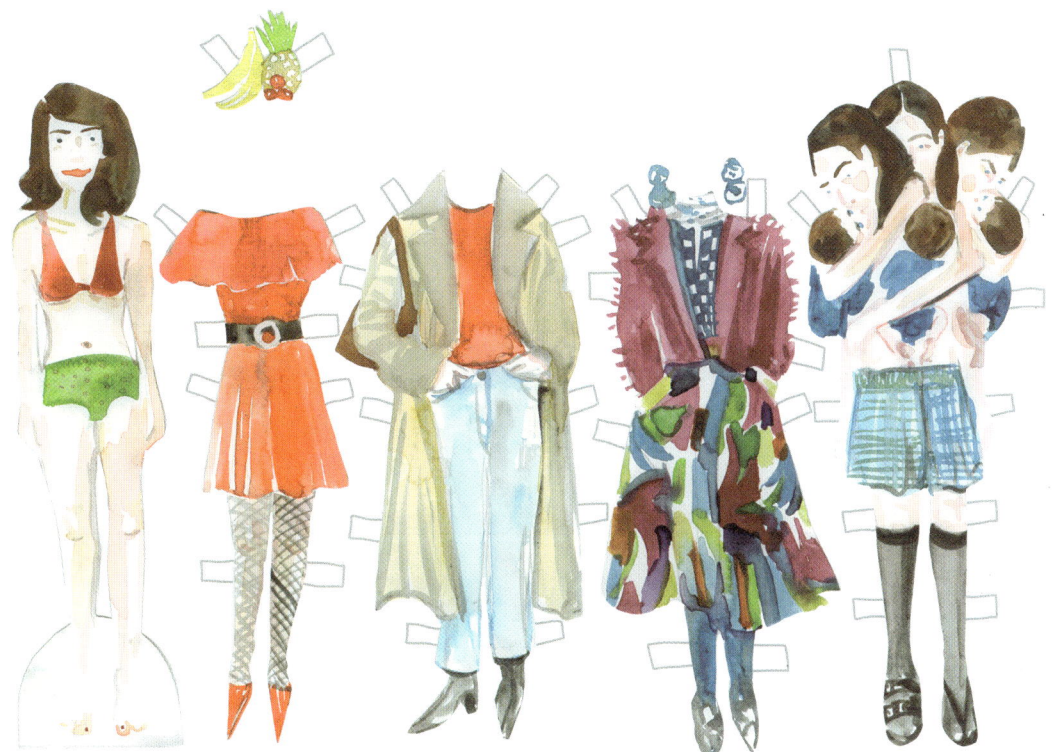

STEP 5
REFLECT

Take a look at your doll collection in full. Were you able to capture the evolution of certain eras by contrasting colors, textures, silhouettes, or even hairstyles? Feel free to cut these out and dress up your doll to your heart's desire.

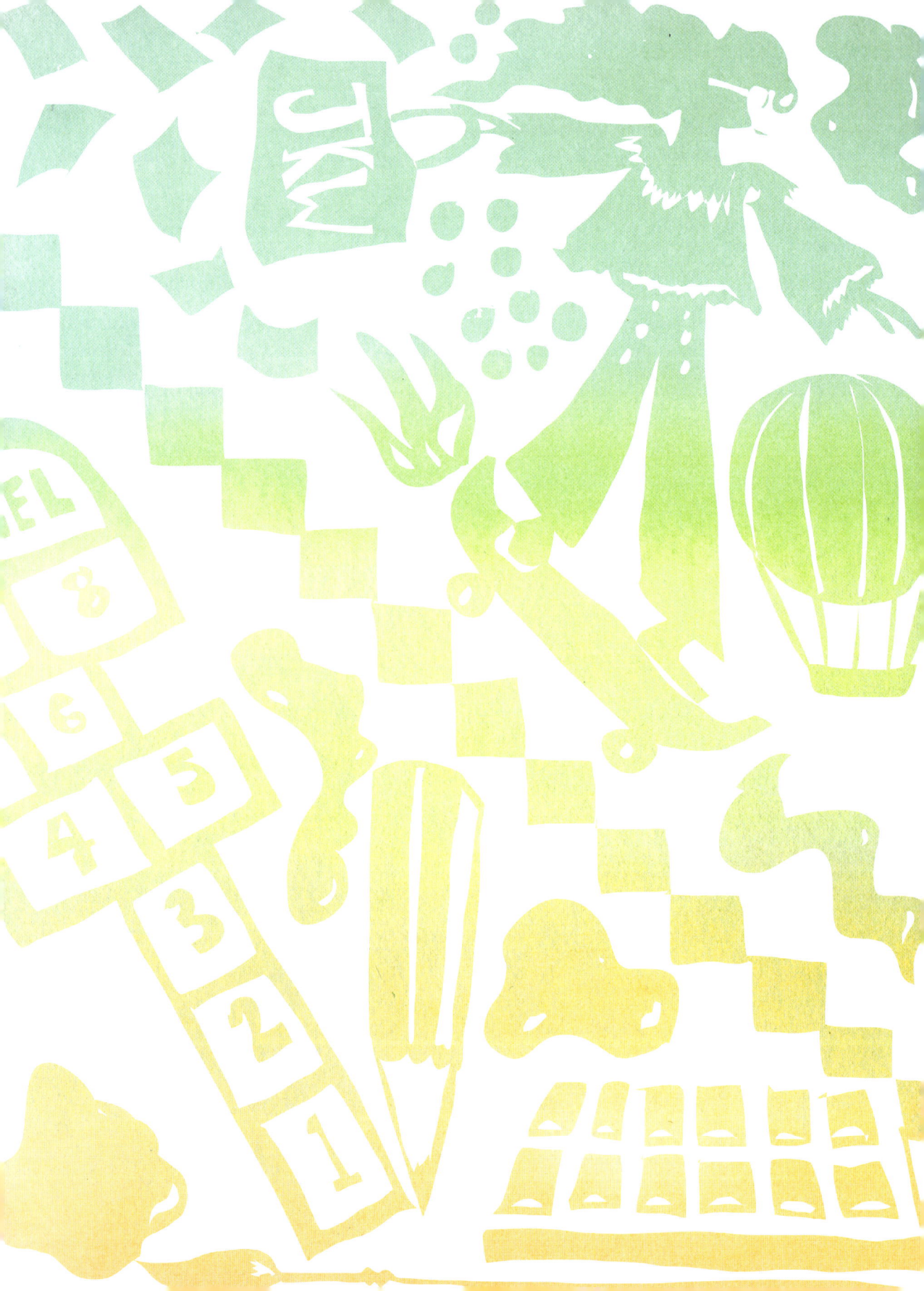

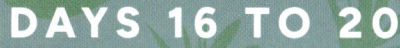

CHILD'S PLAY

Experimentation can easily get brushed off as frivolous, but play is super important to how I develop new styles and ideas. Now that you have a couple of weeks of watercolor exercises under your belt, we are going to take a breather and play around a little bit. This isn't necessarily a goal-oriented chapter; it's about finding wonder in playing with watercolor and expanding what you think it can be. If any of these exercises are particularly fun for you, lean into them! And also lean into the discomfort of getting messy and occasionally feeling lost. This chapter will get you out of your thinking mind and into trusting the process.

DAY 16

PAINT ME A SONG

I am a huge Joni Mitchell fan. The reason I love her music and revisit it often is how visual it is. It's probably because she is a kind of painter, one who can paint pictures with her songs, and they make me listen in color. Today you will paint an album cover inspired by one of your favorite songs. You don't need to say everything, just suggest the essentials of the song, channeling it through your experiences, your imagination, your style, and your cultural references with your use of color.

STEP 1
BRAINSTORM

Quickly jot down some of your favorite songs. Which one has the most visual potential? Does it speak to a certain moment in time? Was that song there for you during a difficult moment? What colors do you see when you listen to this song? How can you use color to recap the emotion you feel when you listen to it?

Today I'll be illustrating "Chelsea Morning" by Joni Mitchell, which I used to sing to my son before he was born, being intentional about conveying the detailed descriptions captured in the song. This song is the ultimate mash-up of a bustling cityscape and a "cocoon" inside a hotel. Remember, you don't need your illustration to say everything; it should just suggest the essentials.

STEP 2
SKETCH

Start sketching out the visual building blocks of the song—and remember that an album cover has a square format. Mine will be a view of both the noisy exterior of the Chelsea Hotel in New York City (pigeons hovering, cars honking their horns, people walking) and the jewel-toned bliss inside (a bowl of oranges, milk and honey, a rainbow on the wall).

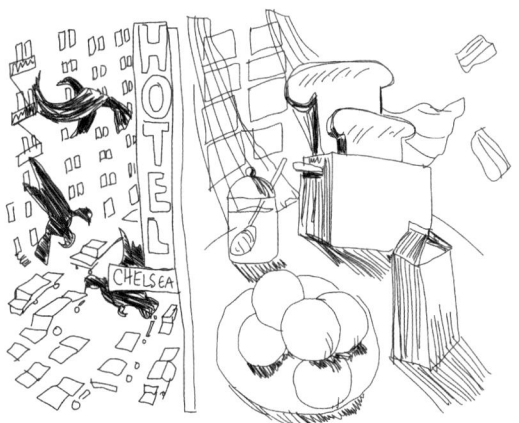

I am feeling ambitious today and want to challenge myself to be less figurative, finding a more abstract entry point. Since this is an homage to my son's Joni Mitchell in utero education, could I tell the story in evocative sound waves? Once I have my primary sketch (in red), I draw concentric circles on top (in blue) to give myself an idea of how to distribute the paint.

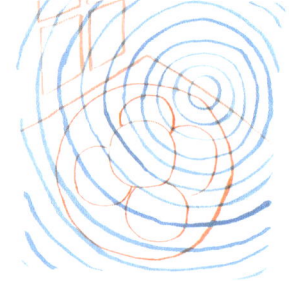

Since this is a new idea, I take a moment to do a watercolor test. I quickly paint the colors that I see when I am thinking of this song. Since it's during the golden hour, I want to have the jewel-toned items mentioned in the song bathed in butterscotch tones of light. Once I have my structure in place, I can start painting section by section. Once the first quadrants are dry, I can fill in the rest.

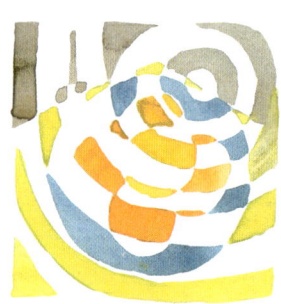

I clean up my final sketch, removing any excess pencil lines and creating concentric circles to build up the structure.

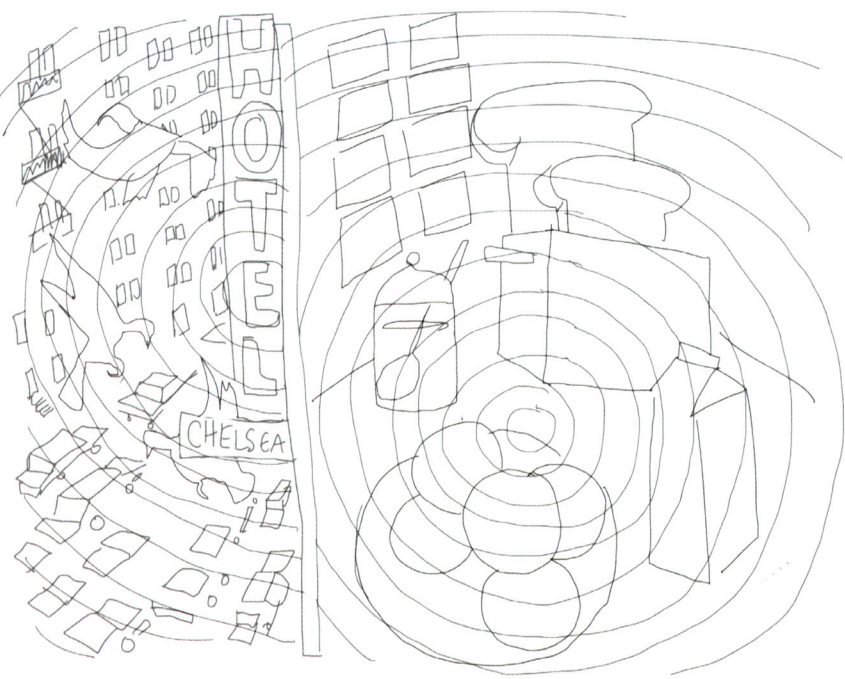

STEP 3
PAINT

I start building the paint, quadrant by quadrant. Because
I don't want two wet quadrants to bleed together, I skip
a quadrant before painting the next. Once my first layer
has dried, I fill in the blanks with the missing portions. Just
because I am working in quadrants doesn't mean I can't mix
techniques. Depending on when I want to add shadow or
contrast, I build washes and drop in extra color when needed
(e.g., more orange to the right of the yellow quadrant shown at right).

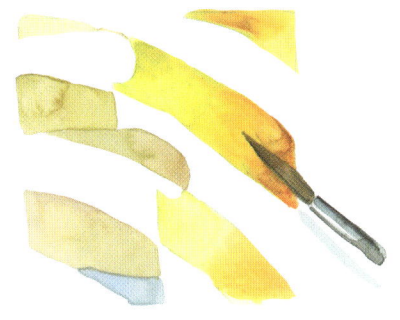

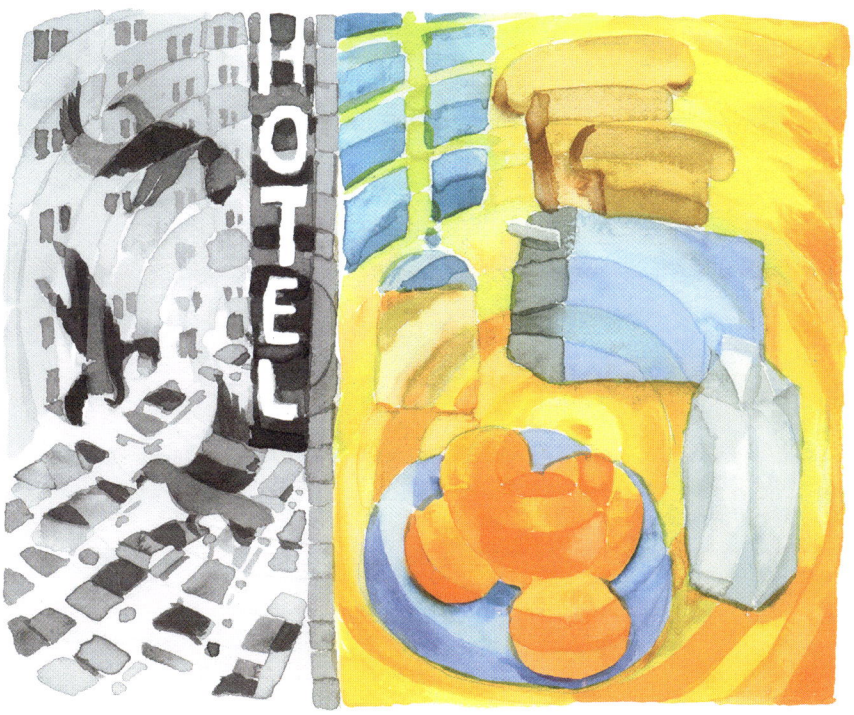

STEP 4
REFLECT

How did your use of color influence the emotional charge of this watercolor?
Pass your work on to a friend and ask what they see and how it makes them feel.
Can they identify the song? If not, were you able to expand on the ideas of the
song and reveal something new?

Snap Out of It

I have a confession to make: My young son has been using my watercolors for some time now. I purchased a grocery store kit when he was still a baby, but the pigments were barely visible, and I didn't want to deprive him of the joy of playing with real watercolor before he's indoctrinated with stick-figure anatomy and the dos and don'ts of art making, which seem to leave a discouraging mark on almost everybody. For now, he just sits down, activates his paint, and sees what happens. What if it was this easy for everybody?

These micro exercises are about reconnecting with that childlike wonder of sitting down and putting your imagination onto paper, the perfect antidote if you need to loosen up or hit your creative reset button. Give yourself permission for it to not be good. Tell yourself that your goal is just to make colors and fill the whole page. If you take something away from this practice, great. If not, at least you had a little bit of fun.

are painting with the movement of your wrist, elbow, or entire arm. Try standing up and see how it changes how you navigate painting. Forget about saving the white space or avoiding muddy colors: Let loose and see how one color merges into the next by painting long, sweeping strokes.

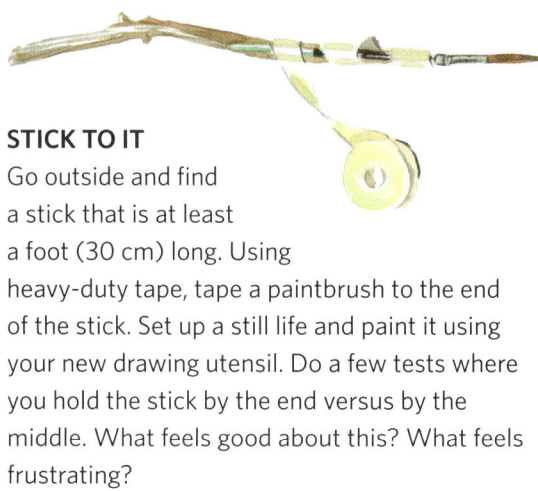

STICK TO IT

Go outside and find a stick that is at least a foot (30 cm) long. Using heavy-duty tape, tape a paintbrush to the end of the stick. Set up a still life and paint it using your new drawing utensil. Do a few tests where you hold the stick by the end versus by the middle. What feels good about this? What feels frustrating?

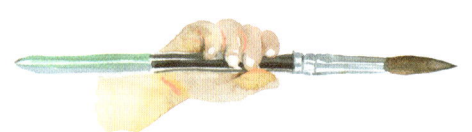

LOOSEN UP

Want to tap into that childhood joy of knowing you are finger painting and the world (aka your home) is your canvas? Set up your watercolor materials. But today you will be painting with your nondominant hand. Try using the biggest brush you have and see how this changes your relationship to the paper. Notice if you

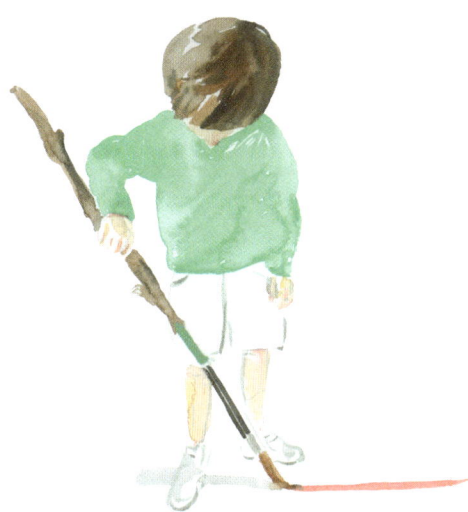

You will notice you aren't painting with your wrist like you would with a normal paintbrush. Depending on where you hold the brush, you are painting with either your elbow or your whole arm—you may even need to stand up. Energetically, it's a much different method of painting, and it could help you to loosen up.

DOODLE WITH WATERCOLOR

Take out a sheet of watercolor paper and start doodling freely with a watercolor brush and paint. Use a contrasting color to add details and see what happens.

MAKE IT LIKE MATISSE

Using the largest brush you have, paint a whole sheet of watercolor paper with one color. (This is a good time to use the reverse side of any botched paintings that you may have collected.) Repeat until you have five sheets, all painted with different colors. Use scissors to cut out geometric forms. Overlap the pieces until you create a graphic and abstract composition. You can set up a still life if you need a primary reference, or just use your imagination. How does it feel working only with forms instead of lines? Once you have an arrangement you're happy with, use a glue stick or double-sided tape to attach the shapes to a clean sheet of paper.

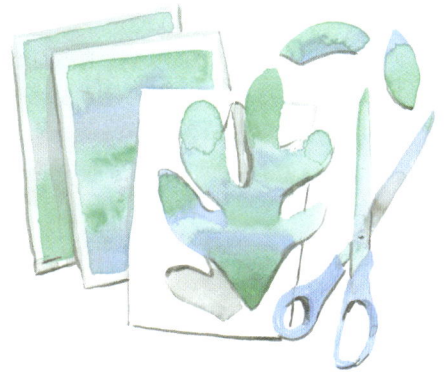

Did you enjoy these mini exercises? How did they push you to see differently? How can you adapt any of these to your regular practice?

DAY 17

GIF ME UP

Today you will create a series of sequential watercolors
that can be grouped together to make a gif (a quick digital
animation that plays on a loop). The reason I am challenging
you to take your watercolors into the next dimension is to
continue broadening your expectations of what watercolor can
be. While previous exercises have nudged you to pay attention
to color in the world around you, now you'll have a greater
eye toward movement: You'll notice things like the nuances of
a tree swaying in the wind, a choreography of branches, and
shimmering leaves.

STEP 1

BRAINSTORM

Find inspiration in something in the real world—this isn't the time for fantasy scenarios—and keep it simple. A thumb going up and down. A portrait of yourself blinking. Your cat sleeping in the sun, its belly rhythmically moving up and down. When you are dreaming up your gif, remember that it will be saved on a loop, meaning the action will be replayed into infinity. So make sure the movement is logical when replayed.

STEP 2

SKETCH

This is an exercise in minimalism. Limit your gif to two to five "frames." Because the goal is to communicate movement, you won't be doing precise, detailed line work. Instead, try graphically highlighting the action of what is moving.

Sketch out the frames, ensuring that all of the drawings are more or less the same size so that they can easily overlap when you make the gif later.

Today I'll be animating a pigeon pecking for crumbs. I look up a few videos on YouTube to closely observe the movement. Does the pigeon's tail move upward as it lowers its head to the ground?

Remember, this isn't Disney animation; you don't need twenty-four frames per second to understand the essential movement. How can you choose a few frames to communicate the motion?

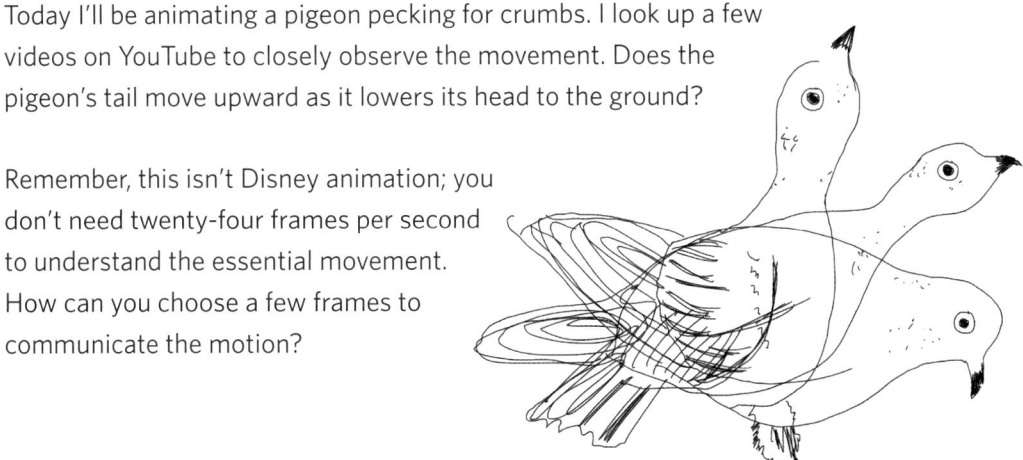

PAINT

How can color add another storytelling element to your gif? The color doesn't need to be true to life but should suggest what the thing is that's in motion.

Since I want my colors to stay consistent, I break down the pigeon into sections and paint the same part on all the sketches before moving on to the next. I mix a light blue wash and paint the bodies of the pigeons wet on dry, leaving the white space of the wing. While the first layer is still wet, I load up my brush with turquoise and dot the neck and head of the pigeon to add texture. To add shadow, I paint a darker blue under the wing and add some lines on the tail to suggest the feathers. I alternately paint blue and gray lines to add texture to the wings. The same orange is painted for the eyes and feet. A final stroke of black watercolor adds the finishing touch to the beak and pupil.

Remember that when you group together variations of the same watercolor, the differences will automatically add some supplementary movement.

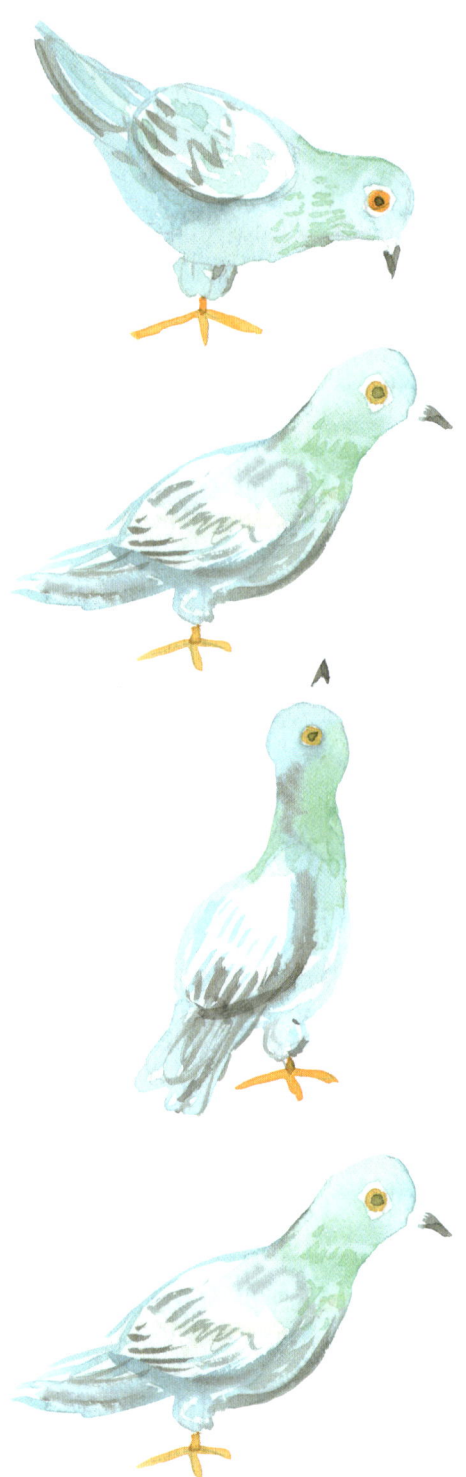

STEP 4

SHARE

Now that you've got the frames, how do you make the gif? I choose to scan my watercolors and build the gif in Photoshop for a clean, professional look. The cheap-and-dirty method is to take a picture of each frame, ideally with natural lighting, and keep the frame consistent so the movement is fluid when the images are grouped together. These pics can then be uploaded to the Giphy app or a social media platform like Instagram or TikTok. Just be sure the frames move quickly; otherwise the viewer won't know that your work is intended to be an animation.

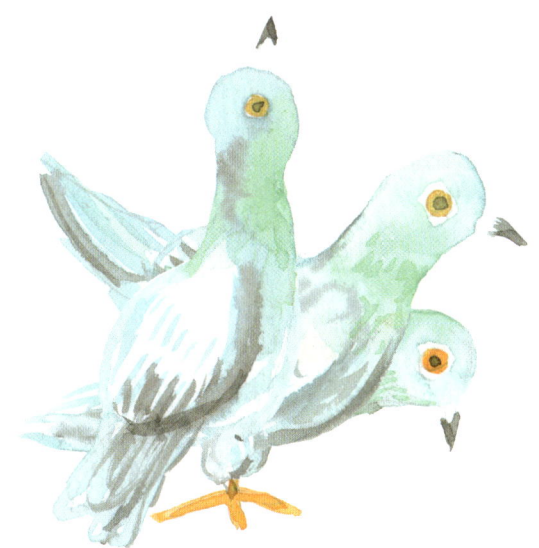

STEP 5

REFLECT

You've done enough exercises now to know that drawing is all about seeing. Animation requires an even closer look at the world and all its moving parts. I once animated a self-portrait with my eyes blinking every couple of seconds. The result, with just my eyes moving, was robotic. The more I looked at myself blinking in the mirror, the more nuances I observed: an occasionally furled eyebrow, the flare of my nostrils, and a pursing of the lips. I re-created the gif with all these micromovements and it was much more lifelike. But this never would have happened had I not spent the time observing with intention. If you're not happy with the final result of this exercise, take a closer look at how your chosen subject moves.

DAY 18

FORGET ME NOT

I've always loved using a Sharpie when sketching. I like how instantly graphic it is, but it grants no leeway for softness; it is the exact opposite of watercolor. When I am sketching in the wild, I always aspire to marry the instant gratification of a Sharpie with the nuance of watercolor. The result is a zigzag technique that I use when I am drawing or painting live. Sketching directly with watercolor, I get the impact of a Sharpie without getting lost in the endless details that I *could* draw.

Today you will be using this zigzag technique to recap something from your memory that you never want to forget. Giving yourself the restriction of working in a completely new way will hopefully unlock your ability to draw off the top of your head.

BRAINSTORM

I can't help but want to put the first year with my little one in a time capsule. The milestones, the ups and downs, the tender and funny moments. I love how a newborn is an appendage of their mother in a baby carrier until their third month, when they pop their little head out like a turtle and life truly begins.

SKETCH

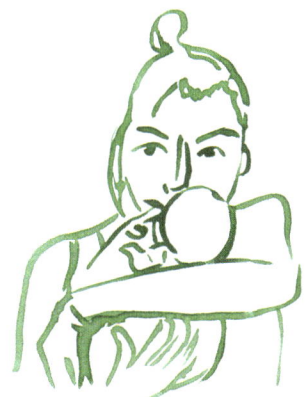 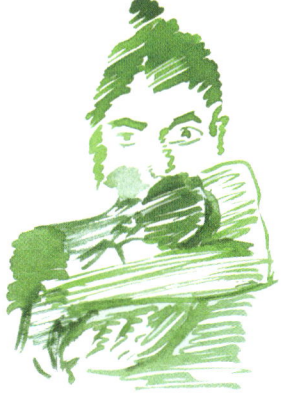

This is a different entry point to watercolor. You will be focused on the form instead of the outline, which leads to a greater sense of volume. To demonstrate, above you see sketches of the same mother and child. The watercolor on the left outlines the figures, while the one on the right renders them energetically with zigzagged lines.

Take out a pencil and sketch a few of your ideas to get the hang of this technique. Remember that you are rendering the shapes and forms instead of the details.

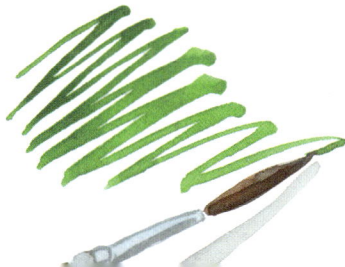

PAINT

Today I would like you to work exclusively with one color, to create continuity among the images. I'll be using green because it suggests harmony and growth. Activate the color of your choice in your watercolor palette. Feel free to mix several versions of the color by adjusting the transparency and opacity or mix in another neighboring color from the color wheel. As you can see, I added a little bit of yellow to mix a warmer green. Load up your paintbrush with color and start building the forms in a zigzag motion. While the paint is wet on the paper, you can always go back with a darker hue to drop in more color if you need to suggest shadows or details.

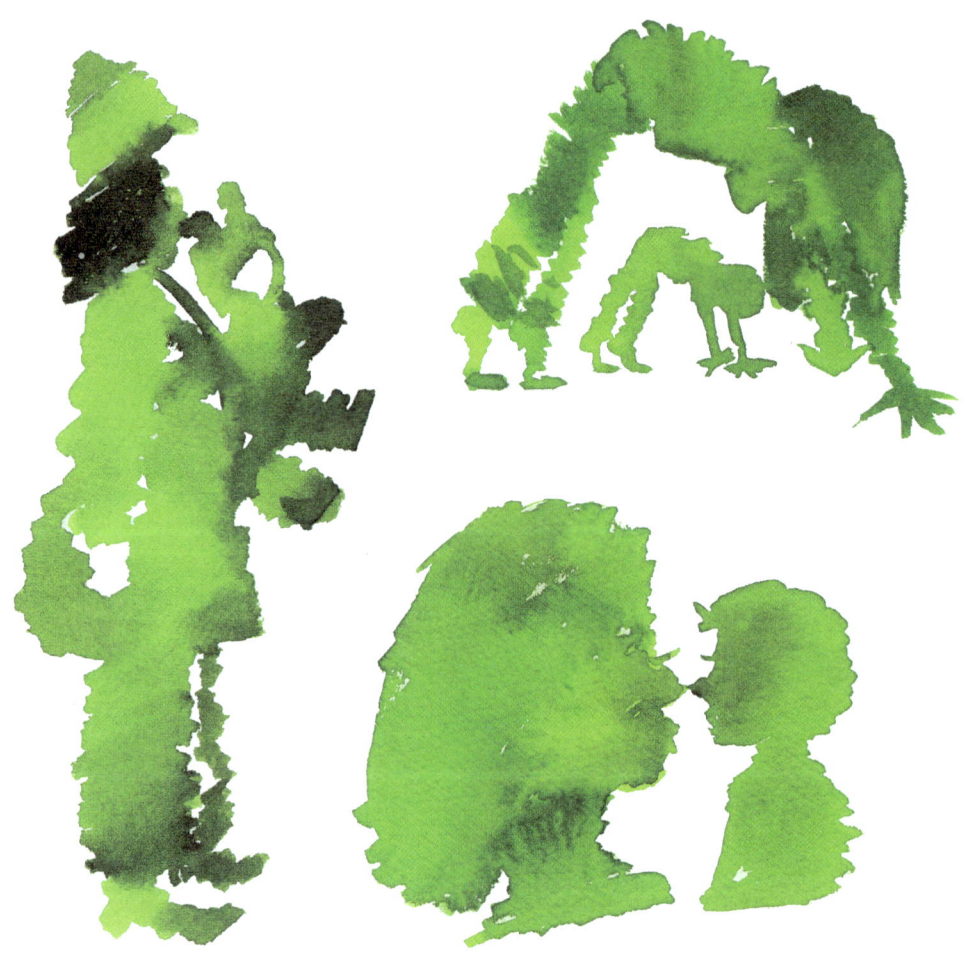

STEP 4

REFLECT

Does working in this style reveal anything new within you? How did identifying forms versus outlines change how you work? What do you think of the final result? Can you include this in your regular sketching practice?

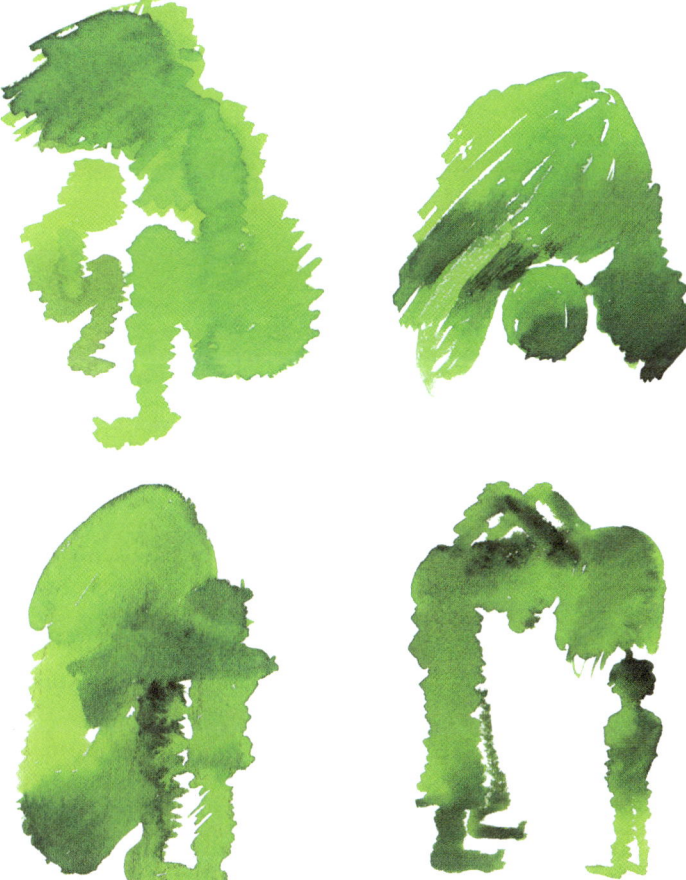

NOW DON'T MESS IT UP!

When we were converting my husband's library into a nursery, he suggested taking the boxes of my watercolor archives to store indefinitely in the basement. What came out of my mouth was a Franglais screech so loud, the building trembled. Since watercolor is water soluble, a humid basement could damage my life's work—and I won't even mention the risk of flooding. Here are a few more hard-won lessons to preserve and protect your watercolors.

- Store your watercolors in a cool, dry place. I store my big watercolor paintings in flat cardboard portfolios. If you have ambitions of becoming a professional artist or saving your work for future generations, you may wish to use archival-quality paper and invest in some acid-free boxes.

- Beware humidity. Do not hang your beautiful watercolor under a boiling tea kettle or in a steamy bathroom.

- Avoid hanging a watercolor in direct sunlight, which can lighten your colors or make your paper yellow. (If you're framing a piece, consider investing in UV-sensitive glass to preserve the colors.)

DAY 19

CROP JOB

When I've had lulls in my workflow or lightning bolts of inspiration, I've often thought of writing a graphic novel. But I always got mired in a laborious process of overwriting, overthinking, and overillustrating. That is, until I ordered a foundational text for visual storytellers, *Understanding Comics: The Invisible Art* by Scott McCloud. He brilliantly recounts the history of graphic novels while sharing the building blocks of the art form.

What defines graphic novels is their use of sequential art. For example, a picture of a coffeepot is just that if it stands alone. But if the same illustration is placed next to a pouring coffeepot, it becomes a story.

Today you will paint a four-to-six-frame storyboard communicating the process for something you know how to do. The twist is that you'll do this while showing the bare minimum, focusing in on the gestures required to execute said task. Not only is this a way to be more poetic in your approach to storytelling, but it will also challenge you to concentrate on rendering texture in your watercolor.

BRAINSTORM

Think of a practical task you do with your hands that you can take pictures of yourself doing—frying an egg, soothing a screaming baby, wrapping a present. This isn't the time to paint something like unlocking your creativity or unleashing your inner goddess. Once you choose a task, write down all the steps required to complete it. Then determine how those steps can be broken down into the smallest number of visuals. Think about the gif exercise on day 17—reduce this down to as few frames as possible to tighten the narrative. I'll be painting "How to make coffee in an Italian percolator."

SKETCH

Take pictures of yourself doing this task. Don't feel like you need to get yourself in each shot—focus more on just the action in the step. Sketch out each step and draw a rectangle on top to crop until you have pared the step down to its bare minimum. I sketch the following steps:

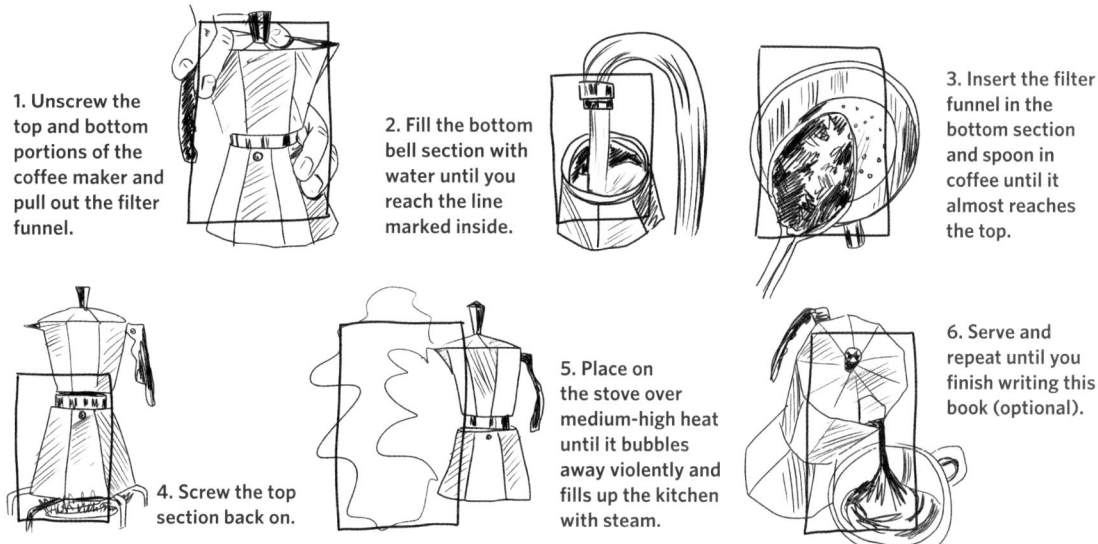

1. Unscrew the top and bottom portions of the coffee maker and pull out the filter funnel.

2. Fill the bottom bell section with water until you reach the line marked inside.

3. Insert the filter funnel in the bottom section and spoon in coffee until it almost reaches the top.

4. Screw the top section back on.

5. Place on the stove over medium-high heat until it bubbles away violently and fills up the kitchen with steam.

6. Serve and repeat until you finish writing this book (optional).

PAINT

Before you begin painting, take a second to think about color. Since I am working on a series of several images, they need to be consistent individually and collectively. The cool steel of the coffee maker complements the warm coffee, giving me a good sense of contrast to build upon.

For the sake of visual consistency, I mix three shades of paint between black and blue to render the percolator. Studying my reference images, I identify where the light source is coming from and then build the blue layers to represent the lightest portions of the coffeepot using the wet-on-dry method.

To render the contrast in the coffee in the third panel, I mix a red-brown and begin painting it on the spoon, being sure to reserve some white spots to suggest the texture. While the layer is still wet, I add a darker brown to the right side of the spoon to give it volume. Once the layer is dry, I use wet on dry to apply some dark brown stippling on the bottom right to reinforce the visual of the coffee grounds.

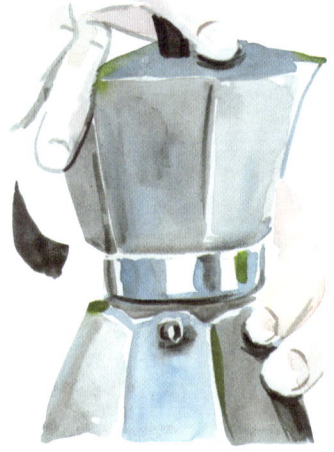 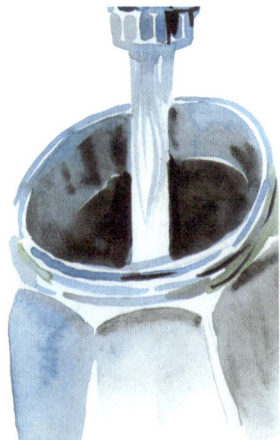 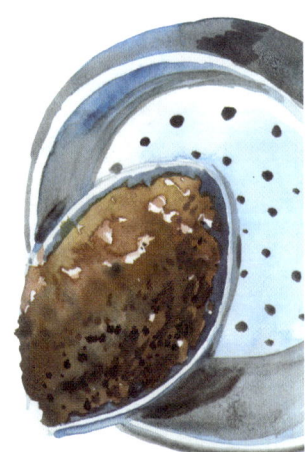

To suggest the steam of a boiling coffeepot for the fifth panel, I employ a technique I often use for rendering skies and clouds: Much like prepping the paper for 50% flood, I dip my paintbrush in water and blot it lightly on a paper towel before lightly dampening the surface I want to paint. I add the color I want on my brush and apply it to the prepped surface by twirling the brush, which creates a soft, irregular effect.

STEP 4
REFLECT

Were you able to tightly crop each frame while still communicating the action? Did your use of color unify the action or draw attention to certain frames more than others? If you were to pass on this drawing to someone else, would they understand how to do the task you illustrated?

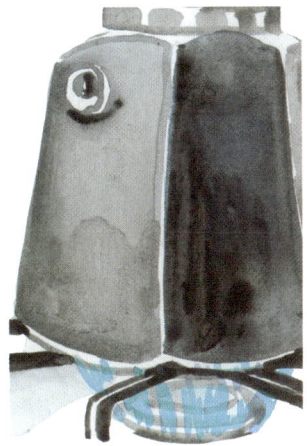
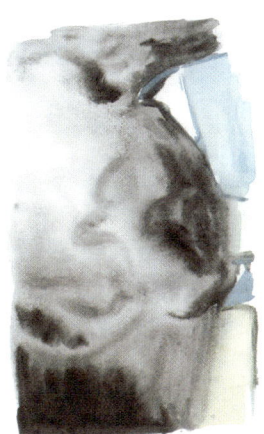
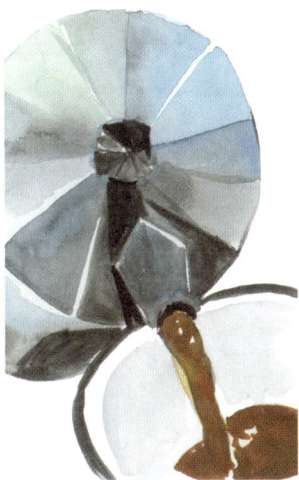

DAY 20

PAINT ME A UTOPIA

Illustration is all about communicating big ideas with the least amount of information. In the Netflix documentary series *Abstract: The Art of Design*, which follows the creative processes of artists and designers at the top of their fields, *New Yorker* cover artist and illustrator Christoph Niemann offers a brilliant example of the power of abstraction: If you were to draw a human heart pumping blood pierced by an arrow, it would be gory and horrifying—far from representing romantic love. If you abstract this idea to its bare minimum, a red square with a diagonal line through it, it doesn't say enough. A good abstraction is the solution found in the middle: a red heart pierced by an arrow. If you need to find an abstract version of a recognizable symbol like a heart, identify the two extremes and then find the middle ground.

In this exercise, you will paint an abstract idea of utopia by breaking everything down into circles and squares. Anyone can paint a circle and a square!

STEP 1
BRAINSTORM

What does utopia mean to you? Is it an island paradise? A green future? And what would you like *your* future to be? Who would you like to be with? How would you like to feel? Where would you like to be, and what speaks of that place? Still stumped? Find a few research images or create a mood board. I'm going to paint a city that is in perfect harmony with nature.

Once you land on your initial idea, how will you represent it while working within the restrictions of painting only squares and circles? This will challenge you to consider space, form, scale, and composition using a limited number of visual elements.

In my case—painting a green city—the circles represent organic shapes, like vegetation and plants. The squares and rectangles suggest man-made material, like the buildings and vehicles. Notice how I was still able to draw inspiration from the typical Parisian windows but stripped them of any excess details.

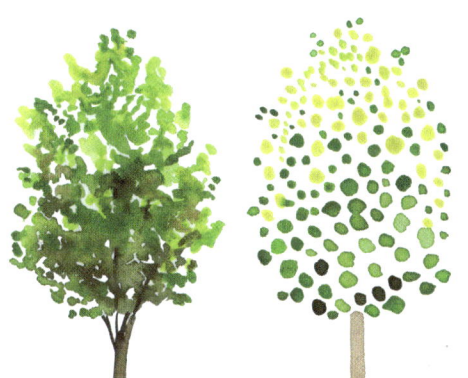
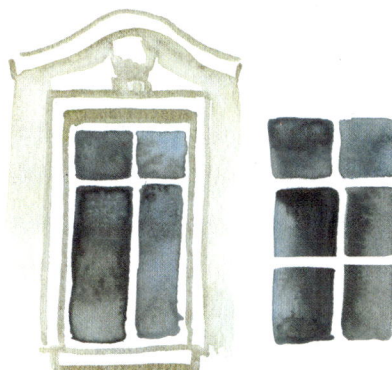

SKETCH

I do a sketch test with black watercolor to see how to balance the elements. I like how the vegetation occasionally overlaps with the windows. This will work well when it's repainted with transparent washes. Since I am taking such a radically abstract left turn here, I want to make sure that I have enough details to represent all the intricacies of city life: public transportation, public space, urban planning, etc.

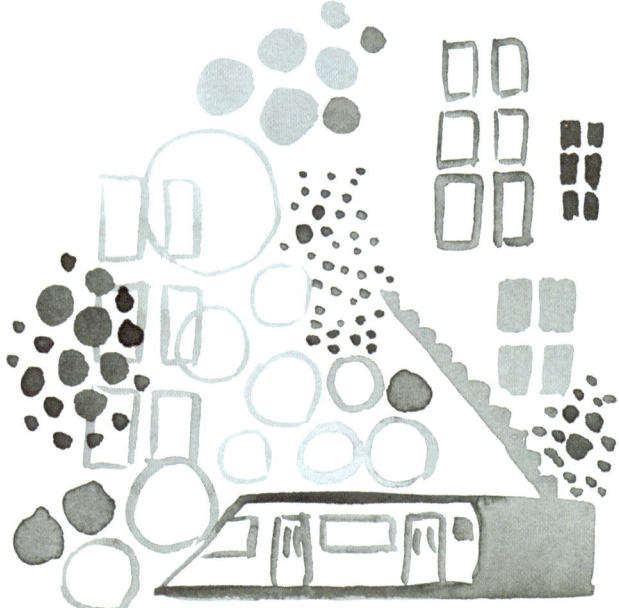

PAINT

Now it is time to activate your watercolor paint. How will color help tell your story? To suggest growth and harmony, I choose shades of yellow and green. I plan to use them interchangeably when I start painting.

My goal is for the final painting to read almost like a pattern. It doesn't have an intentional focal point because I want the overall feel to be harmonious since

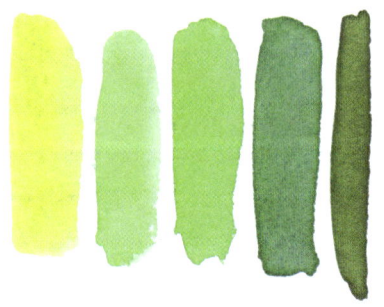

I am using so few colors. I start building windows and overlapping greenery. I play with the scale of the windows to suggest dense city life. Notice how the overlapping transparency of each layer creates new nuances of the color, too.

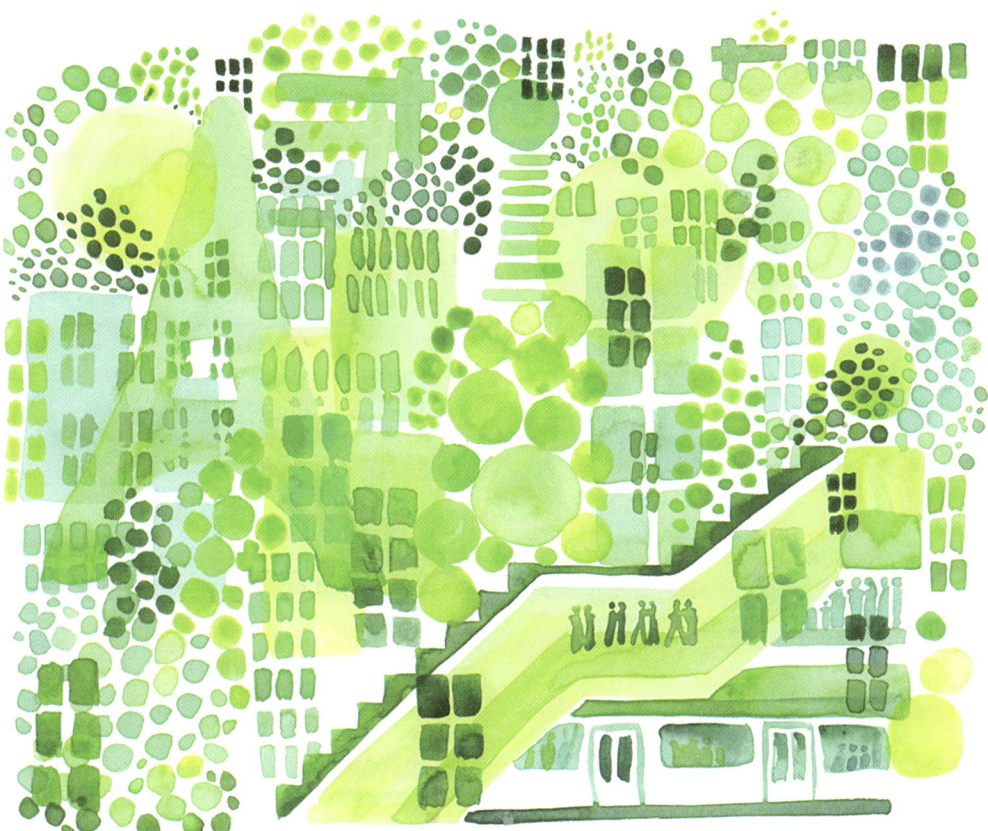

STEP 4
REFLECT

What did you think of this exercise? Was it easier or more difficult to paint something abstract? If you especially enjoyed this one, consider painting with geometric shapes. Looking at the final piece, how do the colors and composition make you feel? Do you feel transported to this utopic place? If not, what would you change to create a greater sense of harmony?

IDEA GENERATION

With the endless chatter about artificial intelligence and its potential effects on every facet of human life, it occurred to me that being an artist is a lot like being an AI model—you are fed variables and information, which then get "processed" through your life experience, references, and personal taste barometer, and what comes out is the visual synthesis of all these variables. (This is not a pro-AI metaphor; I am pro-human till the end!) This chapter is all about minimizing the roadblocks to creativity by feeding you the right variables and interesting constraints so that you can create deeply human work.

DAY 21

DON'T STRESS, DRAW!

Ever feel like you are carrying the weight of your world on your shoulders? Especially if you have an overactive brain like mine, it can be helpful to get down on paper all the stressors you're feeling on a given day.

Sometimes I marvel at how I can push a stroller, carry a week's worth of groceries, wrangle a tiny tot, and leave a sane-sounding voice message about ancillary rights for a client. On top of that, there's the crushing weight of global warming, increasing food costs, and simply hanging on for dear life. But in today's exercise, we'll find the fun in digesting all that life throws at us.

BRAINSTORM

What's weighing you down today? Write down three to five things that are stressing you out. Next, decide how you will represent each one, whether it is an emotion, a complex concept, or an act of God.

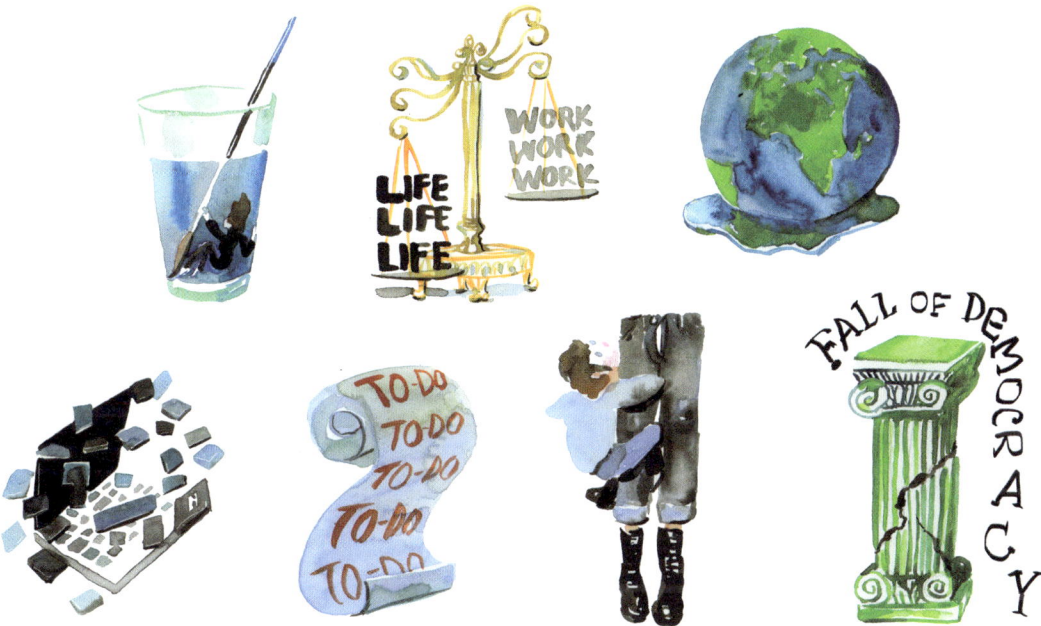

If you are thinking about broad concepts, they may not be easy to visualize and synthesize in a drawing. Something I recommend when trying to visualize complex concepts is to do a Google image search of the topic at hand. For example, when I search "fall of democracy," I see a lot of falling pillars and crumbling Grecian structures. Of course, the point isn't to copy another artist's work but to explore how this topic has been envisioned in the past, so from an image search I think about ways to interpret the concept in my own visual language.

SKETCH

Once you've identified today's stressors, it's time to incorporate yourself into the concept. Ask yourself how your body carries daily stress and how it could impact a visual representation of yourself. Are you so weighed down that you can't lift your head? Are you looking up in awe at all your troubles? Are you completely crushed by stress? Then maybe you are lying on the ground under your stressors. Also consider how you might exaggerate the scale of the most stressful elements. Sketch out two or three rough ideas on scrap paper, choose your favorite, and then lightly draw the final idea on watercolor paper.

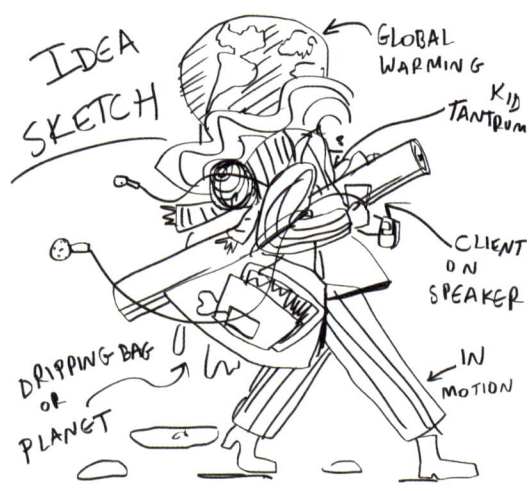

The sketch above is a slice of my daily life, balancing the demands of being a working parent and artist. Stopping isn't really an option, so I'm holding on for dear life with various objects flying behind me.

PAINT

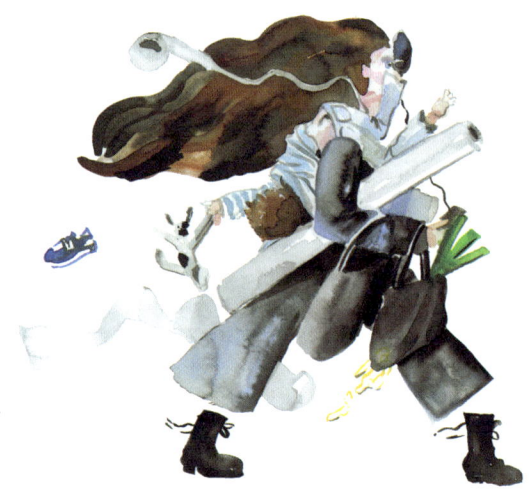

Before you get out your paints, ask yourself how you're going to use color to reinforce your concept while keeping the final watercolor easy to understand and visually impactful. Consider how you can differentiate the body from the load you are carrying. Is there a way to use complementary colors or mix two watercolor techniques (wet on dry, wet on wet) to create contrast? I want the focus to be on the movement of the body carrying the weight, creating contrast between the blue-gray washes of the body and the flowing brown hair.

Notice how the saturated brown hair is the focal point, sending the eye from the top of the figure to the bottom. I did not draw each strand of hair; rather, I broke it down into striped planes, which I painted individually to create flow.

STEP 4
REFINE

Although I like the action and movement in what I've done so far, I want to add one more wink at carrying the weight in motion. I quickly paint a border of color on the left side of the figure. Using the palm of my hand, I smear the paint toward the left side of the page. This final watercolor evokes the extremity of carrying the world on my shoulders while in a constant state of motion.

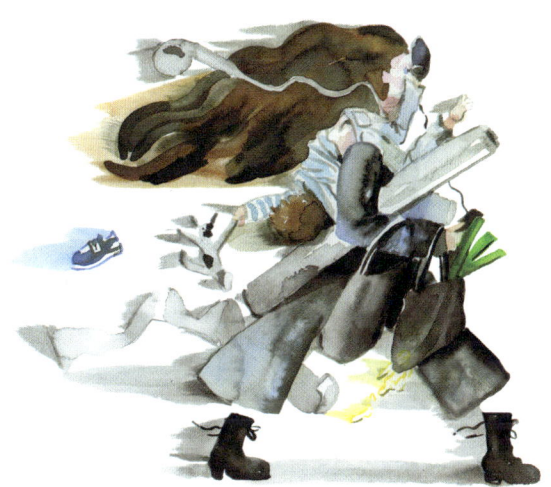

STEP 5
REFLECT

How does it feel seeing yourself loaded up with all of life's stressors? Are you carrying something that is far beyond your control? Can you identify and shed any of these unnecessary burdens?

DAY 22

SURREAL-O-METER

Editorial illustrators (those of us who create illustrations for magazines, newspapers, etc.) don't just capture the essence of an article in one captivating 2D image. We're also professional idea generators and problem solvers. When a client wants a visual concept, I rely on a surreal-o-meter to take my ideas from Granny Smith apple to Magritte-style dandy apple.

In this exercise, we will find humor and a little absurdity in something so mundane you may not even notice it anymore. The challenge will be to develop a logical narrative progression from ordinary to extraordinary in three tight images, otherwise known as a triptych.

BRAINSTORM

To start generating an idea, choose something mundane from your daily life (think: dirty dishes in the sink, gum on your shoe, empty coffee cups). My idea? I'm looking at a pigeon pecking at a stale slice of baguette—nothing new in the streets of Paris.

Now that I have my idea, it's time to take it to two surreal extremes. I'm going to expand on the relationship between the pigeon and the bread. If pigeons are birds of prey, they hover over abandoned baguettes. How can I play with this relationship?

SKETCH

Once you have your initial ideas in place, it's time to start visualizing them. Sketch out three ideas, progressing from the most ordinary to the most surreal.

In the first sketch, I re-create the moment of inspiration. In the second, the pigeon is in flight clutching a whole baguette, a little less likely but not unheard of if you've lived in Paris long enough.

What's the next extreme I can take? Since pigeons are known to hover, the pigeon in the last sketch is a Mylar balloon floating over a baguette. And we get a little nod to the location, with the Eiffel Tower in the background.

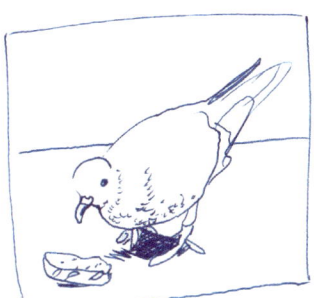 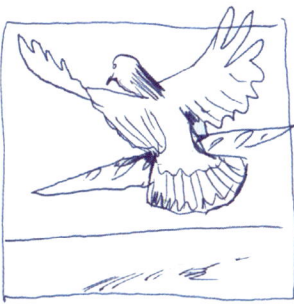 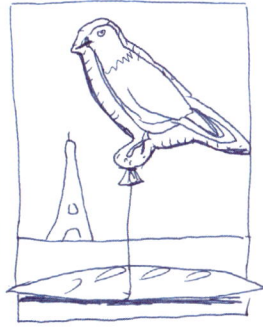

REFINE

Now it is time to clean up your concept. Ask yourself if the trio is effective in telling the story. Perhaps there's a visual way to connect the three? Since height and flight are of such narrative importance to this trio, I'm going to push myself to find a better solution to connect these.

What about including a universal horizon line? Because the eye travels continuously from left to right, this will make it immediately easier to understand the story.

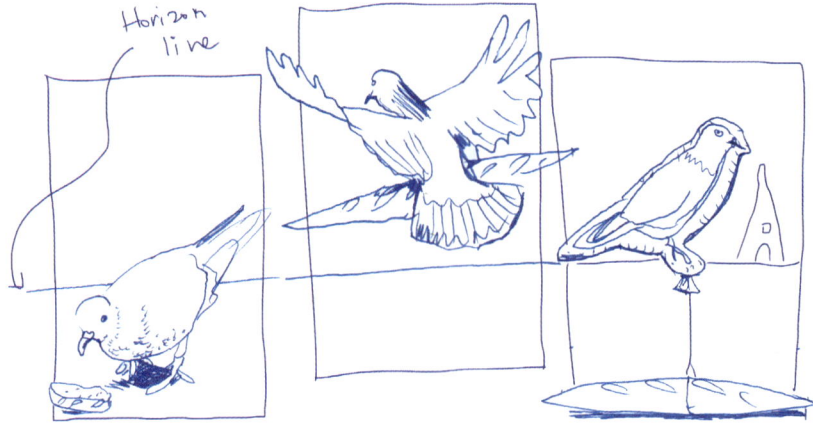

I add some shadows to my sketches before I commit to watercolor. Adding shadow to the top of the middle image brings the eye upward.

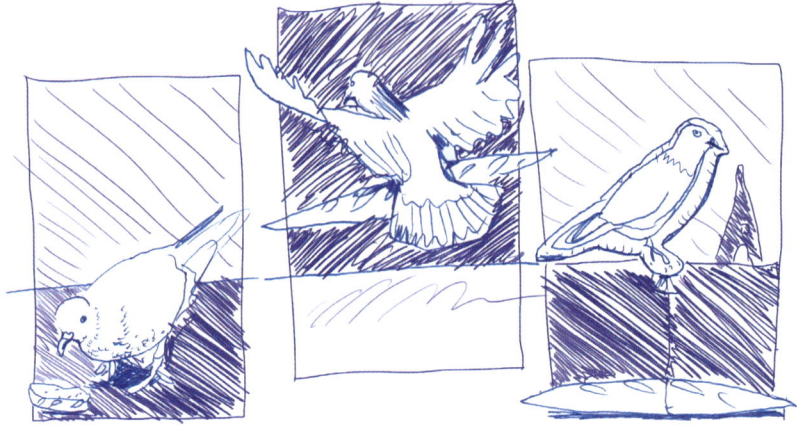

PAINT

Before executing in watercolor, ask yourself a few questions: How can color connect or differentiate the three frames? (Since I have two major elements to render, sky and baguette, I'll highlight two complementary color washes, blue and orange.) How will you optimize the use of washes to suggest the ambiance versus using dry on wet to reinforce the action? Can color and shading be used to reinforce the overall weight and balance of the three images individually and as a triptych?

Here's the final watercolor. Though I ultimately adjusted the horizon line so that it varies from panel to panel, it still transitions smoothly from frame to frame, and each pigeon's action is easily understood. See how I used wash to add extra details like the silhouette of other pigeons in the first frame and the Eiffel Tower in the third? The focus is still very much on the action, but the wash says just a little bit more without competing with the narrative.

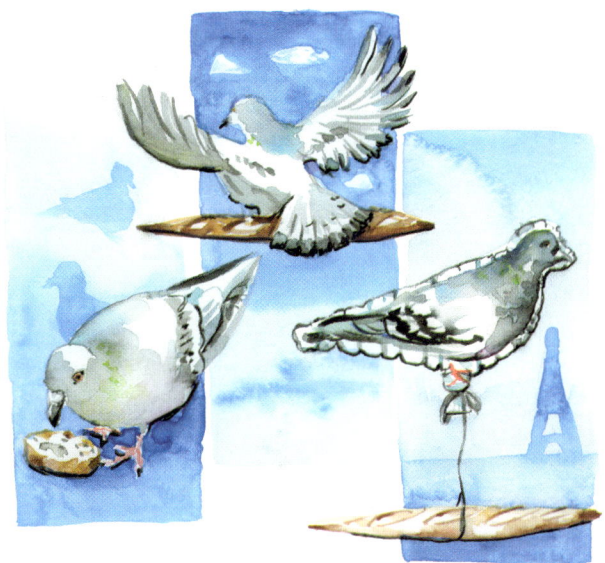

REFLECT

Were you able to use color harmoniously while also drawing attention to what was necessary? How did you find working with three frames instead of one? How did your use of color reinforce the visual story and help unify the frames?

DAY 23

RANDOM SPOT GENERATOR

A spot illustration is a small drawing that reinforces an idea or concept. If you read *The New Yorker*, you will be familiar with the little random line drawings that delve into a theme throughout an entire issue. They need to be efficient and instantly understandable to keep the reader's attention. In this assignment, I challenge you to make a series of spots inspired by a concept or an expression.

What's different about today's exercise is that you will replace a traditional sketch with a mind map: a visual representation of a thought process that breaks down a complex idea into a digestible diagram.

STEP 1

BRAINSTORM

To get the ideas flowing this time around, we'll find a theme and make a mind map. First, write a theme at the top of a piece of paper, then draw three lines underneath it and come up with three subcategories for that theme. I'm going to delve into the timely and unfortunate theme of global warming, with the subcategories of timeliness, planet, and overheating.

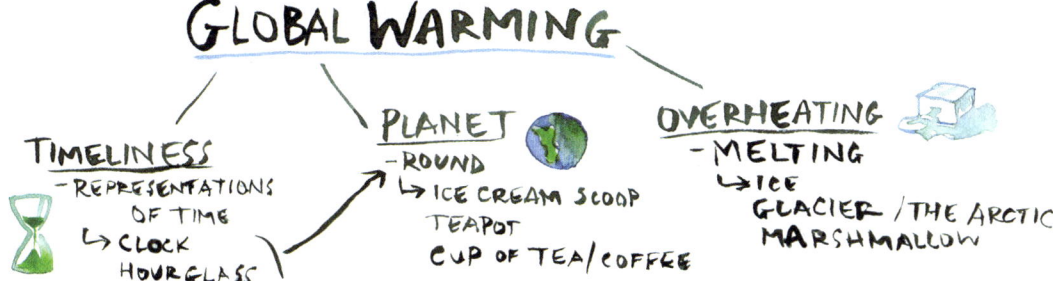

Below the subcategories, draw and/or write a few symbols that come to the top of your mind for each one. Feel free to Google the concepts to see any existing visualizations; it can help jump-start the process. For example, when I think of timeliness, I write out representations of time, like a clock and an hourglass.

Now that you have symbols for each subcategory, can you find a way to merge them together to suggest your theme? Try coming up with eight different spot illustrations. There are two routes I can take here, inspired by my mind map. I can merge the Earth and representations of time to evoke the timeliness of the subject (read: a planet sliding down an hourglass). Or I can merge overheating and the planet. I opt for the latter, so I'm going to find ways to merge the hot Earth with cold objects or associations (read: a melting Earth ice cream cone). When I think of a planet, I think of a sphere, which could represented by a scoop of ice cream, a teapot, or a cup of tea or coffee.

SKETCH

I put together eight sketchy watercolor spots fueled by my research. Which one is the most effective? Some strictly suggest the heating planet (Earth teapot and cuppa), but they don't have a sense of action. The Earth hourglass is the strongest call to action, while the Earth fan is a nod to overheating with a sense of motion. I scrap the two least-effective ideas before I move on to the final six watercolors. Which ones are the most effective? Which ones would you eliminate?

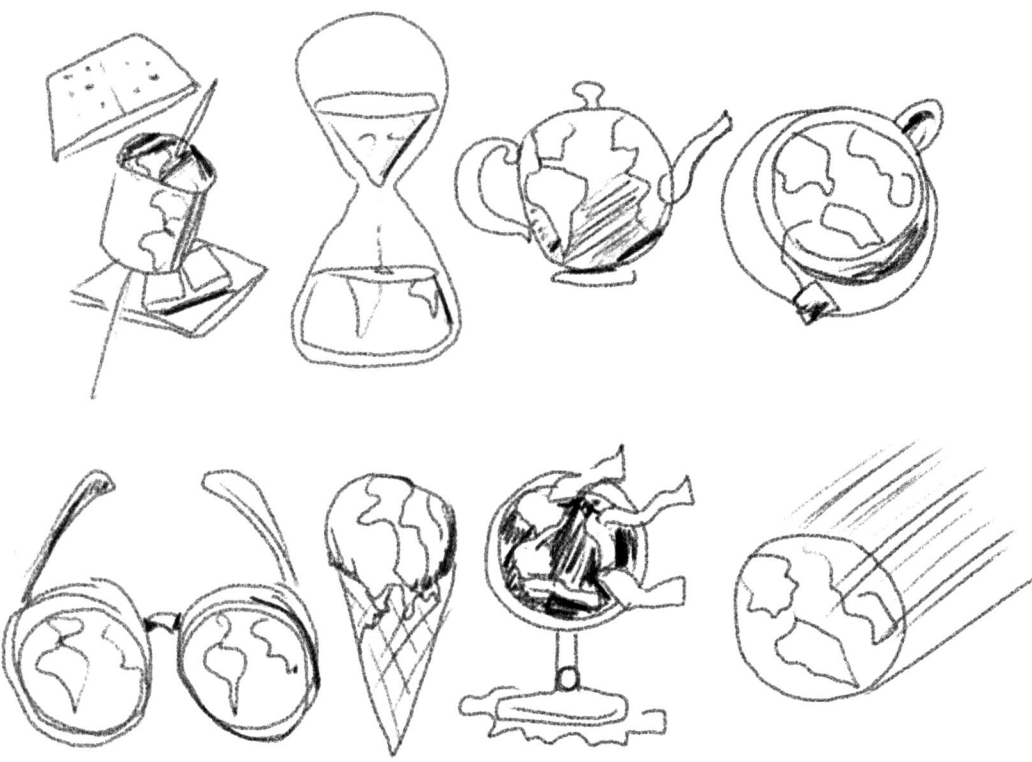

STEP 3
PAINT

Now that your concept is set in stone, it is time to paint your top six. Which technique best serves your concept? Loose and gestural, like in the previous step? Or more detailed and controlled, like in your usual watercolor practice? If there was no context, would you understand the concept at first glance? Should you keep a consistent color palette to reinforce the idea, like I did below?

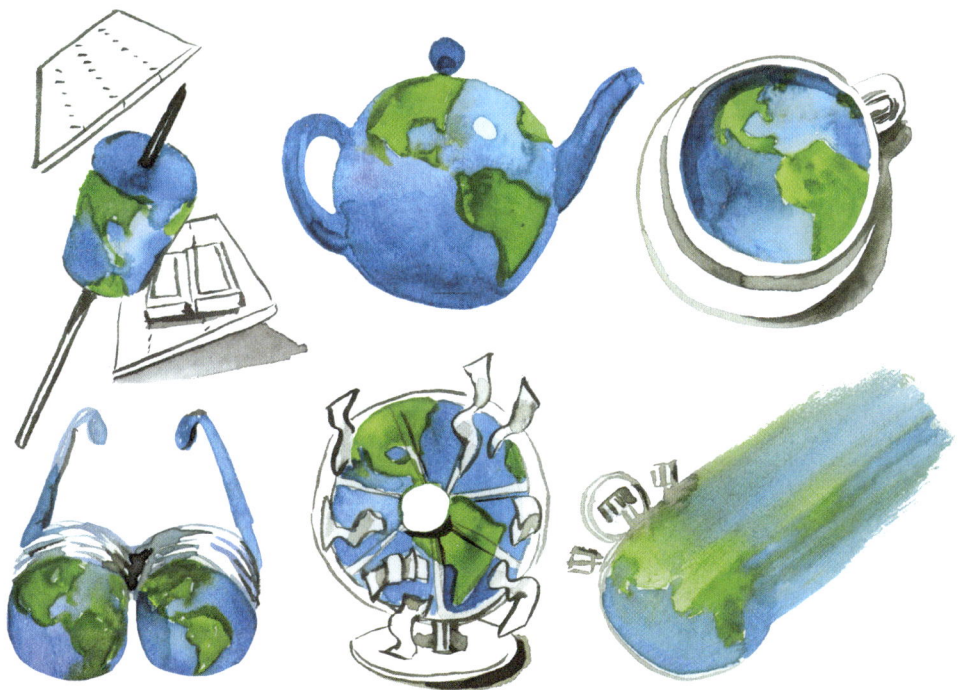

STEP 4
REFLECT

I always like to say that if you think about a lauded artist's work, you probably call to mind two or three of their most famous pieces. But you don't think about the lifetime of lost, scrapped, failed, and repurposed sketches and final products that got them to creating those iconic pieces. Being an artist is not only about producing work, but also about editing. We edit down to the good ideas worth pursuing and scrap the bad. Did you produce enough options in this exercise to be selective?

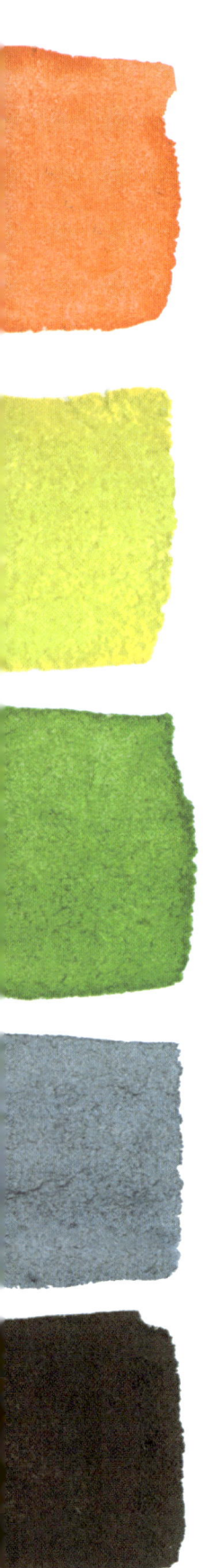

DAY 24

C'EST MOI
SELF-PORTRAIT

I cherish flipping through old sketchbooks and observing how I've represented myself throughout the years. The emergence and ubiquitousness of selfie culture led to a lot of duck-lipped self-portraits in my early Paris days. Once my watercolor technique strengthened, though, so did my visual imagery.

Today you will take a good look in the mirror and capture your current context by exploring an "emotion" element, an "audience" or connection (or lack of one) to the outside world, and an "ambiance" or spatial component. This will establish a framework to expand on the idea of a self-portrait and give it a more emotional edge.

BRAINSTORM

To begin, take a moment to ask yourself how you are feeling. What emotion would you use to describe yourself? Next, consider how would you describe your current setting, or ambiance. Finally, imagine a hypothetical audience observing all of this. Are they a "fly on the wall" or someone on the other end of your smartphone? How would these two different viewpoints change the perspective of your composition? My answers are "overwhelmed," "an iPhone screen," and "a client."

SKETCH

Look at your answers, and quickly create two or three sketches of the first things that come to your mind, being sure to render your drawing from the perspective of your audience. (I have a comic artist friend who has a little doll on her desk she uses to find more cinematic angles when building a composition. This is an interesting device to play around with when you need to inject a point of view into an illustration.) Take a close look at your sketches and select the strongest option. I like the clever framing device of having an infinite number of open windows in the last sketch, so I commit to developing it further.

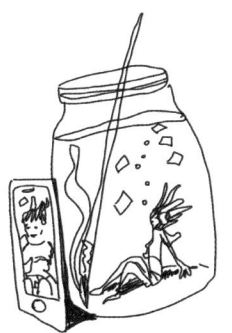 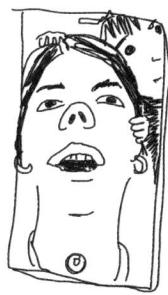 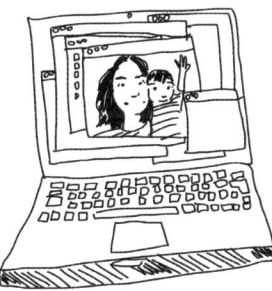

STEP 3
REFINE

Flesh out your concept further in your final sketch, until the desired emotion is achieved.

Before you begin painting, take a second to decide how color will reinforce the emotion of your concept and bring focus to the composition. Feel free to paint your sketch if you're hesitant about what colors to choose.

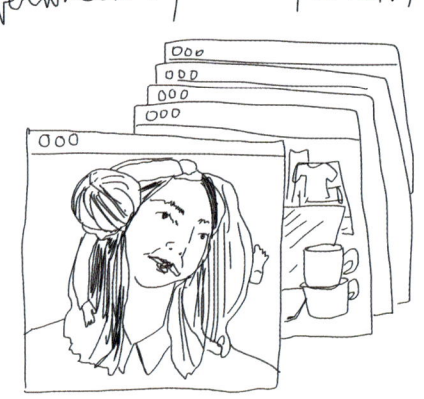

Since my audience is a client, I look at my computer screen for some visual cues to suggest that my portrait is within a Zoom call. The red, yellow, and green circles at the top left corner are a good visual nod to the tech. Perhaps I can reuse these colors as the pattern of my shirt?

STEP 4
PAINT

I decide which layers to attack first. Because there is a good amount of light reflecting from my computer screen, I want my face to have a halo effect. I wet the surface of the paper around my hair with 50% flood. I load up my paintbrush with blue paint and apply it in a circular motion around the head **(A)**.

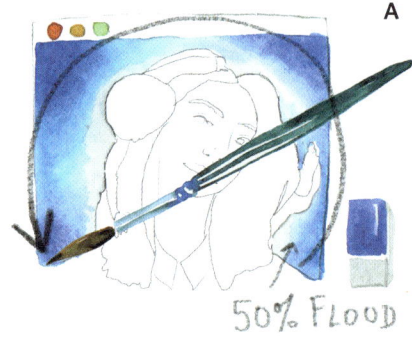

Hair is best rendered when it reflects the light source and the strands aren't laboriously rendered one by one. I break the hair down into sections and paint each one individually to reflect the light **(B)**. (For more on this, refer to page 145.)

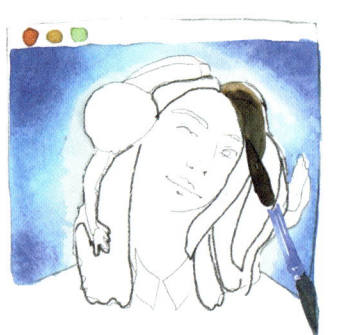

To complete my illustration **(C)**, I add the facial features (for tips on this see page 72), bring in my pops of colors, and paint the background windows.

C

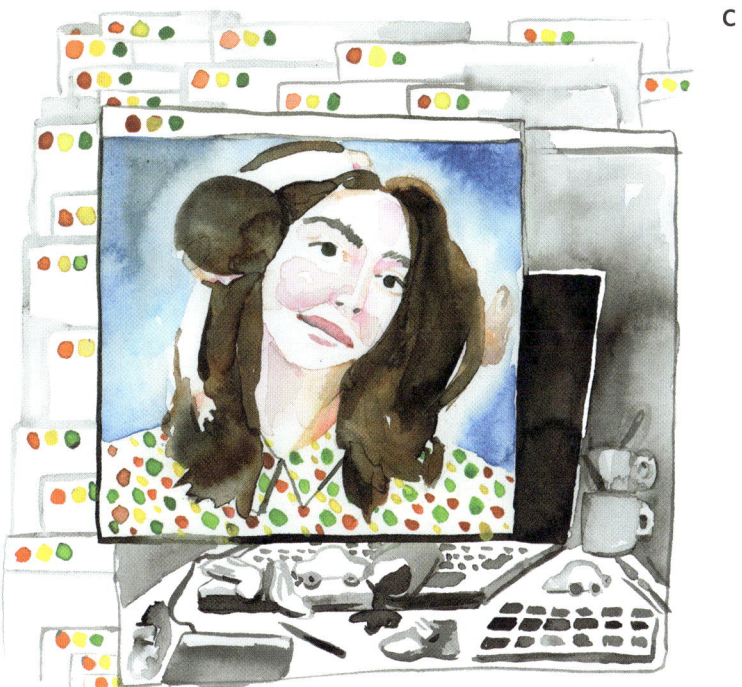

STEP 5
REFLECT

How does it feel seeing yourself personified in this very specific moment? Were you able to use color to communicate a strong emotion while keeping the composition harmonious? How did identifying an audience impact the overall interest of your composition? If you squint, what do you see first in the composition? If need be, add more contrast or shadow to draw attention to the desired focal point.

DAY 25

IP MASH-UP

The greatest secret to any creative work is . . . you don't have to reinvent the wheel. The more of yourself you put into your work (your generational references, accumulated life experiences, cutting humor, etc.), the more you can adapt your source of inspiration into something completely new.

This is often how my own story ideas are fueled. I think of a current event and mash it up with some kind of cultural movement or other existing piece of intellectual property (IP), such as a book, movie, or toy. How about an upcoming election as the next installment of *The Hunger Games*?

In this exercise, I challenge you to mash up two different cultural properties that you know and love into a humorous multiframe story. This exercise is a little bit different because there is some writing involved—just think of the text as another way to reinforce your visual ideas.

STEP 1

BRAINSTORM

Think of something that you loved when you were young and ask yourself how it's aged. Is there a trend from your teenage years you'd want to revive? Is there a remake you'd want to see of a TV show from your youth? How would it be perceived? Would it need to be made more politically correct for today? Can you mash this up with a franchise, auteur, book, or film from this time? The more recognizable and universal the IP, the easier it will be to merge the visuals.

After a few years of living in Paris, I finally returned to my childhood home and an attic full of boxes with my name on them. Being far, far away, I'd overdramatized the prized possessions awaiting me: the bespoke vintage gowns I'd collected in high school, my study-abroad sketchbooks recounting unrequited loves on several (okay—two) continents, and all my childhood treasures. Much to my chagrin, what I found was a bunch of dusty boxes filled with mass-produced junk I should never have kept. Isn't it funny how nostalgia can make you see everything through rose-colored glasses? This story evolved into a mash-up of *Goodnight Moon* retold from my childhood 1990s bedroom, "Goodnight Caboodle: A Bedtime Story for Nostalgic Millennials."

Create a list of words, characters, or objects that you associate with your two chosen properties. If you've chosen a property from another time period, are there ways to reinforce it? Consider the color palette, and look up typography, furniture design, or pop culture juggernauts. Mix and match until you have at least five ideas that you are happy with. Here are a few ways I'll adapt the classic children's story to my own childhood:

- I think of my own prized possessions from that time and insert them into the format of *Goodnight Moon*. The more specific, the better! I look up some millennial clickbait on BuzzFeed to remind myself of some toys of that time.
- Goodnight . . . goodnight, what? I land on something indisputably nineties: the Caboodle. The sacred place where I kept all my FIMO experiments and empty Lip Smacker tubes.
- I'll make sure that the text rhymes, in the same spirit as *Goodnight Moon*.

SKETCH

Once you have your concept fleshed out, sketch at least five visuals. Think about what is essential for telling the story and what you can cut to clean up the narrative. To begin my "Goodnight Caboodle" mash-up, I sketch some iconic nineties things I either coveted or owned myself.

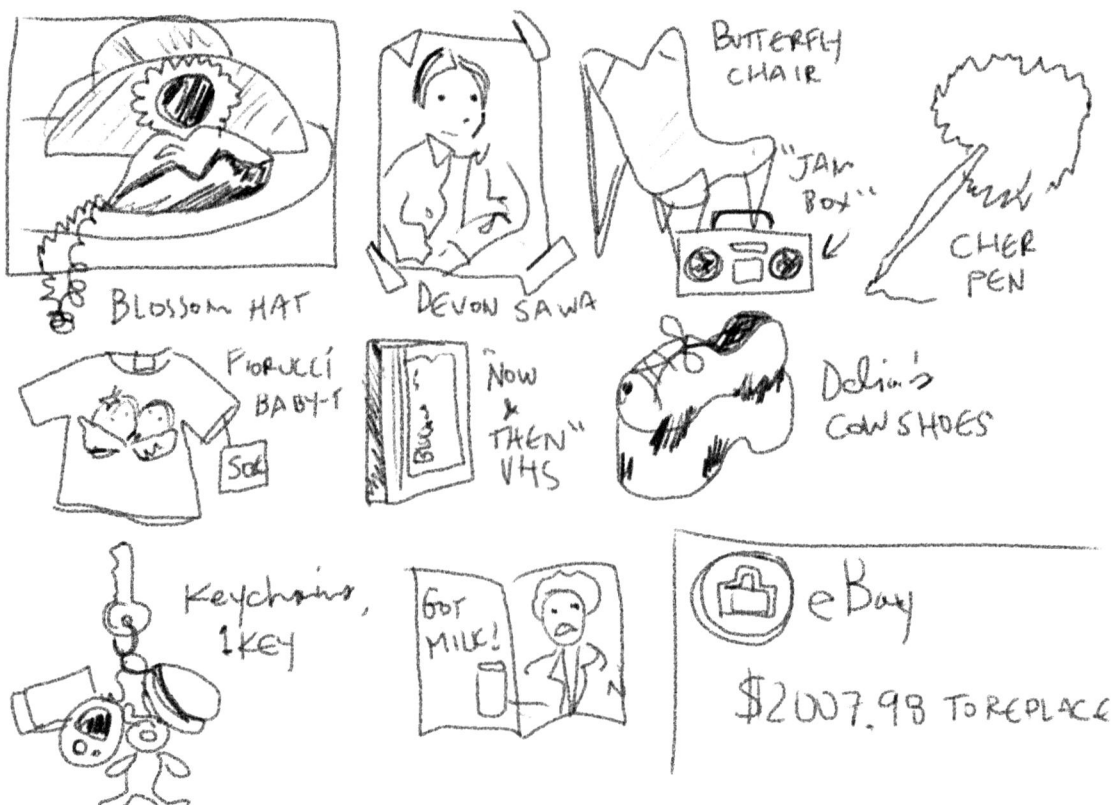

STEP 3

PAINT

One of the aha moments I had while rediscovering childhood treasures was realizing how tackily nineties everything was. I'm going to replace the primary and secondary colors of *Goodnight Moon* with a totally nineties palette of yellow, magenta, baby blue, and turquoise. Following the style of the original illustrations from the book, I am going to use this set palette and paint everything in graphic blocks of color. I won't be mixing the colors; instead, I'll let them define the shapes on their own. This will keep the story consistent and pack an extra millennial punch.

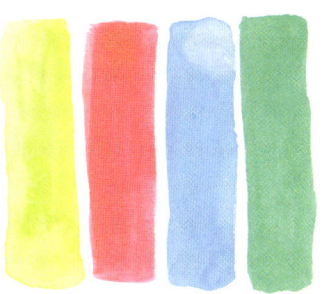

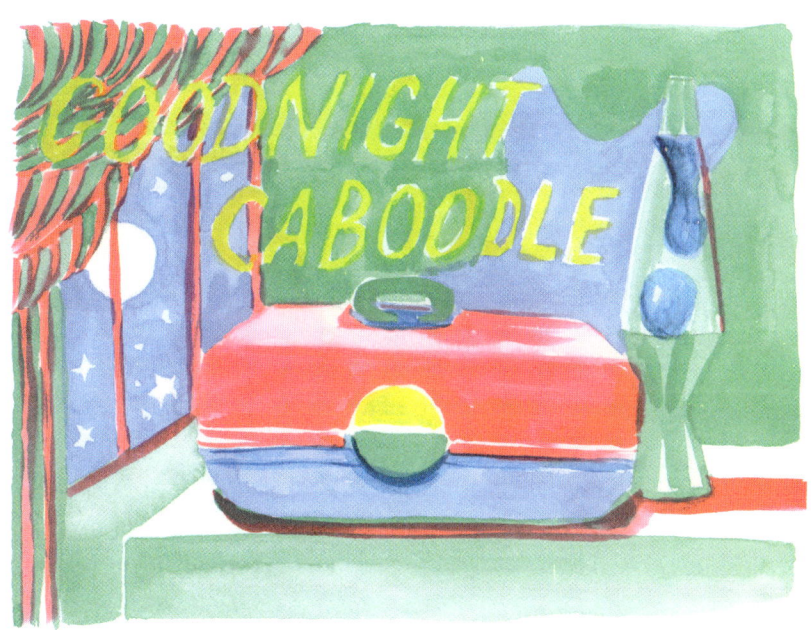

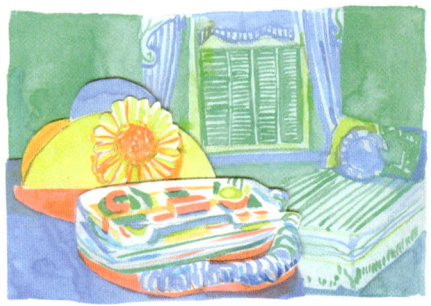

In the great green room there was a clear phone and a hat with a *Blossom* bloom.

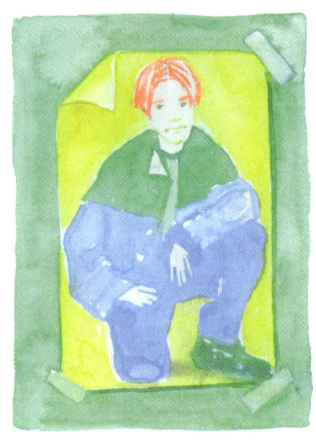

And a portrait of Devon Sawa, my future groom.

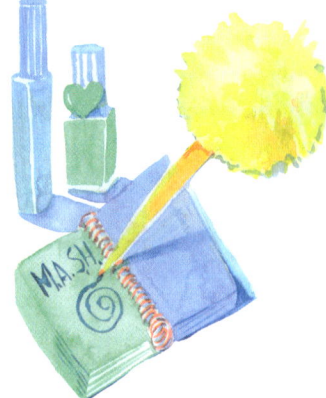

Goodnight feathered pen, signature Cher Horowitz.

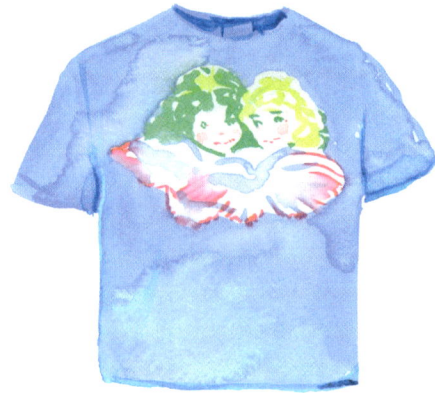

Goodnight baby tee. Extra-small? Don't think it fits.

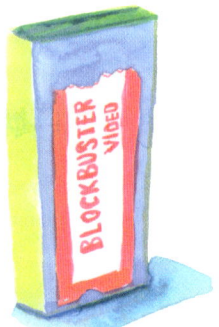

Goodnight *Now and Then*. $200 fine, overdue.

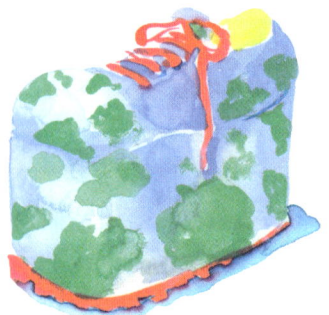

Goodnight Delia's cow-print shoes.

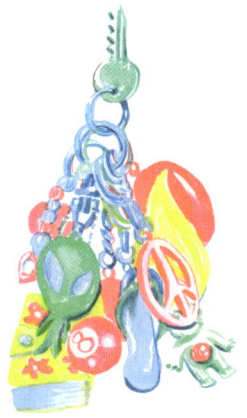

Goodnight keychains
hanging from a key.

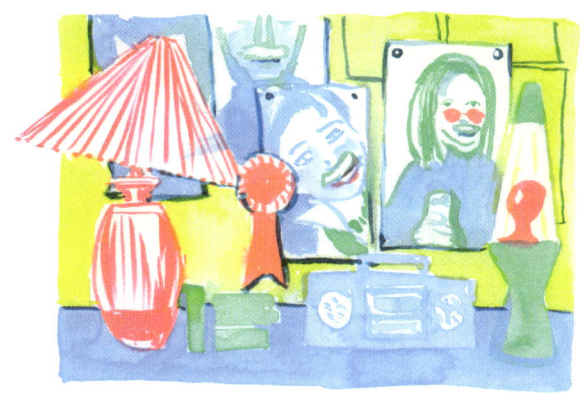

Goodnight "Got milk?" gallery.

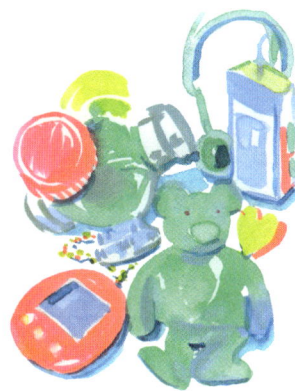

Goodbye Mom, for tossing
all this to make space.

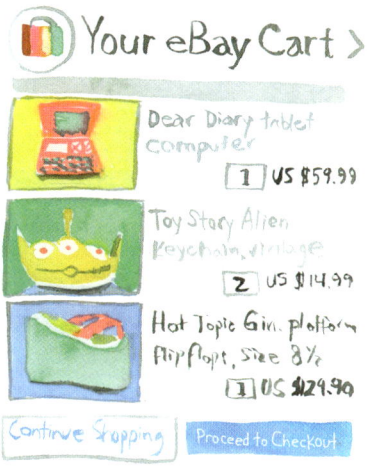

Goodnight eBay.
$1,000 to replace.

STEP 4

REFLECT

Nostalgia is always a good entry point, especially for fellow millennials who swoon with longing at any mention of a Trapper Keeper or a lip-shaped landline phone. Were you able to identify a few things that take you back to your childhood or adolescence? How did you use color to reinforce the style of a very specific decade? Narratively speaking, could you add or take away a frame?

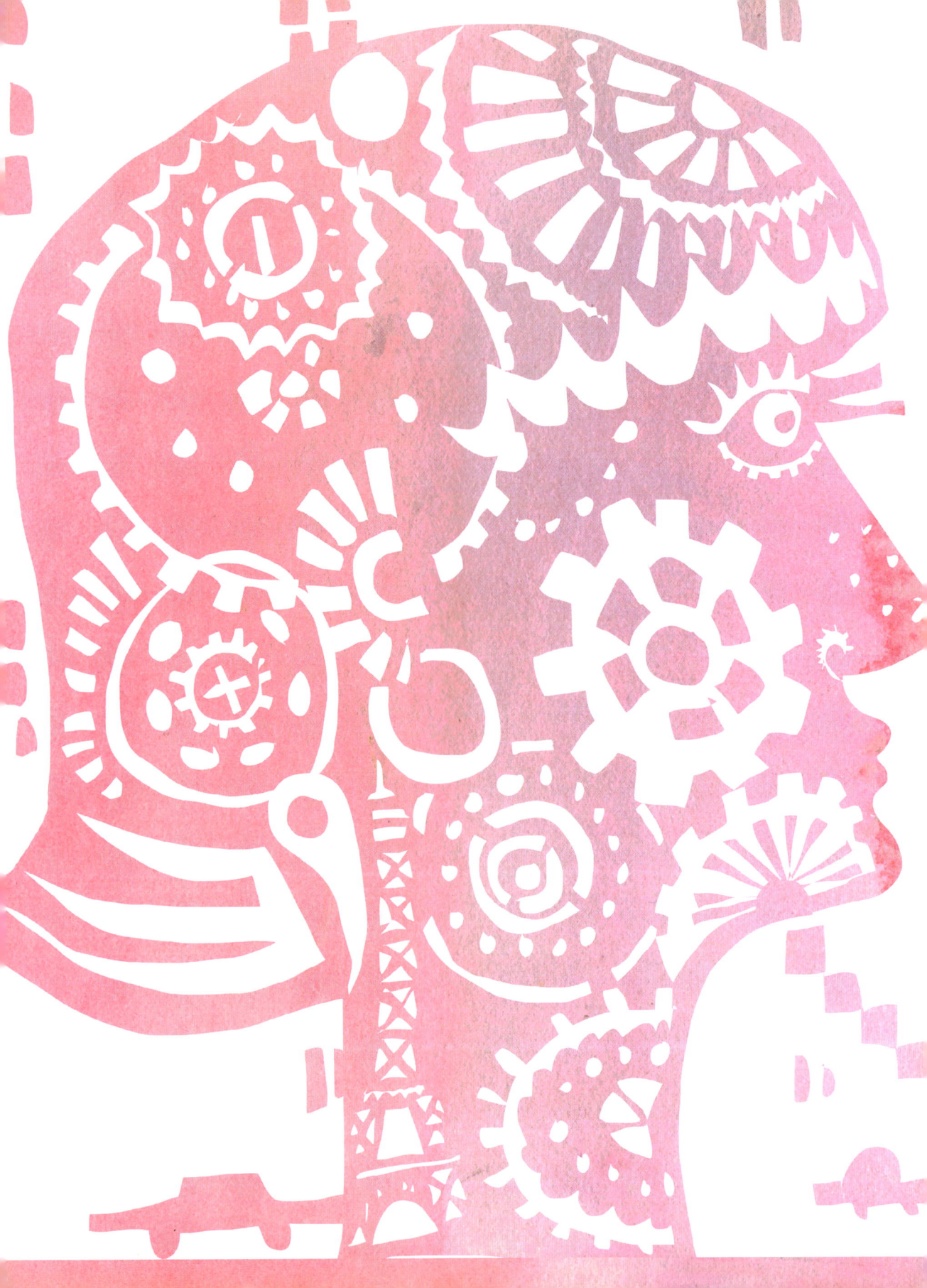

IT'S PERSONAL

Now that your watercolor skills are up to snuff, it's time to take a deep dive into your psyche. I never thought I had much of an imagination—it was always easier for me to recount my own life than imaginary ones. But much like I had to sketch from life to learn how to draw, telling your own story is the natural first step in accessing those of others. These final five exercises give you some building blocks to apply your own narrative, whether to recap a wonderful moment in your life or rewrite an experience that was less than pleasant.

DAY 26

COAT OF ARMS

One of the most underrated and inspiring museums in Paris is the newly renovated Musée Carnavalet, dedicated to Parisian history from prehistory to the present. Before the streets were given names and before most Parisians were literate, shops and artisans advertised with intricate metal signs merging symbols representing their services and enough decorative flair to attract passersby. I love this intersection between decorative art and function. Today's exercise will challenge you to think about the symbols that represent you, using the structure of a medallion or a coat of arms.

STEP 1

BRAINSTORM

Jot down a quick list of what matters to you: your values, how you identify yourself, what you aspire to be. Be as precise as possible. Now research images of coats of arms and their meanings. Can you find a symbol, object, animal, or plant that can represent each of the things you listed?

I commit to creating a coat of arms for my first year in Paris. The high-low realities of living in the city as a humble jeune fille au pair will give me plenty of material to play with. This includes the one-Nespresso-capsule ration I received daily from my host family, the pigeons nesting on my bedroom windowsill, my mission to find the best croissant in Paris (the only simple pleasure I could afford), and a French translation of a quote from Margaret Atwood's novel *The Handmaid's Tale*: "Don't let the bastards grind you down."

STEP 2

SKETCH

Start sketching out the visuals from your list and playing with a design for your coat of arms. Something I do in my own work when I am still deciding on a composition is to cut out each of the elements individually and overlap them to find the best solution, as if I am making a collage.

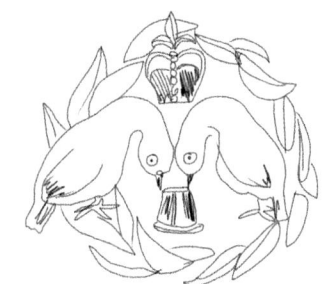

When building a composition, it is always worth thinking about scale. If you have a dominant force in your narrative, consider enlarging it to give it more visual weight. If I were to exaggerate the size of the pigeons or the Nespresso capsule, for example, how would it change the overall concept and intention of my coat of arms?

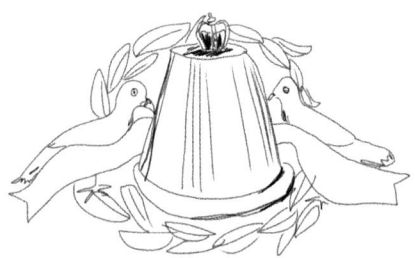

To tie all my symbols together, I use a branch of bay leaves to not only wink at the culinary ambitions that Paris sparked in me but also reference the plant's historical connotations of courage and strength.

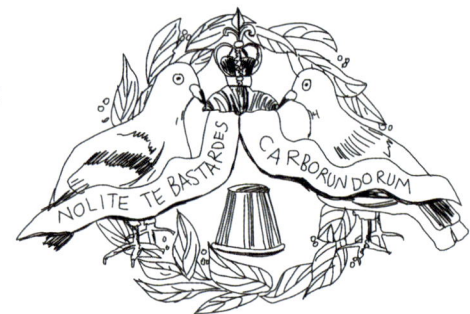

STEP 3
PAINT

Now it's time to start building layers. If there is an overpowering emotion that is dominating everything else in your life, how might you use color to evoke it?

Because I had not yet adapted to Paris's monthslong gray season, I use blue to symbolize the seasonal sadness of my first year. I mix two hues of blue wash to maintain the balance of the overall coat of arms by dosing out the intensities. Even if you are using several different hues of the same color, consider how you might use the more saturated hues and the white of the paper to create a strong focal point and a sense of balance.

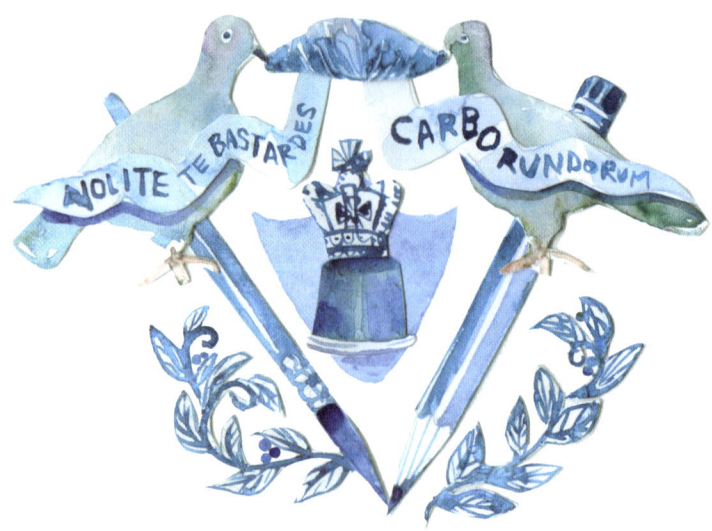

STEP 4

REFLECT

There's a moment when it is important to start sharing your work with others. It's easy to self-isolate as an artist and cocoon yourself off from unwanted criticism and opinions. Pass your final coat of arms along to a friend or family member without any context. Ask them what they see and how they interpret all the choices you made. Ask them to dig deeper and find ways that it relates to you specifically. You can take or leave their remarks, but perhaps they will share something with you that you can use to strengthen the watercolor.

HOT TIP

DEVELOPING TASTE

How do you cultivate taste? It's easy to say that you've either got it or you don't. Instead, think of taste as your internal mood board, reflecting your beliefs, your background, and your culture. As contradictory as it may seem, good and bad taste can be used hand in hand.

Taste *impacts* style, but they are not interchangeable. Taste is what's *inside* you. Style is what comes *out* of you. One thing leads to another.

If you're still frustrated with the work you are making, your taste level may not meet your own visual expectations. Take some time to understand what you like and how you can apply principles that you appreciate (color, emotion, and composition) to your watercolors.

Begin by identifying what you like. What kinds of paintings are

you drawn to at a museum? What are some other major cultural influences that have impacted your life (music, movies, etc.)? How do they make you feel? Is that emotion communicated through color or subject matter? I think my love of color is inspired by my childhood favorite film, *The Wizard of Oz*, and the rabbit hole of other Technicolor films I watched religiously. If I am looking for a color palette, I still go back to rewatch some of those movies.

Then, start collecting. An artist is a collector of inspirations for their internal image bank. If I see an exhibition that I love, I always buy a few postcards of my favorite pieces. I've amassed a little collection throughout the years, and when I'm looking for inspiration for a color palette or technique, I can flip through these

to my heart's content. As the world becomes more and more digitized, I've gotten into the habit of collecting vintage stationery, postcards, flea market mementos, and any magazine clippings I find visually appealing. Although you can always head to Google to search for an image, a lot of these little fragments may never be digitized and may disappear forever. Start collecting and think of this as your own personal primary reference archive.

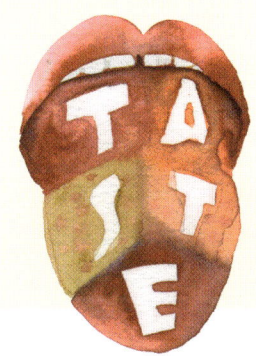

DAY 27

BOOK COVER OF
YOUR LIFE

In this exercise, you will visualize a cover for the book of
your life. Of course, that's a lot of information to convey in
one image! You can't pack it all in. And remember, this is
the selling point of the book. Imagine browsing through
a bookstore—each cover is designed to seduce you into
thumbing through the book and, ideally, buying it. This isn't
the time for delicate line work. It's time to be bold, impactful,
and easily understood.

STEP 1
BRAINSTORM

Before you can illustrate the cover, you need to decide what kind of book it is. Is it women's fiction? A horror novel? A celeb-style autobiography? Once you've made a decision, take a look at a few existing covers from the genre. You will see patterns. Celebrity memoirs have the author front and center. A horror novel usually isn't illustrated with pastel colors; it's dark and brooding.

Next, decide on a title and subtitle. The images and text should complement and enhance each other. For example, if the book is called *Edge of Seventeen: An Ode to an Eighties Adolescence*, the reader will know automatically which decade the book evokes. Perhaps an eighties-inspired color palette could give another nod to the concept without overexplaining it?

I'm going to start thinking about a visual for *Born Again French*. I like this idea because I can play with religious iconography and the tropes of living in France.

STEP 2
SKETCH

Before you begin sketching, decide on a format (square, landscape, or portrait) for the finished piece. This will force you to be more intentional and assure a stronger composition. Your assignment today is to paint a 5-by-7-inch (13 by 18 cm) vertical cover. As you start working out your composition, don't forget to consider how the title, subtitle, and author name will nestle into the watercolor as well.

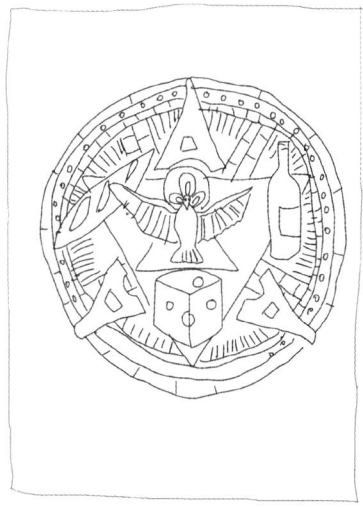

I sketch a few rough visuals and a cover concept, including a nod to the iconic stained glass windows of Notre Dame and the Eiffel Tower.

REFINE

I can already sense that the image is too busy, because my eye isn't drawn to any one area in particular. And because this book is meant to be a memoir, I realize that I need to continue sketching to find a solution to incorporate a sense of myself within the image.

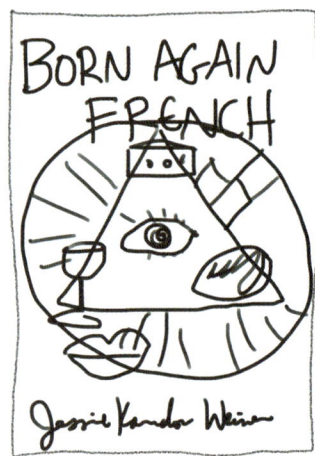

I keep the framework of wine, bread, and cheese as the French holy trinity. As I research stained glass windows, I notice the use of a watchful eye, which is a good option for the focal point. I sketch one in the middle of the trinity and balance it out with a pair of lips on the bottom—it implies the female perspective and French flair without the heavy-handed clichés of my first attempt. I lightly sketch out my final composition on watercolor paper, along with a rough idea of how I envision the title within the image. You can see that even if I didn't nail the sketch of the first idea, I can still evolve it into a more successful cover idea in its second incarnation.

PAINT LAYER 1

How will you use colors to make an impactful cover? Will you opt for primary or complementary colors? Can color bring attention to the action or the focal point? Because of the simplicity of my final sketch, I choose a simple color palette of red, white, and blue to reinforce the stained glass concept and draw attention to the focal point, the eye in the center of the image.

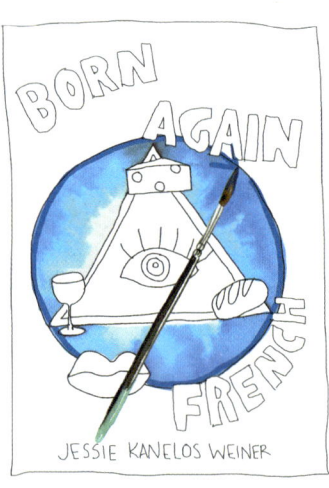

Studying stained glass windows, I noticed a halo effect that I will use to bring emphasis to the central eye. To do this, I lightly dampen the circle to prepare for 50% flood.

While the layer is slightly damp, I load up my brush with blue and paint around the circumference of the circle. I also paint a few blue details to render the wine, bread, and cheese icons.

STEP 5
PAINT LAYERS 2 AND 3

Red can be a dominant color, so I paint this layer after the blue, adding in the triangle, lips, glass of wine, and title text.

Once my wash layers are completely dry, I paint black watercolor with a small round brush to add the stained glass shapes and final fine details.

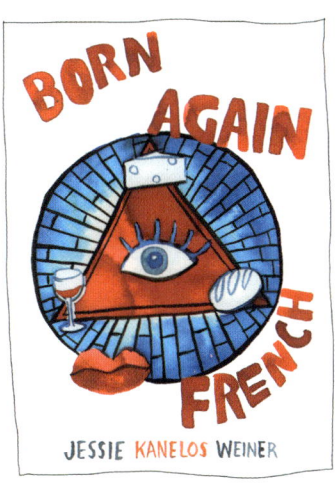

STEP 6
REFLECT

Would this book stand out on a shelf at a bookstore? If you were to show this to a friend, would they understand the genre of the book and get an immediate idea of what it is about?

A MOMENT WHEN EVERYTHING CHANGED

One of my favorite museums in Paris is a secluded oasis in the middle of Montmartre, Musée de la Vie Romantique. No, it's not a museum dedicated to long-stemmed red roses and teenagers smooching on Parisian park benches. It's dedicated to Romanticism, the late-eighteenth-century European art and intellectual movement. Romantic art is all about visualizing the emotion preceding a big, dramatic moment, like a sky filling with gray clouds before a torrential downpour. Rather than trying to say everything, these artists minimized the drama, leaving the viewer to fill in the blanks.

Today, via a six-frame comic, you will tell the story of a moment when everything in your life changed. This could be a breakup, a birth, a death, an unexpected fork in the road, or a failure that shifted everything. In the spirit of Romanticism, don't paint the big bang but rather the suspenseful unraveling of what happened ahead of time. (Think cause and effect, but hold the effect.)

STEP 1

BRAINSTORM

When choosing your moment, do you have any emails, journals, or sketchbooks from the time you would like to reference? Jot down a few sentences about this moment in time.

I've decided to draw the moment when I moved to Paris after graduation with a few hundred dollars and an unconfirmed one-year visa. I found the Eiffel Tower notebook my aunt Carol gave me as a graduation gift. I remember cracking open the first page during my thirty-six hours of air travel to Paris. My story was still unwritten, but I was dying to write something legendary and groundbreaking. A few details from this moment include:

- Writing in my Eiffel Tower journal about how everyone at home was completely gaga about my adventure in Paris. But I was terrified and slightly embarrassed to not have a tangible life plan set up. What would this year abroad bring? Would I ever find love?
- Being overloaded with luggage at Charles de Gaulle and knowing I didn't have the budget for a taxi.
- Clutching *French for Dummies* and still not mastering "Où sont les toilettes?" after days of repetition.
- Hoping my suitcase full of vintage clothes and Forever 21 finds would hold up in the fashion capital of the world. Would I be able to fully integrate or look like an American tourist?

SKETCH

It is overwhelming to break down a complete story into just a few visuals. Sketch freely in the first phase and feel free to scrap the least-essential ideas.

Though my finished watercolor will have only six frames, I start by sketching nine. I want to recap the pressure I felt filling in the first page of the first journal on my one-way trip to Paris. Would this flight change my life? How can you document the potential first day of the rest of your life?

In the third sketch, I want to make reference to the fact that I knew absolutely no French, so I include *French for Dummies* and index cards covered with basic phrases.

In the fourth sketch, the flight attendant asks if I want flat or sparkling water and my response is "Okay!" I was trying so hard to keep cool and not embarrass myself, while also being totally clueless.

In the fifth sketch, I draw a cricket to represent the quiet suspense of opening up a virgin notebook and waiting for inspiration.

In the seventh sketch, the customs agent asks for my passport and I give her my Paris journal by mistake. This didn't actually happen, but it gives extra emotional weight to the journal that set me on my path. What is the ultimate way to signify the beginning of a crazy adventure? In the ninth sketch, I imagine myself walking to Paris from the airport, completely wrecking myself before the story even begins. Stretch the truth if you need to, especially if it's funny.

I scrap the sketches of the flight attendant and scribbling hand because they don't add much to the story.

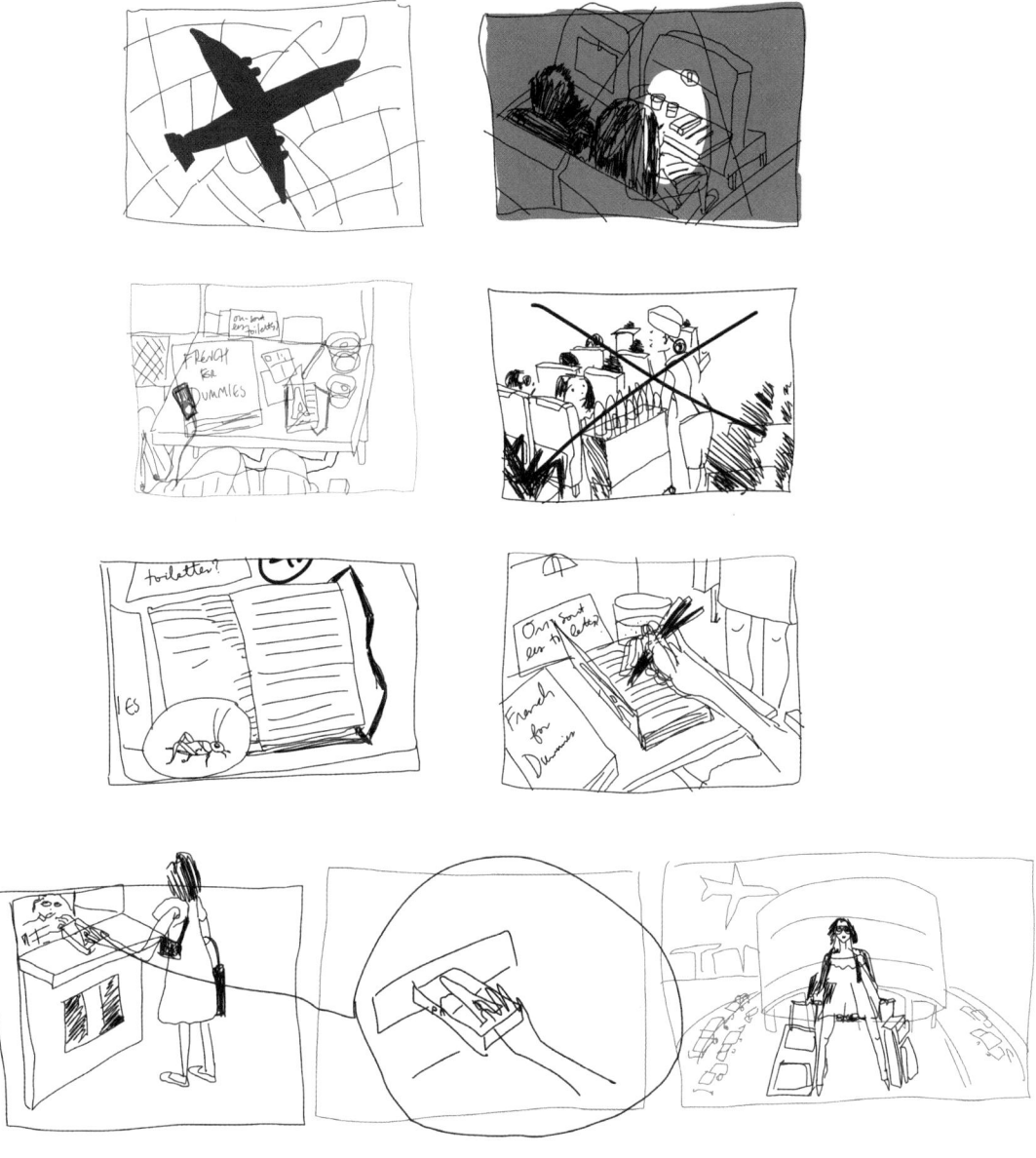

PAINT

Before you activate your paint, consider how color can be used systematically (or not) to create harmony and draw attention to certain frames. Be sure to leave sufficient white space for contrast.

I remember wearing this distinctly red polyester vintage dress on the airplane. I am the main character of this story, and the red will make me the focal point—especially if I stick to cooler tones elsewhere.

In the first frame, I draw a horizon line. I use a wet paintbrush to lightly dampen the top half of the sky. I still want to be able to control the horizontal stripes of the sky, so I choose 50% flood. Working quickly while the layer is wet, I load up my paintbrush with orange and paint the stripe above the horizon line. Then I repeat the process with yellow. I use a slightly bigger brush to start painting horizontal lines of sky blue until I reach the top of the lightly dampened surface area. I mix blue and black together to create a dark blue, which I then paint on the very top of the dampened surface and watch as the water pulls the color downward. I continue adding the dark blue until I am happy with the contrast. Once the top layer is completely dry, I load up my paintbrush with dark blue and paint the bottom half. I add more black to the dark blue and add one final stripe at the bottom.

In the final frame, I will use the same colors but a lot of white space, which will automatically create contrast with the first frame.

REFLECT

Were you able to create a story with a solid beginning, middle, and end? Is there anything in particular that isn't working that you can either update or accept for what it is? Are you saying too much or too little? Could you crop any of the images to remove any unnecessary information? Did you save enough white on the paper during the process?

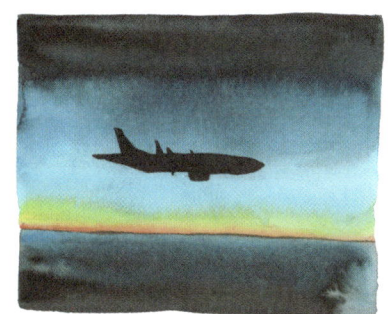
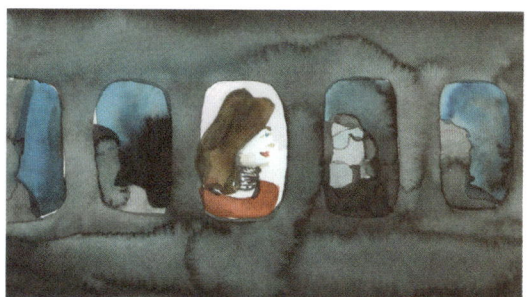
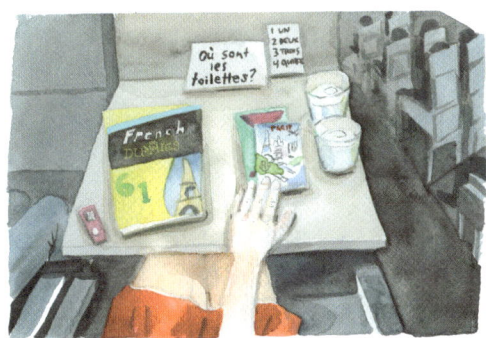
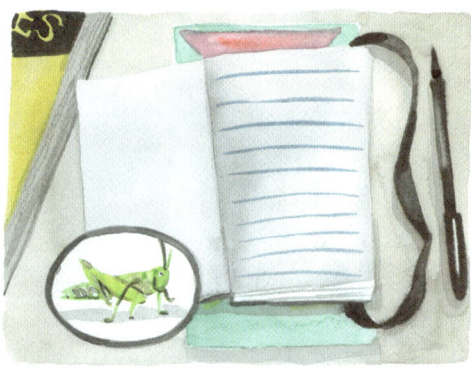
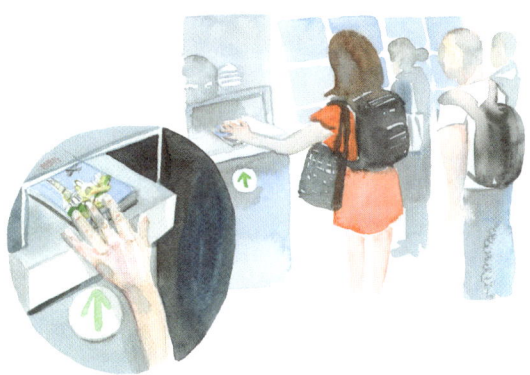
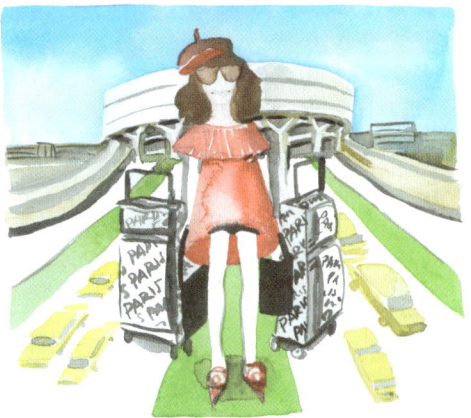

DAY 29

A WALK IN MY SHOES

Like a lot of creative breakthroughs, my mapmaking style was the product of needing to solve a problem. I was developing the concept for my book *Paris in Stride*. It needed to strike a balance between being evocative of the iconic city and being a usable guide to a neighborhood. How do you share just enough to suggest a neighborhood but not get lost in the centuries' worth of fine details? Thanks to Google Maps and trial and error, I found a way to create a map that was evocative of the place while also being pragmatic enough to follow.

Today we will flesh out an engaging map that's both usable and aesthetically pleasing. I'll help you use different tips and tricks to understand the color story of the place, incorporating enough detail to make it evocative but not overwhelming.

BRAINSTORM

Before we begin, imagine that this map will be passed on to someone to use. This drawing is good for something! Maybe it will show the route from your home to the grocery store, from your bed to your first cup of coffee, or from the Earth to the moon. The important thing is to identify a point A and a point B. You may want to look at vintage maps to find inspiration in color combinations or other navigation tools, such as the compass rose and scale.

Today I am creating a map from my home to my son's school, which I will pass on to my mother-in-law. Since she only uses her phone for voice calls, I'll have to be strategic about including easy-to-read street names and other visual cues so she doesn't get lost. I'll also draw a lined path for her to follow.

SKETCH LAYER 1

You may want to use Google Maps as a reference for understanding the overhead geography and collecting essential details like street names, monuments, and other visual cues. Before I begin a new map, I always pin the places on a Google Map and draw a line connecting them to understand the path.

Looking at my Google Map, I sketch out the essential streets to give structure to the map. I also add a few references to local monuments to help my mother-in-law get the lay of the land. There's a main street and the Eiffel Tower far away in the distance, just to give some overall context and location.

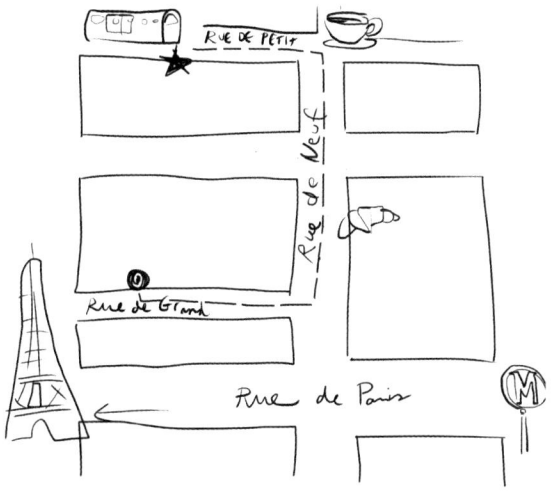

SKETCH LAYER 2

In the second layer of my sketch, I add the
neighborhood château, the corner café,
the best croissant to buy along the way,
the train station, and a few more details
to up the charm factor. I also sketch out
the direct path from home to the school.
Imagine yourself using the map and
following the path. What are the essential
landmarks to keep an eye out for?

Trace out the final sketch and path on
watercolor paper.

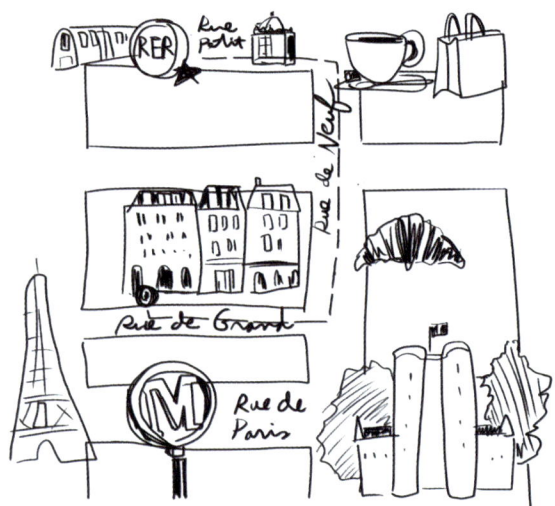

PAINT

Remember to ask yourself what the purpose of the map is. Is it to take someone
from point A to point B? How can it be as functional as possible? If the map
has a greater purpose, it will have greater intention. How will you use color to
communicate your idea? How will you include as much information as possible
without overloading the visuals?

Since this map is more functional than decorative,
I'm going to keep my use of colors minimal and
French. Red and blue for obvious reasons, and beige
to represent the limestone Parisian buildings. I'll
consistently use color for designated purposes so the
map is as simple and easy to understand as possible.

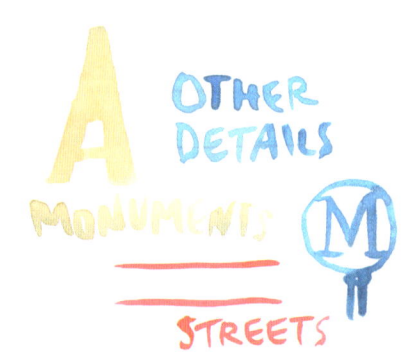

I mix my beige paint by watering down a light brown and start building the visual cues: the croissant, the newspaper stand, the château. Blue will be used to mark the path, so I paint it boldly between the starting point and the starred final destination. Red is strictly for streets and their names, which I paint with a fine-tipped round brush.

Colorwise, my composition begins to feel unbalanced because of the bold presence of red. I add a few more blue details in the roof of the château and the metro signs. A tiny French flag atop the château brings my eyes all the way around the page.

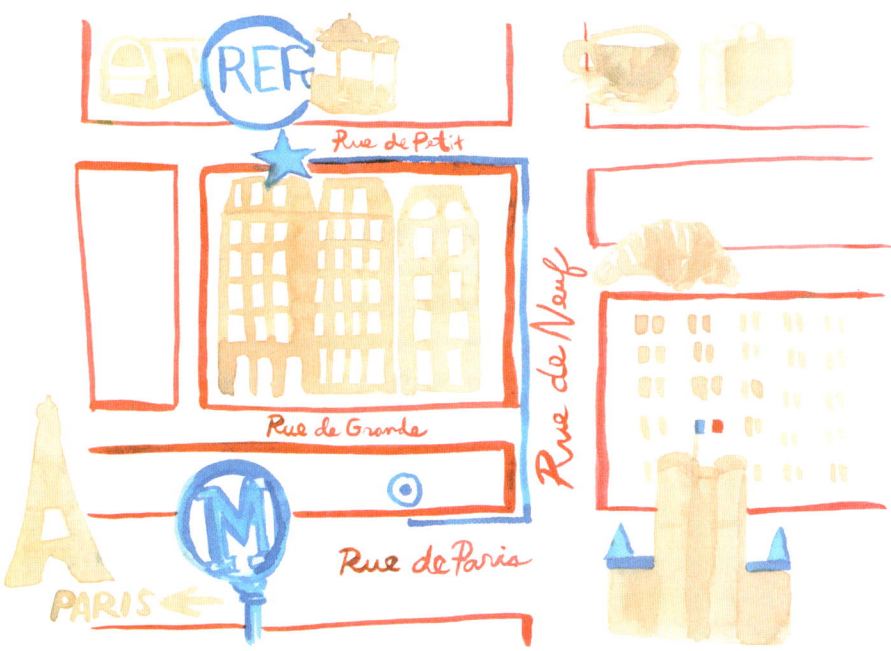

STEP 5
REFLECT

If you handed off your map to someone with no explanation, would they be able to follow the suggested path and identify all the visual cues on the map?

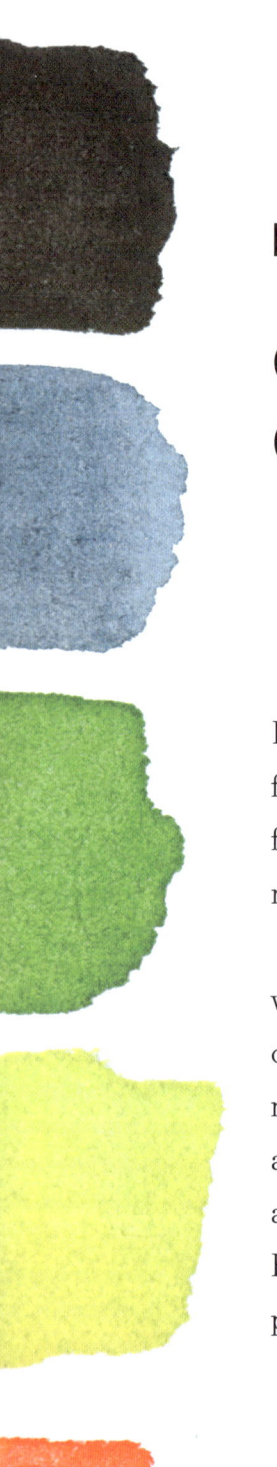

DAY 30

COMPASSION FOR OTHER SELVES

In this final exercise, I'd like you to pinpoint a difficult moment from your life that you didn't initially give yourself credit for getting through. Is there a story within you that you can rewrite?

For my illustration, I want to acknowledge the young artist who was always within me, whether I knew it or not. A lot of the emotional roadblocks I confronted were very much reflections of my hypersensitivity. Even if I didn't always have a daily practice or wasn't a professional artist, the way I saw and understood the world has shaped my path and trajectory. How can I show my younger self grace by reimagining my past, present, and future selves?

STEP 1
BRAINSTORM

Today you will challenge yourself to identify a throughline in your life. My inner world as a child was so colorful and complex that I didn't always find it easy to connect with other kids. Is there a metaphor I can think of to communicate this? On days when I am under-rested, over-caffeinated, and straight-up clumsy, it is easy to make the visual metaphor of me walking with a cloud of colorful, squiggly lines around my head. The colors are emotions in constant motion, distracting my attention, never letting me see in perspective.

It's not a terrible thing to feel all these colors—being able to access emotions is a side effect of being an artist. But I don't have to let them dominate every waking moment of my day. That's exhausting and unproductive. What if there was an easier way to access them only when needed?

Sorting through these colors is the burden and superpower of being someone who feels and processes emotions deeply. How can I capture the evolution from being completely overwhelmed by the colors to channeling them strategically? Now that I have a base metaphor, how can I use it to create some compassion for my younger self? I'll see what is revealed while sketching.

SKETCH

When you begin sketching, you may already have an idea and run with it, or something may be revealed when you put pencil to paper. In this case, I just start sketching to see what comes out of me. I sketch the internal gears (slash color wheels) of a young me's brain. I like the idea of her slowly opening a curtain of squiggly lines, stepping into a life in extreme color until the color becomes a cloud enrobing her. I remember crying on my family dog's shoulder because I didn't feel like anyone understood me. I draw a color vortex and a figure falling down it. I sketch my adult self with the young me on my shoulders, accepting my inner young artist and graciously taking her with me.

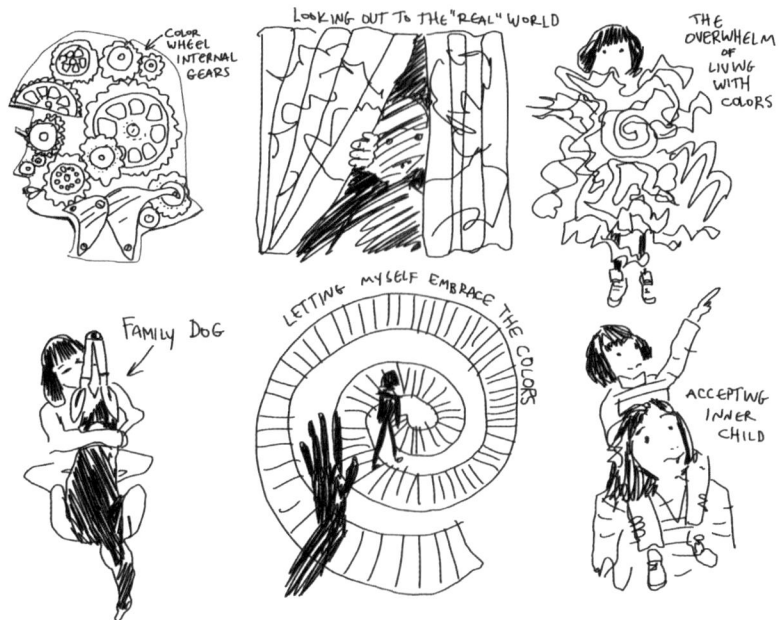

PAINT

Now, dear reader, it is time to paint. Once again, the stronger and more personal the point of view, the stronger the final work will be. Since this is our last exercise, think about how you can apply all the micro and macro lessons on color theory, harmony, perspective, and composition you've learned over these thirty days of discovery.

Since my story is all about color, I'm not going to be shy with it. I don't want rainbows, because they are a loaded symbol themselves, but I'd like to work with bold, striped patterns and some black elements when I need something graphic. I decide not to add text because I'm hoping whoever sees this connects the dots.

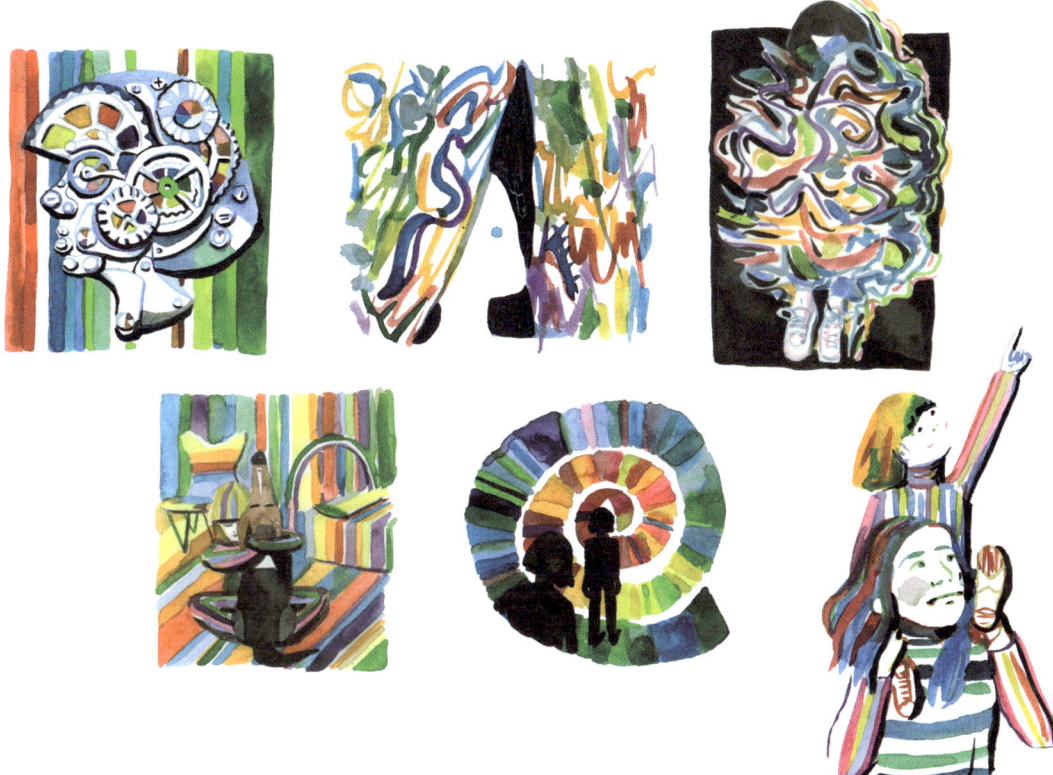

STEP 4
REFLECT

How does it feel looking at your final watercolors? Does this series of images give you a greater sense of self-understanding? If so, can this image become an emotion reset button when you are feeling down or unsettled?

Looking at my illustration, I reflect on how the colors make me unique, and think about how I might hone them into something less destabilizing moving forward. How can I accept these colors and celebrate the power they give me?

EPILOGUE

Congratulations! You've made it to the end of this thirty-day odyssey. Whether you choose to write a graphic novel or just park yourself in front of a beautiful sunset, my wish is that you've gotten to know watercolor on a deeper level and feel liberated to express yourself both literally and abstractly. And even if watercolor won't ultimately be your medium of choice, I hope that you are better equipped with myriad ways to conceptualize and visually articulate your story.

So now what? Keep this book handy and return to the exercises every so often to inspire you. And if you're still struggling with your watercolors, flip back to the Watercolor Hotline (page 34) to troubleshoot any issues you may be experiencing.

The journey doesn't end here. Share on Instagram how you are thinking in watercolor by tagging me @jessiekanelosweiner and including a hashtag with the book title and day of the exercise (e.g., #thinkinginwatercolorday5). And for more insights into the creative process, watercolor techniques, and all things illustration, please follow along and subscribe to my Substack, *La Vie en Watercolor / Jessie Kanelos Weiner*.

Remember, perfection is never the goal. Creativity is not a passive act, so give yourself credit for sitting down and doing the work, day in and day out. Take care, dear reader. And don't drink the watercolor water.

RESOURCES

These recommended reads and references greatly inspired me during the writing of this book, and I hope they will guide you on your own journey.

BOOKS

Big Magic: Creative Living Beyond Fear
by Elizabeth Gilbert
This book highlights the sacred power of inspiration and creativity.

How to Draw: Sketch and Draw Anything, Anywhere
by Jake Spicer
If you've found a passion for observational drawing, this book is filled with exercises to continue pushing you to draw from life.

Keys to Drawing with Imagination: Strategies and Exercises for Gaining Confidence and Enhancing Your Creativity **by Bert Dodson**
If you're looking for more ways to inject your watercolors with imagination, this book is filled with creative exercises and artist references.

Steal Like an Artist: 10 Things Nobody Told You About Being Creative **by Austin Kleon**
No creative work is inherently original. Good artists borrow, while great artists steal.

Understanding Comics: The Invisible Art
by Scott McCloud
This is a fascinating and brilliant meta-breakdown of comics past and present.

OTHER RESOURCES

Illustration Department **podcast**
Interviews with illustrators, agents, editors, and other professionals in the illustration world.

Abstract: The Art of Design
A documentary series on Netflix that follows the lives and works of artists and designers at the top of their fields.

ACKNOWLEDGMENTS

I'd like to thank my wonderful editor, Bridget Monroe Itkin, and everyone at Artisan—Lia Ronnen, Laura Cherkas, Abby Knudsen, Jane Treuhaft, Elissa Santos, Zach Greenwald, Nancy Murray, Allison McGeehon, Abigail Sokolsky, and Diana Griffin—for understanding my ambitious book idea, and Judy Linden of Stonesong for her continual support. Thank you to my friends and fellow artists—Crystal, Asha, Amanda, Camille, Jane, Marianne, Emily, Irené, Mathilde, Virginie, Isabelle, Zeva, Nathalie, and Christine—for your unfailing friendship. Thank you, Cyrille and Sol. Thanks, Dave and Beth, for your unconditional affection and sandwich signs.

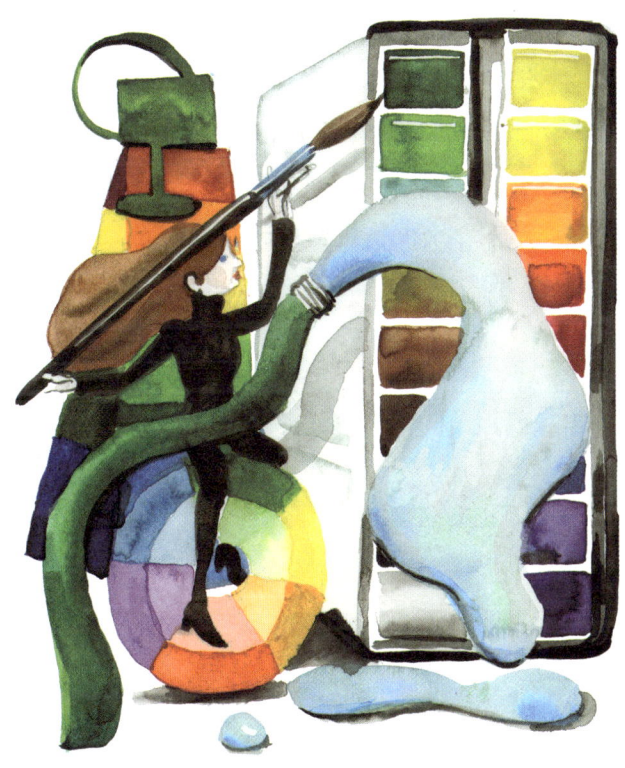

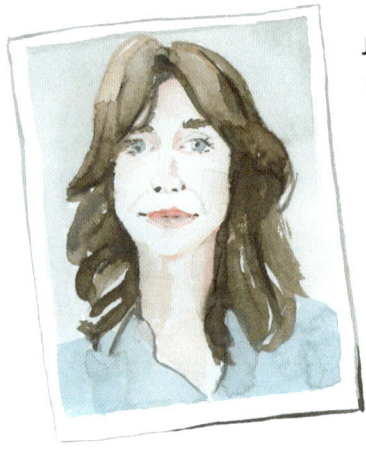

Jessie Kanelos Weiner is a Franco-American watercolor illustrator, author, and stand-up comedian whose work explores gastronomy, travel, architecture, and Paris in a distinctly whimsical and witty watercolor style. She is the coauthor of *New York in Stride* and bestseller *Paris in Stride* and the author of *Edible Paradise: A Coloring Book of Seasonal Fruits and Vegetables* and *The New Victory Garden Wall Calendar* series. Her work has been featured in *The New Yorker*, *Vogue*, *T: The New York Times Style Magazine*, the *New York Times*, and *Cherry Bombe*, and she was named a rising star in food illustration by *Food & Wine*. She regularly collaborates with brands like Chevrolet, LVMH, Fragonard, and Nespresso. Born and raised in Chicago, Illinois, she has been based in Paris for more than fifteen years, where she teaches drawing at several art schools and hosts watercolor workshops and retreats for brands and students of all levels. See her work at jessiekanelosweiner.net and subscribe to her Substack newsletter, *La Vie en Watercolor / Jessie Kanelos Weiner*.